The Princeton Review®

MCAT®

Organic Chemistry Review

The Staff of The Princeton Review

D0126862

Random House, Inc. New York

The Princeton Review, Inc.
2315 Broadway
New York, NY 10024
E-mail: editorialsupport@review.com

Terms of Service: The Princeton Review Online Companion Tools ["Online Companion Tools"] for the *Cracking* book series and *MCAT Organic Chemistry Review* are available for the most recent edition. Online Companion Tools may be activated only once per eligible book purchased. Activation of Online Companion Tools more than once per book is in direct violation of these Terms of Service and may result in discontinuation of access to Online Companion Tools Services.

ISBN 978-0-375-42793-0
ISSN 2150-8887

Editor: Heather Brady
Production Editor: Meave Shelton
Production Coordinator: Mary Kinzel

Printed in China.

10 9 8 7

Editorial

Robert Franek, VP Test Prep Books, Publisher
Seamus Mullarkey, Editorial Director
Laura Braswell, Senior Editor
Rebecca Lessem, Senior Editor
Heather Brady, Editor
Selena Coppock, Editor

Production Services

Scott Harris, Executive Director, Production Services
Kim Howie, Senior Graphic Designer
Ryan Tozzi, Production Manager

Production Editorial

Meave Shelton, Production Editor
Jennifer Graham, Production Editor
Kristen O'Toole, Production Editor

Research & Development

Ed Carroll, Agent for National Content Directors
Liz Rutzel, Project Editor

Random House Publishing Team

Tom Russell, Publisher
Nicole Benhabib, Publishing Manager
Ellen L. Reed, Production Manager
Alison Stoltzfus, Associate Managing Editor
Elham Shabahat, Publishing Assistant

CONTRIBUTORS

Peter J. Alaimo, Ph.D.
    Senior Author

TPR MCAT O-Chem Development Team:

Bethany Blackwell, M.S., Senior Editor, Lead Developer

Kristen Brunson, Ph.D.

William Ewing, Ph.D.

Karen Salazar, Ph.D.

Edited for Production by:

Judene Wright, M.S., M.A.Ed.
    National Content Director, MCAT Program, The Princeton Review

The TPR MCAT O-Chem Team and Judene would like to thank the following people for their contributions to this book :

Farhad Aziz, B.S., Brian Butts, B.S., B.A., Douglas S. Daniels, Ph.D., Amanda Edward, H.BSc, H.BEd, Carlos Guzman, Omair Adil Khan, Adam Johnson, Stefan Loren, Ph.D., Joey Mancuso, D.O., M.S., Janet Marshall, Ph.D., Katherine Miller, B.A., Tenaya Newkirk, Ph.D., Jason Osman, M.S., Daniel J. Pallin, M.D., Tyler Peikes, Chris Rabbat, Ph.D., Jayson Sack, M.D., M.S., Sina Shahbaz, B.S., Christopher Volpe, Ph.D.

In addition, The Princeton Review would like to thank Kim Howie, Mary Kinzel, Sheena Paul, and Meave Shelton, for their hard work on the production of this book.

Periodic Table of the Elements

1 **H** 1.0																	2 **He** 4.0
3 **Li** 6.9	4 **Be** 9.0											5 **B** 10.8	6 **C** 12.0	7 **N** 14.0	8 **O** 16.0	9 **F** 19.0	10 **Ne** 20.2
11 **Na** 23.0	12 **Mg** 24.3											13 **Al** 27.0	14 **Si** 28.1	15 **P** 31.0	16 **S** 32.1	17 **Cl** 35.5	18 **Ar** 39.9
19 **K** 39.1	20 **Ca** 40.1	21 **Sc** 45.0	22 **Ti** 47.9	23 **V** 50.9	24 **Cr** 52.0	25 **Mn** 54.9	26 **Fe** 55.8	27 **Co** 58.9	28 **Ni** 58.7	29 **Cu** 63.5	30 **Zn** 65.4	31 **Ga** 69.7	32 **Ge** 72.6	33 **As** 74.9	34 **Se** 79.0	35 **Br** 79.9	36 **Kr** 83.8
37 **Rb** 85.5	38 **Sr** 87.6	39 **Y** 88.9	40 **Zr** 91.2	41 **Nb** 92.9	42 **Mo** 95.9	43 **Tc** (98)	44 **Ru** 101.1	45 **Rh** 102.9	46 **Pd** 106.4	47 **Ag** 107.9	48 **Cd** 112.4	49 **In** 114.8	50 **Sn** 118.7	51 **Sb** 121.8	52 **Te** 127.6	53 **I** 126.9	54 **Xe** 131.3
55 **Cs** 132.9	56 **Ba** 137.3	57 ***La** 138.9	72 **Hf** 178.5	73 **Ta** 180.9	74 **W** 183.9	75 **Re** 186.2	76 **Os** 190.2	77 **Ir** 192.2	78 **Pt** 195.1	79 **Au** 197.0	80 **Hg** 200.6	81 **Tl** 204.4	82 **Pb** 207.2	83 **Bi** 209.0	84 **Po** (209)	85 **At** (210)	86 **Rn** (222)
87 **Fr** (223)	88 **Ra** 226.0	89 **†Ac** 227.0	104 **Rf** (261)	105 **Db** (262)	106 **Sg** (266)	107 **Bh** (264)	108 **Hs** (277)	109 **Mt** (268)	110 **Ds** (281)	111 **Rg** (272)	112 **Cn** (285)		114 **Uuq** (289)		116 **Uuh** (289)		

*Lanthanide Series:

58 **Ce** 140.1	59 **Pr** 140.9	60 **Nd** 144.2	61 **Pm** (145)	62 **Sm** 150.4	63 **Eu** 152.0	64 **Gd** 157.3	65 **Tb** 158.9	66 **Dy** 162.5	67 **Ho** 164.9	68 **Er** 167.3	69 **Tm** 168.9	70 **Yb** 173.0	71 **Lu** 175.0

†Actinide Series:

90 **Th** 232.0	91 **Pa** (231)	92 **U** 238.0	93 **Np** (237)	94 **Pu** (244)	95 **Am** (243)	96 **Cm** (247)	97 **Bk** (247)	98 **Cf** (251)	99 **Es** (252)	100 **Fm** (257)	101 **Md** (258)	102 **No** (259)	103 **Lr** (260)

MCAT ORGANIC CHEMISTRY REVIEW CONTENTS

Chapter 1
MCAT Basics

SO YOU WANT TO BE A DOCTOR

So... you want to be a doctor. If you're like most premeds, you've wanted to be a doctor since you were pretty young. When people asked you what you wanted to be when you grew up, you always answered "a doctor." You had toy medical kits, bandaged up your dog or cat, and played "hospital." You probably read your parents' home medical guides for fun.

When you got to high school you took the honors and AP classes. You studied hard, got straight As (or, at least, really good grades!), and participated in extracurricular activities so you could get into a good college. And you succeeded!

At college you knew exactly what to do. You took your classes seriously, studied hard, and got a great GPA. You talked to your professors and hung out at office hours to get good letters of recommendation. You were a member of the premed society on campus, volunteered at hospitals, and shadowed doctors. All that's left to do now is to get a good MCAT score.

Just the MCAT.

Just the most confidence-shattering, most demoralizing, longest, most brutal entrance exam for any graduate program. At 5 hours (including breaks), the MCAT tops the list; even the closest runners up, the LSAT and GMAT, are only about 4 hours long. The MCAT tests significant science content knowledge along with the ability to think quickly, reason logically, and read comprehensively, all under the pressure of a timed exam.

The path to a good MCAT score is not as easy to see as the path to a good GPA or the path to a good letter of recommendation. The MCAT is less about what you know, and more about how to apply what you know—and how to apply it quickly to new situations. Because the path might not be so clear, you might be worried. That's why you picked up this book.

We promise to demystify the MCAT for you, with clear descriptions of the different sections, how the test is scored, and what the test experience is like. We will help you understand general test-taking techniques as well as provide you with specific techniques for each section. We will review the science content you need to know as well as give you strategies for the Verbal Reasoning section. We'll show you the path to a good MCAT score and help you walk the path.

After all, you want to be a doctor. And we want you to succeed.

WHAT IS THE MCAT...REALLY?

Most test-takers approach the MCAT as though it were a typical college science test, one in which facts and knowledge simply need to be regurgitated in order to do well. They study for the MCAT the same way they did for their college tests, by memorizing facts and details, formulas and equations. And when they get to the MCAT they are surprised...and disappointed.

It's a myth that the MCAT is purely a content-knowledge test. If medical school admission committees want to see what you know, all they have to do is look at your transcripts. What they really want to see, though, is how you think. Especially how you think under pressure. And that's what your MCAT score will tell them.

The MCAT is really a test of your ability to apply basic knowledge to different, possibly new, situations. It's a test of your ability to reason out and evaluate arguments. Do you still need to know your science content? Absolutely. But not at the level that most test-takers think they need to know it. Furthermore, your science knowledge won't help you on the Verbal Reasoning section. So how do you study for a test like this?

You study for the science sections by reviewing the basics and then applying them to MCAT practice questions. You study for the Verbal Reasoning section by learning how to adapt your existing reading and analytical skills to the nature of the test (more information about the Verbal Reasoning section can be found in *MCAT Verbal Reasoning Review*).

The book you are holding will review all the relevant MCAT Organic Chemistry content you will need for the test, and a little bit more. Plus, it includes hundreds of questions (printed and online) designed to make you think about the material in a deeper way, along with full explanations to clarify the logical thought process needed to get to the answer. It also comes with access to two full-length online practice exams to further hone your skills.

GO ONLINE!

In addition to the review material you'll find in this book, there is a wealth of practice content available online at **PrincetonReview.com/cracking**. There you'll find:

*   2 full-length practice MCATs
*   Dozens of practice passages and questions covering every topic reviewed in this book
*   Useful information about taking the MCAT and applying to medical school

To register your book, go to **PrincetonReview.com/cracking**. You'll see a welcome page where you can register your book by its ISBN number (found on the back cover above the barcode). Set up an account using this number and your email address, then you can access all of your online content.

MCAT NUTS AND BOLTS

Overview

The MCAT is a computer-based test (CBT) that is *not* adaptive. Adaptive tests base your next question on whether or not you've answered the current question correctly. The MCAT is linear, or fixed-form, meaning that the questions are in a predetermined order and do not change based on your answers. However, there are many versions of the test, so that on a given test day, different people will see different versions. The following table highlights the features of the MCAT exam.

Registration	Online via www.aamc.org. Begins as early as six months prior to test date; available up until week of test (subject to seat availability).
Testing Centers	Administered at small, secure, climate-controlled computer testing rooms.
Security	Photo ID with signature, electronic fingerprint, electronic signature verification, assigned seat
Proctoring	None. Test administrator checks examinee in and assigns seat at computer. All testing instructions are given on the computer.
Frequency of Test	28 times per year distributed over January, March, April, May, June, July, August, and September.
Format	Exclusively computer-based. NOT an adaptive test.
Length of Test Day	5 hours.
Breaks	Optional 10-minute breaks between sections.
Number of Questions and Timing	52 Physical Sciences (PS), 70 minutes. 40 Verbal Reasoning (VR), 60 minutes. 52 Biological Sciences (BS), 70 minutes. 32 optional questions*, 45 minutes.
Scoring	Test is scaled. Several forms per administration. PS, VR, and BS receive scaled scores of 1–15.
Allowed/Not allowed	No timers/watches. No ear plugs. Noise reduction headphones available. Scratch paper and pencils given at start of test and taken at end of test. Locker or secure area provided for personal items.
Results: Timing and Delivery	Approximately 30 days. Electronic scores only, available online through AAMC login. Examinees can print official score reports.
Maximum Number of Retakes	Can be taken a maximum of three times per year, but an examinee can only be registered for one date at a time.

*Beginning in January 2013, the Writing Sample will be eliminated from the MCAT. Test takers will have the option of taking a voluntary unscored trial section including multiple-choice questions from introductory psychology, sociology, and biochemistry. The AAMC states that those who take the optional section and put forth a good faith effort will be compensated. This section will become required and scored in 2015.

Registration

Registration for the exam is completed online at www.aamc.org/students/mcat. The AAMC opens registration for a given test date at least two months in advance of the date, often earlier. It's a good idea to register well in advance of your desired test date to make sure that you get a seat.

Sections

There are four sections on the MCAT exam: Physical Sciences (PS), Verbal Reasoning (VR), Biological Sciences (BS), and an optional psychology/sociology and biochemistry section. All sections consist of multiple-choice questions.

Section	Concepts Tested	Number of Questions and Timing
Physical Sciences	Basic concepts in physics and general chemistry, data analysis, basic non-calculus math, critical reasoning skills.	52 questions, 70 minutes, approximately 50% physics and 50% general chemistry
Verbal Reasoning	Reading comprehension and critical thinking.	40 questions, 60 minutes
Biological Sciences	Basic concepts in biology and organic chemistry, data analysis, critical reasoning skills.	52 questions, 70 minutes, approximately 80% biology and 20% organic chemistry
Voluntary Unscored Trial Section	Basic concepts in psychology, sociology, and biochemistry.	32 questions, 45 minutes

Most questions on the MCAT (39 out of 52 on the science sections, all 40 in the VR section) are **passage-based**, and each section of the test will have a total of seven passages. A passage consists of a few paragraphs of information on which several following questions are based. In the science sections, passages often include equations or reactions, tables, graphs, figures, and experiments to analyze. Verbal Reasoning passages come from literature in the social sciences, humanities, and natural sciences and do not test content knowledge in any way.

Some questions in the science sections are **freestanding questions** (FSQs). These questions are independent of any passage information. These questions appear in three groups of between 3 and 5 questions, and are interspersed throughout the passages. There are 13 freestanding questions in each of the science sections and the remaining 39 questions are passage-based.

Each section on the MCAT is separated by a 10-minute break.

Section	Time
Test Center Check-In	Variable, can take up to 40 minutes if center is busy.
Tutorial	10 minutes
Physical Sciences	70 minutes
Break	10 minutes
Verbal Reasoning	60 minutes
Break	10 minutes
Biological Sciences	70 minutes
Break	10 minutes
Voluntary Unscored Trial Section	45 minutes
Void Option	5 minutes
Survey	10 minutes

The survey includes questions about your satisfaction with the overall MCAT experience, including registration, check-in, etc., as well as questions about how you prepared for the test.

Scoring

The MCAT is a scaled exam, meaning that your raw score will be converted into a scaled score that takes into account the difficulty of the questions. There is no guessing penalty. The PS, VR, and BS sections are scaled from 1–15. Because different versions of the test have varying levels of difficulty, the scale will be different from one exam to the next. Thus, there is no "magic number" of questions to get right in order to get a particular score. Plus, some of the questions on the test are considered "experimental" and do not count toward your score; they are just there to be evaluated for possible future inclusion in a test.

At the end of the test, you will be asked to choose one of the following two options, "I wish to have my MCAT exam scored" or "I wish to VOID my MCAT exam." You have five minutes to make a decision, and if you do not select one of the options in that time, the test will automatically be scored. If you choose the VOID option, your test will not be scored (you will not now, or ever, get a numerical score for this test), medical schools will not know you took the test, and no refunds will be granted. You cannot "unvoid" your scores at a later time.

Even though we can't tell you a specific number of questions to get right in order to receive a particular score, we can tell you the percentile numbers that the scores correspond with. The percentile numbers tell you what percent of examinees scored lower or higher than you. For example, if you are in the 90th percentile, then 90% of examinees scored lower than you did, and 10% scored higher.

Score	Physical Sciences Percentile*	Verbal Reasoning Percentile*	Biological Sciences Percentile*
14–15	100%	100%	100%
13	97%	99%	97%
12	91%	96%	92%
11	82%	91%	80%
10	69%	75%	64%
9	52%	53%	41%
8	37%	35%	23%
7	22%	22%	12%
6	11%	14%	7%
5	4%	7%	4%
4	2%	4%	2%
3	1%	2%	1%
2	0%	1%	0%
1	0%	0%	0%
	Avg score 9.3, std dev 2.3	Avg score 9.0, std dev 2.3	Avg score 9.8, std dev 2.1

*Data from *The Official Guide to the MCAT Exam*, 2009 ed., © 2009 Association of American Medical Colleges

So, what's a good score? Most people would agree that since the average total score on the MCAT is around 28, you want to at least hit that number. To be competitive, you really want scores in the low 30s, and for the top-ranked medical schools, you'll want scores in the high 30s to low 40s. If your GPA is on the low side, you'll need higher MCAT scores to compensate, and if you have a strong GPA, you can get away with lower MCAT scores. But the reality is that your chances of acceptance depend on a lot more than just your MCAT scores. It's a combination of your GPA, your MCAT scores, your undergraduate coursework, letters of recommendation, experience related to the medical field (such as volunteer work or research), extracurricular activities, your personal statement, etc. Medical schools are looking for a complete package, not just good scores and a good GPA.

GENERAL TEST-TAKING STRATEGIES

CBT Tools

There are a number of tools available on the test, including highlighting, strike-outs, the Mark button, the Review button, the Exhibit button, and of course, scratch paper. The following is a brief description of each tool.

1. **Highlighting**—This is done in passage text (including table entries and some equations, but excluding figures and molecular structures) by clicking and dragging the cursor over the desired text. To remove the highlighted portion, just click over the highlighted text. Note that highlights DO NOT persist once you leave the passage.

2. **Strike-outs**—This is done on the various answer choices by clicking over the answer choice that you wish to eliminate. As a result, the entire set of text associated with that answer choice is crossed out. The strike-out can be removed by clicking again. Note that you cannot strike-out figures or molecular structures, and strike-outs DO persist after leaving the passage.

3. **Mark button**—This is available for each question and allows you to flag the question as one you would like to review later if time permits. When clicked, the Mark button turns red and says "Marked."

4. **Review button**—This button is found near the bottom of the screen, and when clicked, brings up a new screen showing all questions and their status (either "answered," "unanswered," or "marked"). You can then choose one of three options: "review all," "review unanswered," or "review marked." You can only review questions in the section of the MCAT you are currently taking, but this button can be clicked at any time during the allotted time for that section; you do NOT have to wait until the end of the section to click it.

5. **Exhibit button**—Clicking this button will open a periodic table. Note that the periodic table is originally large, covering most of the screen. However, this window can be resized to see the questions and a portion of the periodic table at the same time. The table text will not decrease, but scroll bars will appear on the window so you can center the section of the table of interest in the window.

6. **Scratch Paper**—You will be given four pages (8 faces) of scratch paper at the start of the test. While you may ask for more at any point during the test, your first set of paper will be collected before you receive fresh paper. Scratch paper is only useful if it is kept organized; do not give in to the tendency to write on the first available open space! Good organization will be very helpful when/if you wish to review a question. Indicate the passage number in a box near the top of your scratch work, and indicate which question you are working on in a circle to the left of the notes for that question. Draw a line under your scratch work when you change passages to keep the work separate. Do not erase or scribble over any previous work. If you do not think it is correct, draw one line through the work and start again. You may have already done some useful work without realizing it.

Pacing

Since the MCAT is a timed test, you must keep an eye on the timer and adjust your pacing as necessary. It would be terrible to run out of time at the end to discover that the last few questions could have been easily answered in just a few seconds each.

If you complete every question, in the science sections you will have about one minute and twenty seconds (1:20) per question, and in the Verbal Reasoning section you will have about one minute and 30 seconds per question (1:30).

Section	# of Questions in Passage	Approximate time (including reading the passage)
Physical Sciences and Biological Sciences	5	6.5–7 minutes
	6	8 minutes
	7	9–9.5 minutes
Verbal Reasoning	5	7.5 minutes
	6	9 minutes
	7	10.5 minutes

When starting a passage in the science sections, make note of how much time you will allot for it, and the starting time on the timer. Jot down on your scratch paper what the timer should say at the end of the passage. Then just keep an eye on it as you work through the questions. If you are near the end of the time for that passage, guess on any remaining questions, make some notes on your scratch paper (remember that highlighting disappears), "Mark" the questions, and move on. Come back to those questions if you have time.

For Verbal Reasoning, one important thing to keep in mind is that most people will maximize their score by not trying to complete every question, or every passage, in the section. A good strategy for a majority of test takers is to complete six of the seven passages, randomly guessing on one passage. This allows you to have good accuracy on the passages you complete, and to maximize your total percent correct in the section as a whole. To complete six of the passages, you should spend about 8 minutes on a five-question passage, 9 minutes on a six-question passage, and 10 minutes on a seven-question passage. That is, a total of about 3 minutes plus 1 minute for each question ("# of Q + 3").

To help maximize your number of correct answer choices in any section, do the questions and passages within that section in the order you want to do them in. Skip over the more difficult questions (guess and "Mark" them), and answer the questions you feel most comfortable with first.

Process of Elimination

Process of Elimination (POE) is probably the most useful technique you have to tackle MCAT questions. Since there is no guessing penalty, POE allows you to increase your probability of choosing the correct answer by eliminating those you are sure are wrong. If you are guessing between a couple of choices, use the CBT tools to your advantage:

1. Strike out any choices that you are sure are incorrect or do not answer the issue addressed in the question.
2. Jot down some notes on your scratch paper to help clarify your thoughts if you return to the question.
3. Use the "Mark" button to flag the question for review at a later time. (Note, however, that in the Verbal Reasoning section, you generally should not be returning to rethink questions once you have moved on to a new passage.)
4. Do not leave it blank! If you are not sure and you have already spent more than 60 seconds on that question, just pick one of the remaining choices. If you have time to review it at the end, you can always debate the remaining choices based on your previous notes.
5. Special Note: If three of the four answer choices have been eliminated, the remaining choice must be the correct answer. Don't waste time pondering why it is correct, just click it and move on. The MCAT doesn't care if you truly understand why it's the right answer, only that you have the right answer selected.

Guessing

Remember, there is NO guessing penalty on the MCAT. NEVER leave a question blank!

SECTION SPECIFICS

Question Types

In the science sections of the MCAT, the questions fall into one of three main categories.

1. Memory questions: These questions can be answered directly from prior knowledge and represent about 25% of the total number of questions.
2. Explicit questions: These questions are those for which the answer is explicitly stated in the passage. To answer them correctly, for example, may just require finding a definition, or reading a graph, or making a simple connection. Explicit questions represent about 35% of the total number of questions.
3. Implicit questions: These questions require you to apply knowledge to a new situation; the answer is typically implied by the information in the passage. These questions often start "if... then..." (for example, "If we modify the experiment in the passage like this, then what result would we expect?").

In the Verbal Reasoning section, the questions also fall into three main categories:

1. Specific questions: These questions ask you for specific information from the passage, such as a fact (retrieval question), an inference ("which of the following is best supported by the passage?"), or a definition (vocabulary-in-context question).
2. General questions: These questions ask you to summarize themes (main idea and primary purpose questions) or evaluate an author's opinion (tone/attitude questions).
3. Complex questions: These are typically more difficult questions that can ask you to do a number of different things. Generally, Complex questions will ask you to do one of the following: consider how the author constructs his/her argument (structure questions), decide how or how well the author supports his/her argument (evaluate questions), decide which answer most supports or undermines the author's argument (strengthen/weaken questions), evaluate how new facts or scenarios relate to or affect the author's points (new information questions), or apply the author's argument to a new situation (analogy questions).

Remember that for all sections, you should do the questions in the order you want to. In the science sections, it's wise to do all the FSQs first since they are often quick memory questions, and then tackle the passages. Start with the subject you feel the most comfortable with, and then come back to the other subject. This helps keep your brain focused on a single subject at a time, instead of jumping, for example, between biology and organic chemistry randomly. Do the passages within a section in the order that you feel most comfortable with, and within the passages themselves, tackle the easier questions first, leaving the most time consuming ones for last.

In the Verbal Reasoning section, it is best to do the Specific questions within a passage first, then the General questions (after you have learned more about the passage by answering the Specific questions) and to leave the Complex questions (which tend to be more difficult) until the end of the set. For the section as a whole, answer the questions for the easier passages in your first "pass" through the section, and then come back for a second pass, completing some of the more difficult passages.

ORGANIC CHEMISTRY ON THE MCAT

Organic chemistry questions comprise the smallest proportion of any science subject on the test. However, the topics that are tested cover a very broad range of material, equal to two semesters of college organic chemistry. This section should not be overlooked or take a back burner to biology during your studies, since up to 25 percent of the Biological Sciences section could be O-Chem.

Just about all MCAT O-Chem questions will fall into one of these five big categories:

1. Structure (IUPAC nomenclature, isomerism, functional groups, etc.)
2. Stability of intermediates or products of reactions (induction, resonance, steric strain, conjugation, etc.)
3. Recognition of reaction types
4. Lab techniques (separations and spectroscopy)
5. Predicting products of reactions

Keep in mind that O-Chem questions on the MCAT will be more likely to ask you to apply fundamental basics of chemistry to a novel reaction or class of molecules than ask you to regurgitate a factoid. Remember the MCAT tests your analytical abilities and your problem-solving skills, not your ability to remember trivia. If you're stumped on a problem, try to remember your basics, and apply one or more of the specific test taking strategies below.

How to Map the Passage and Use Scratch Paper

1. The passage should not be read like textbook material, with the intent of learning something from every sentence (science majors especially will be tempted to read this way). Passages should be read to get a feel for the type of questions that will follow, and to get a general idea of the location of information within the passage. Use your scratch paper to jot down a few notes and facts before moving to the questions.
2. Highlighting—Use this tool sparingly, or you will end up with a passage that is completely covered in yellow highlighter! Remember that you cannot highlight any part of a chemical structure, and highlighting in equations seems random; sometimes you can highlight them, sometimes not. Keep in mind that highlighting does not persist as you move from passage to passage within the section. If you want to make more permanent notes, use the scratch paper. Highlighting in an O-Chem passage should be used to draw attention to a few words that demonstrate one of the following:
   - The main theme of a paragraph or the passage (e.g., reaction type, class of biologically important molecules, etc.)
   - Details of how a reaction proceeds or how it is similar or different to a reaction you are familiar with
   - An unusual or unfamiliar term that is defined specifically for that passage (e.g., something that is italicized)
3. Pay brief attention to equations, synthetic schemes or mechanisms, figures, and experiments, noting only what information they deal with. Do not spend a lot of time analyzing at this point. Keep in mind, however, that a large percentage of the questions associated with an O-Chem passage will be answered from a quick reference to a chemical structure given in

a synthetic or mechanistic scheme, and very infrequently from the text of the passage itself. Questions will most likely direct you specifically to the numbered structure or reaction step in the figure, so don't worry about paying too much attention to molecules on the first pass through the passage.

4. Scratch paper is only useful if it is kept organized! Make sure that your notes for each passage are clearly delineated and marked with the passage number. This will allow you to easily read your notes when you come back to a review a marked question. Resist the temptation to write in the first available blank space as this makes it much more difficult to refer back to your work.

Organic Chemistry Question Strategies

1. Remember that Process of Elimination is paramount! The strikeout tool allows you to eliminate answer choices; this will improve your chances of guessing the correct answer if you are unable to narrow it down to one choice.

2. Answer the straightforward questions first. Leave questions that require analysis of experiments and graphs for later.

3. Make sure that the answer you choose actually answers the question, and isn't just a true statement.

4. Try to avoid answer choices with extreme words such as "always," "never," etc. In O-Chem, there is almost always an exception and answers are rarely black and white.

5. I-II-III questions: always work between the I-II-III statements and the answer choices. Unfortunately, it is not possible to strike out the Roman numerals, but this is a great use for scratch paper notes. Once a statement is determined to be true (or false) strike out answer choices which do not contain (or do contain) that statement.

6. Ranking questions: Look for an extreme in whatever is being ranked, then look at the answer choices. Use the strikeout feature to eliminate choices as you go. In some cases, you may immediately get the answer as only one choice lists the appropriate option as "least" or "greatest." Usually you will, at minimum, be able to strikeout two answer choices. Then just examine the remaining possibilities to determine which of the items at the other end of the ranking can be correct.

7. LEAST/EXCEPT/NOT questions: Don't get tricked by these questions that ask you to pick that answer that doesn't fit (the incorrect or false statement). It's often good to use your scratch paper and write a T or F next to answer choices A–D. The one that stands out as different is the correct answer!

8. Math: Any questions that involve calculations should be left for last (there aren't many in O-Chem, but they happen). You should always round numbers and estimate while working out calculations on your scratch paper.

9. Again, don't leave any question blank.

A Note About Flashcards

Contrary to popular belief, flashcards are NOT the best way to study for the MCAT. For most of the exams you've taken previously, flashcards were probably helpful. This was because those exams mostly required you to regurgitate information, and flashcards are pretty good at helping you memorize facts. Remember, however, that the most challenging aspect of the MCAT is not that it requires you to memorize the fine details of content-knowledge, but that it requires you to apply your basic scientific knowledge to unfamiliar situations. Flashcards won't help you do that.

There is only one situation in which flashcards can be beneficial, and that's if your basic content knowledge is deficient in some area. For example, if you don't know the hormones and their effects in the body, flashcards can help you memorize these facts. Or, maybe you are unsure of some of the organic chemistry functional groups you need to know; flashcards can help you solidify that knowledge. You might find it useful to make flashcards to help you learn and recognize the different question types or the common types of wrong answers for the Verbal Reasoning section. (And remember that part of what makes flashcards useful is the fact that *you make them yourself.* Not only are they then customized for your personal areas of weakness, the very act of writing down information on a flashcard helps stick that information in your brain.) But other than straight, basic fact-memorization in your personal weak areas, you are better off doing and analyzing practice passages than carrying around a stack of flashcards.

TEST-DAY TIPS

On the day of the test, you'll want to arrive at the test center about a half-hour prior to the starting time of your test. Examinees will be checked in in the order they arrive at the center. You will be assigned a locker or secure area in which to put your personal items. Textbooks and study notes are not allowed, so there is no need to bring them with you to the test center. Nothing is allowed at the computer station except your photo identification, not even your watch. Your ID will be checked, a digital image of your fingerprint will be taken, and you will be asked to sign in. You will be given scratch paper and a couple of pencils, and the test center administrator will take you to the computer on which you will complete the test. (Note that if there is a white-board and erasable marker is provided, you can specifically request for scratch paper at the start of the test.) You may not choose a computer; you must use the computer assigned to you.

If you choose to leave the testing room at the breaks, you will have your fingerprint checked again, and you will have to sign in and out. You are allowed to access the items in your locker except for notes and cell phones. At the end of the test, the test administrator will collect your scratch paper and shred it.

GENERAL TEST-DAY TIPS

- Take a trip to the test center a day or two before your actual test date so that you can easily find the building and room on test day. This will also allow you to gauge traffic, and see if you need money for parking or anything like that. Knowing this type of information ahead of time will greatly reduce your stress on the day of your test.
- Don't do any heavy studying the day before the test. Try to get a good amount of sleep on the days leading up to the test.
- Eat well. Try to avoid excessive caffeine and sugar. Ideally, in the weeks leading up to the actual test you should experiment a little bit with foods and practice tests to see which foods give you the most endurance. Aim for steady blood sugar levels; sports drinks, peanut-butter crackers, trail mix, etc. make good snacks for your breaks.
- Definitely take the breaks! Get up and walk around. It's a good way to clear your head between sections and get the blood (and oxygen!) flowing to your brain.
- Ask for new scratch paper at the breaks if you use it all up.

Chapter 2
Organic Chemistry
Basics

2.1 BACKGROUND AND INTRODUCTION

This section covers the fundamentals of nomenclature in organic chemistry. Although this section will require memorization as your primary study technique, it is in your best interest to be comfortable reading, hearing, and using this terminology. Although most of the terminology that appears on the MCAT is IUPAC, some common nomenclature is also used.

Basic Nomenclature

Carbon Chain Prefixes and Alkane Names			
Number of carbon atoms in a row	Prefix	Alkane	Name
1	meth-	CH_4	methane
2	eth-	CH_3CH_3	ethane
3	prop-	$CH_3CH_2CH_3$	propane
4	but-	$CH_3CH_2CH_2CH_3$	butane
5	pent-	$CH_3(CH_2)_3CH_3$	pentane
6	hex-	$CH_3(CH_2)_4CH_3$	hexane
7	hept-	$CH_3(CH_2)_5CH_3$	heptane
8	oct-	$CH_3(CH_2)_6CH_3$	octane
9	non-	$CH_3(CH_2)_7CH_3$	nonane
10	dec-	$CH_3(CH_2)_8CH_3$	decane

In the case of an all-carbon containing ring, these are preceded by the prefix **cyclo-**. Hence, a six-membered ring containing all $-CH_2-$ units is called *cyclohexane*.

Nomenclature For Substituents	
Substituent	Name
$-CH_3$	methyl
$-CH_2CH_3$	ethyl
$-CH_2CH_2CH_3$	propyl
$H_3C-\overset{\overset{\displaystyle H}{\vert}}{\underset{\vert}{C}}-CH_3$	isopropyl
$-CH_2CH_2CH_2CH_3$	butyl (or *n*-butyl)
$CH_3\underset{\vert}{C}HCH_2CH_3$	*sec*-butyl
$\overset{\displaystyle CH_3}{\underset{\displaystyle CH_3}{\overset{\vert}{\underset{\vert}{-C}}-CH_3}}$	*tert*-butyl (or *t*-butyl)

Common Functional Groups

R = alkyl group = hydrogen substituents group (or H), X = halogen (F, Cl, Br, I)

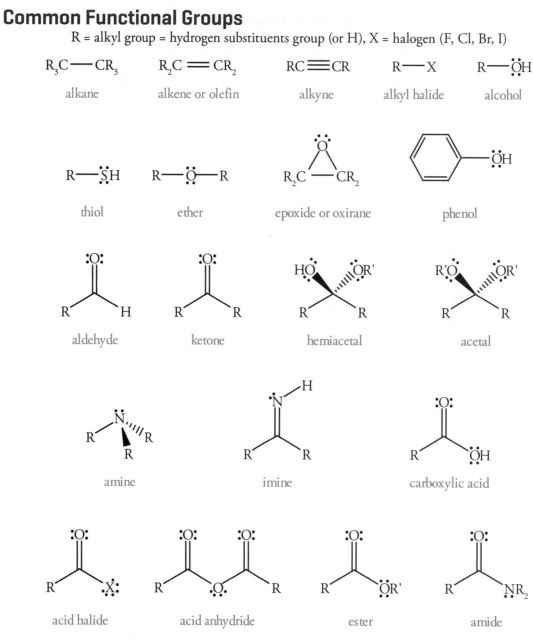

2.2   ABBREVIATED LINE STRUCTURES

The prevalence of carbon-hydrogen (C—H) bonds in organic chemistry has led chemists to use an abbreviated drawing system, merely for convenience. Just imagine having to draw every C—H bond for a large molecule like a steroid or polymer! Abbreviated line structures use only a few simple rules:

1. Carbons are represented simply as vertices.
2. C–H bonds are not drawn.
3. Hydrogens bonded to any atom *other* than carbon must be shown.

To illustrate rules 1 and 2, pentane can be represented using the full Lewis structure,

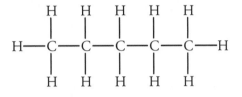

or using the abbreviated line structure.

Although C—H bonds are not drawn, the number of hydrogens required to complete carbon's valency are assumed. To clarify this, let's look more closely at the abbreviated line structure of pentane:

These three carbon atoms are each bonded to two other carbon atoms. In order to complete carbon's valency, we assume there are two hydrogens bonded to each of these carbons.

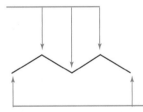

These two carbon atoms are each bonded to one other carbon atom. In order to complete carbon's valency, we assume there are three hydrogens bonded to each of these carbons.

This must be correct, because if we draw out all of the hydrogens in pentane, we get the full Lewis structure shown above.

To illustrate rule 3, consider dimethyl amine:

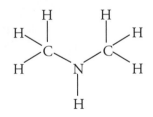

full Lewis structure

abbreviated line structure

2.2

Remember that hydrogens bonded to carbon can be assumed (the methyl groups in dimethyl amine, for example), but hydrogens bonded to any other atom must be shown. Lone pairs of electrons are often omitted.

Example 2-1: Translate each of the following Lewis structures into an abbreviated line structure:

(a)

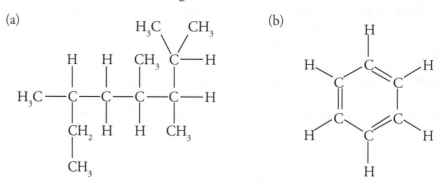

(b)

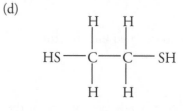

(c)

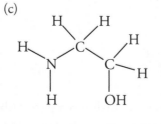

(d)

Solution:

(a)

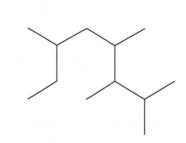

(b)

(c)

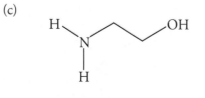

(d)

Example 2-2: Translate each of the following abbreviated line structures into a Lewis structure:

(a)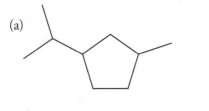

(b)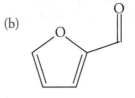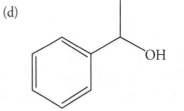

(c)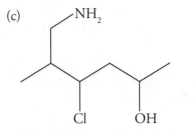

(d)

Solution:

(a)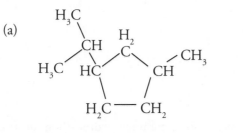

(b)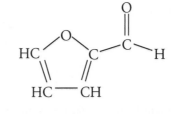

(c)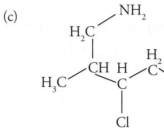

(d)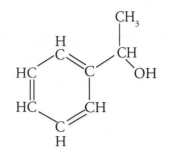

2.3   NOMENCLATURE OF ALKANES

Alkanes are named by a set of simple rules. One particular alkane (shown below) will be used to illustrate this process:

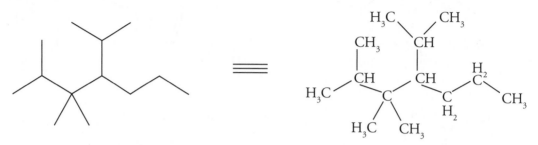

1.   Identify the longest continuous carbon chain. The names of these chains are given in the first table in this chapter ("Carbon Chain Prefixes and Alkane Names").

The longest chain in the compound above is a 7-carbon chain, which is called *heptane*. (This chain is shown below, outlined by dashed lines.)

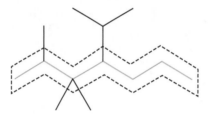

2.   Identify any substituents on this chain. The names of some common hydrocarbon substituents are given in the second table in this chapter ("Nomenclature for Substituents").

There are four substituents in this example: three methyl groups and one isopropyl group.

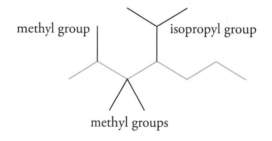

3.   Number the carbons of the main chain such that the substituents are on the carbons with lower numbers.

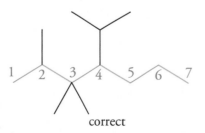

correct

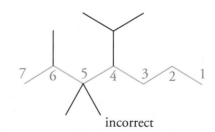

incorrect

Now each substituent can be associated with the carbon atom to which it's attached:

    2 – methyl
    3 – methyl
    3 – methyl
    4 – isopropyl

4.   Identical substituents are grouped together; the prefixes **di-**, **tri-**, **tetra-**, and **penta-** are used to denote how many there are, and their carbon numbers are separated by a comma.

In this case we have

    2 – methyl
    3 – methyl   ⟶   2,3,3-trimethyl
    3 – methyl

5.   Alphabetize the substituents, ignoring the prefixes di-, tri-, etc. and *n-*, *sec-*, *tert-*, and separate numbers from words by a hyphen and numbers from numbers by a comma. Note that "iso" is not a prefix but is part of the name of the substituent, so it is NOT ignored when alphabetizing.

The complete name for our molecule is therefore **4-isopropyl-2,3,3-trimethylheptane.**

Let's do another example and find the name of this molecule:

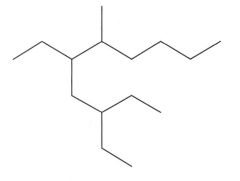

1.   The longest continuous carbon chain is a 10-carbon chain, called **decane.**

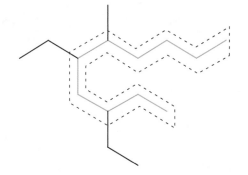

2. There are three substituents on this chain: two ethyl groups and a methyl group.

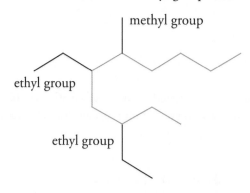

3. The correct numbering of the carbons in the main chain is as follows:

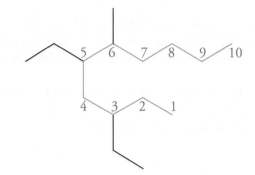

4. The substituents are now identified as:
    3,5-diethyl
    6-methyl

5. The complete name of the molecule is therefore **3,5-diethyl-6-methyldecane**.

Example 2-3: Name each of the following alkanes:

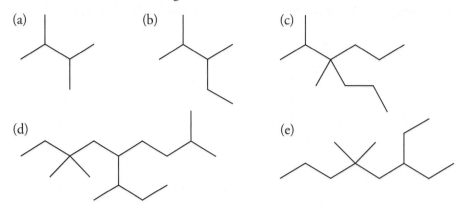

Solution:

- (a) 2,3-dimethylbutane
- (b) 2,3-dimethylpentane
- (c) 4-methyl-4-isopropylheptane
- (d) 5-*sec*-butyl-2,7,7-trimethylnonane
- (e) 3-ethyl-5,5-dimethyloctane

2.4   NOMENCLATURE OF HALOALKANES

Alkanes with halogen (F, Cl, Br, I) substituents follow the same set of rules as simple alkanes. Halogens are named using these prefixes:

Halogen	Prefix
fluorine	fluoro-
chlorine	chloro-
bromine	bromo-
iodine	iodo-

By applying the same rules as for naming simple alkanes, verify the following names:

Structure   Name

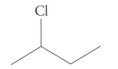

2-chlorobutane

2-chloro-1-fluoro-4-methylpentane

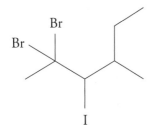

2, 2-dibromo-3-iodo-4-methylhexane

Example 2-4: Name each of the following haloalkanes:

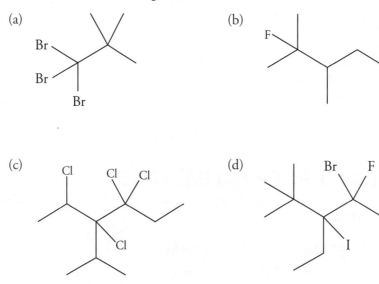

(a)

(b)

(c)

(d)

Solution:

(a)   1,1,1-tribromo-2,2-dimethylpropane
(b)   2-fluoro-2,3-dimethylpentane
(c)   2,3,4,4-tetrachloro-3-isopropylhexane
(d)   4-bromo-3-ethyl-4-fluoro-3-iodo-2,2-dimethylhexane

Example 2-5: For each name, draw the structure:

(a)   3-chloro-2,2-dimethylbutane
(b)   3-bromo-4-chloro-5,5-diethylnonane
(c)   2,3-dibromo-1,1-diiodopropane
(d)   3,4-difluoro-2,2,3-trimethylpentane

Solution:

(a)

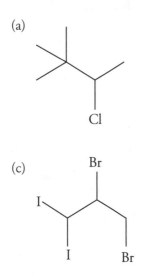

(b)

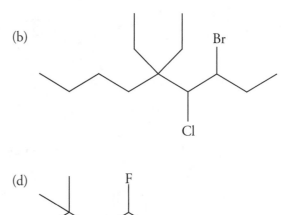

(c)

(d)

2.5 NOMENCLATURE OF ALCOHOLS

Alcohols also follow many of the same nomenclature rules as alkanes. Hydroxyl groups (–OH), however, are typically denoted by a suffix to the main alkyl chain. The table of straight-chain alcohols given below shows that to denote a hydroxyl group, the suffix **–ol** replaces the last **–e** in the name of the alkane.

Alkanes		Alcohols	
Structure	Name	Structure	Name
CH_4	methane	CH_3OH	methanol
CH_3CH_3	ethane	CH_3CH_2OH	ethanol
$CH_3CH_2CH_3$	propane	$CH_3CH_2CH_2OH$	propanol
$CH_3CH_2CH_2CH_3$	butane	$CH_3CH_2CH_2CH_2OH$	butanol

When the position of the hydroxyl group needs to be specified, the number is placed after the name of the longest carbon chain and before the –ol suffix, separated by hyphens. For example:

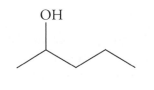

butan-2-ol
(or 2 butanol)
or *sec*-butanol

pentan-2-ol
(or 2-pentanol)

Priorities are assigned (the way the main carbon chain is numbered) to give the lowest number to the hydroxyl group. For example:

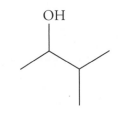

3-methylbutan-2-ol
not
2-methylbutan-3-ol

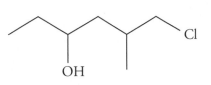

6-chloro-5-methylhexan-3-ol

Example 2-6: Name each of the following molecules:

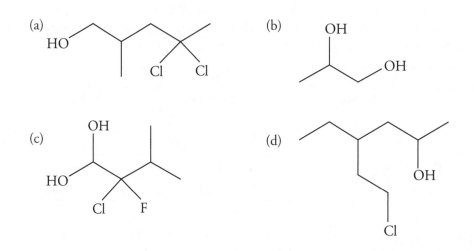

(a)

(b)

(c)

(d)

Solution:

(a) 4,4-dichloro-2-methylpentanol (the "-1-" is assumed if no number is given)
(b) propan-1,2-diol (or 1,2-propandiol)
(c) 2-chloro-2-fluoro-3-methylbutan-1,1-diol
(d) 6-chloro-4-ethylhexan-2-ol

Other organic functional groups have small nuances to their nomenclature, but this introduction to nomenclature should allow you to interpret chemical names on the MCAT.

Chapter 3
Structure and Bonding

3.1 BONDING IN ORGANIC MOLECULES

The chemistry of organic molecules is dominated by the reactivity of covalent bonds. An understanding of the fundamentals of covalent bonding can provide the intuitive grasp necessary to answer a wide range of questions in organic chemistry. This chapter will briefly outline the basic principles that must be mastered in order to successfully complete organic chemistry passages on the MCAT. These include hybridization, sigma (σ) bonding, pi (π) bonding, structural formulas, electron delocalization, resonance stabilization, bond length, bond energy, isomerism, chirality, and optical activity.

Hybridization

In order to rationalize observed chemical and structural trends, chemists developed the concept of orbital hybridization. In this model, one imagines a mathematical combination of atomic orbitals centered on the same atom to produce a set of composite, **hybrid** orbitals. For example, consider an s and a p orbital on an atom.

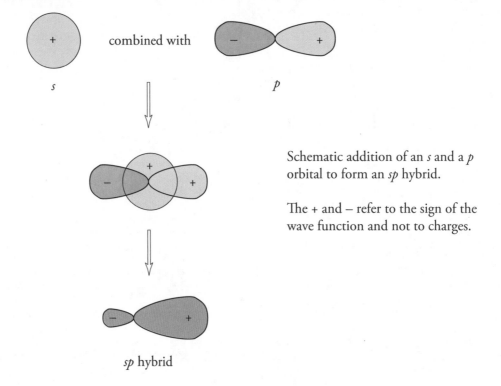

Schematic addition of an s and a p orbital to form an sp hybrid.

The + and − refer to the sign of the wave function and not to charges.

Notice that the new orbital is highly directional; this allows for better overlap when bonding.

There will be two such sp hybrid orbitals formed because two orbitals (the s and the p) were originally combined; that is, the total number of orbitals is conserved in the formation of hybrid orbitals. For this reason, the number of hybrid orbitals on a given atom of hybridization sp^x is $1 + x$ (1 for the s, x for the p's), where x may be either 1, 2, or 3.

The percentages of the *s* character and *p* character in a given *sp^x* hybrid orbital are listed below:

sp^x hybrid orbital	*s* character	*p* character
sp	50%	50%
sp^2	33%	67%
sp^3	25%	75%

To determine the hybridization for most atoms in simple organic molecules, add the number of attached atoms to the number of non-bonding electron pairs (non-delocalized) and use the brief table below (which also gives the ideal bond angles and molecular geometry). The number of attached atoms plus the number of lone pairs is equal to the number of orbitals combined to make the new hybridized orbitals.

# of attached atoms + # of lone pairs	Hybridization	Bond Angles [ideal]	Molecular Geometry
2	*sp*	180°	linear
3	*sp^2*	120°	trigonal planar
4	*sp^3*	109.5°	tetrahedral

sp hybridization:

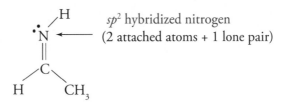

sp^2 hybridization:

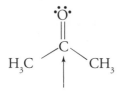

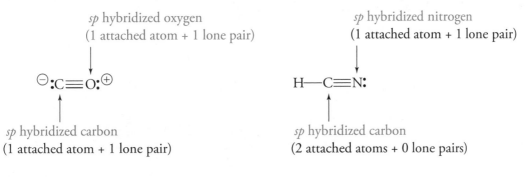

sp³ hybridization:

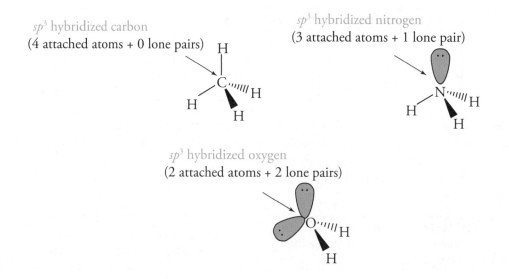

sp³ hybridized carbon
(4 attached atoms + 0 lone pairs)

sp³ hybridized nitrogen
(3 attached atoms + 1 lone pair)

sp³ hybridized oxygen
(2 attached atoms + 2 lone pairs)

Sigma (σ) Bonds

A **σ bond** consists of two electrons that are localized between two nuclei. It is formed by the end-to-end overlap of one hybridized orbital (or an *s* orbital in the case of hydrogen) from each of the two atoms participating in the bond. Below, we show the σ bonds in ethane, C_2H_6:

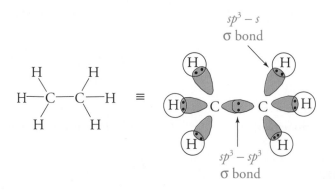

$sp^3 - s$
σ bond

$sp^3 - sp^3$
σ bond

Remember that an *sp³* carbon atom has 4 *sp³* hybrid orbitals, which are derived from one *s* orbital and three *p* orbitals.

Example 3-1: Label the hybridization of the orbitals comprising the σ bonds in the molecules shown below:

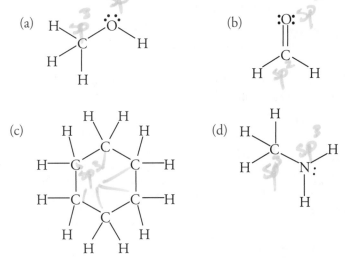

(a)

(b)

(c)

(d)

Solution:

(a) Bonds to H are sp^3-s σ bonds. The C—O bond is an sp^3-sp^3 σ bond.
(b) The bonds to H are sp^2-s σ bonds. The C=O bond contains an sp^2-sp^2 σ bond. (It's also composed of a π bond, which we'll discuss in the next section.)
(c) All C—C bonds are sp^3-sp^3 σ bonds, while all C—H bonds are sp^3-s σ bonds.
(d) All bonds to H are sp^3-s σ bonds. The C—N bond is an sp^3-sp^3 σ bond.

Pi (π) Bonds

A π **bond** is composed of two electrons that are localized to the region that lies on opposite sides of the plane formed by the two bonded nuclei and immediately adjacent atoms, not directly between the two nuclei as with a σ bond. A π bond is formed by the proper, parallel, side-to-side alignment of two unhybridized p orbitals on adjacent atoms. (An sp^2 hybridized atom has three sp^2 orbitals—which come from one s and two p orbitals—plus one p orbital that remains unhybridized.) Below, we show the π bonds in ethene, C_2H_4:

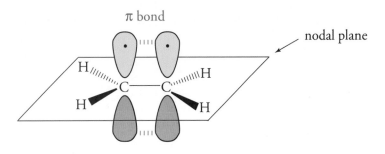

In any multiple bond, *there is only one* σ *bond; the remainder are* π *bonds*. Therefore:

a single bond: composed of 1 σ bond
a double bond: composed of 1 σ bond and 1 π bond
a triple bond: composed of 1 σ bond and 2 π bonds

Example 3-2: Count the number of σ bonds and π bonds in each of the following molecules. (Don't forget to count all of the C–H σ bonds!)

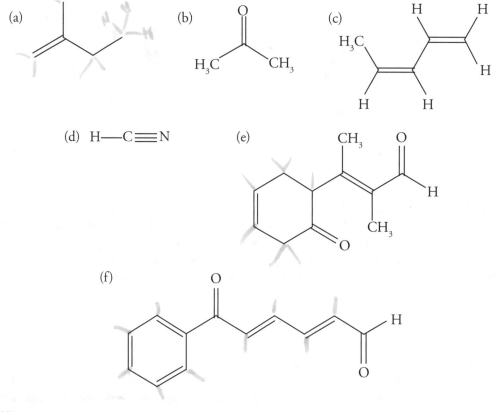

(d) H—C≡N

Solution:

(a)   14 σ, 1 π
(b)   9 σ, 1 π
(c)   12 σ, 2 π
(d)   2 σ, 2 π
(e)   27 σ, 4 π
(f)   24 σ, 7 π

3.2 STRUCTURAL FORMULAS

By definition, an organic molecule is said to be **saturated** if it contains no π bonds and no rings; it is **unsaturated** if it has at least one π bond or a ring. A saturated compound with n carbon atoms has exactly $2n + 2$ hydrogen atoms, while an unsaturated compound with n carbon atoms has fewer than $2n + 2$ hydrogens.

The formula below is used to determine the **degree of unsaturation** (d) of simple organic molecules:

$$\text{degree of unsaturation} = \frac{(2n+2) - x}{2}$$

n = number of carbons
x = number of hydrogens*

* x represents the number of hydrogens and any monovalent atoms (such as the halogens: F, Cl, Br, or I).
Since the number of oxygens has no effect, it is ignored.
For nitrogen-containing compounds, replace each N by 1 C and 1 H when using this formula.

One degree of unsaturation indicates the presence of one π bond or one ring; two degrees of unsaturation means there are two π bonds (two separate double bonds or one triple bond), or one π bond and one ring, or two rings, and so on. The presence of heteroatoms can also affect the degree of unsaturation in a molecule. This is best illustrated through a series of related molecules that all have one degree of unsaturation.

Butene (C_4H_8) has one degree of unsaturation, since $d = [2(4 + 2) - 8]/2 = 1$, in the form of a double bond:

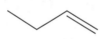

4-Chlorobutene (C_4H_7Cl) also has one degree of unsaturation, but the number of hydrogens is different. Each halogen atom (fluorine, chlorine, bromine, iodine) or other monovalent atom "replaces" one hydrogen atom, so $d = [(2\cdot4 + 2)-(7 + 1)]/2 = 1$:

Methoxyethene (C_3H_6O) also has one degree of unsaturation. Each oxygen (or other divalent atom) "replaces" one carbon and two hydrogen atoms (CH_2 groups are sometimes referred to as methylene groups), so $d = [2(3 + 1) + 2)-(6 + 2)]/2 = 1$. Since a divalent atom can take the place of a methylene group, it doesn't affect the degree of unsaturation, and can be ignored.

Methyl vinyl amine (C_3H_7N) has one degree of unsaturation as well. Each nitrogen (or other trivalent atom) "replaces" one carbon and one hydrogen atom. The formula thus gives $d = [(2(3 + 1) + 2)-(7 + 1)]/2 = 1$:

Example 3-3: Determine the degree of unsaturation of each of these molecules. Which, if any, are saturated?

(a) C_6H_8
(b) C_4H_6O
(c) $C_{20}H_{30}O$
(d) C_3H_8O
(e) C_3H_5Br

Solution:

(a) $d = [(2\cdot6 + 2)-8]/2 = 3$.
(b) Just ignore the O, and find that $d = [(2\cdot4 + 2)-6]/2 = 2$.
(c) Ignoring the O, we get $d = [(2\cdot20 + 2)-30]/2 = 6$.
(d) Ignore the O, and find that $d = [(2\cdot3 + 2)-8]/2 = 0$. *This molecule is saturated.*
(e) Since Br is a halogen, we treat it like a hydrogen, so $d = [(2\cdot3 + 2)-(5 + 1)]/2 = 1$.

3.3 BOND LENGTH AND BOND DISSOCIATION ENERGY

While the term *bond length* makes good intuitive sense (the distance between two nuclei that are bonded to one another), **bond dissociation energy (BDE)** is not quite as intuitive. Bond dissociation energy is the energy required to break a bond *homolytically*. In **homolytic bond cleavage**, one electron of the bond being broken goes to each fragment of the molecule. In this process two radicals form. This is *not* the same thing as **heterolytic bond cleavage** (also known as *dissociation*). In heterolytic bond cleavage, both electrons of the electron pair that make up the bond end up on the same atom; this forms both a cation and an anion.

$$(H_3C)_3C \longrightarrow H \longrightarrow C(CH_3)_3{}^\bullet + H^\bullet$$

homolytic bond cleavage

$$(H_3C)_3C \longrightarrow Cl \longrightarrow C(CH_3)_3{}^{\oplus} + Cl^{\ominus}$$

heterolytic bond cleavage

These two processes are very different and hence have very different energies associated with them. Here, we will only consider homolytic bond dissociation energies.

When one examines the relationship between bond length and bond dissociation energy for a series of similar bonds, an important trend emerges: For similar bonds, *the higher the bond order, the shorter and stronger the bond*. The following table, which lists the bond dissociation energies (BDE, in kcal/mol) and the bond lengths (r, in angstroms, where 1 Å = 10^{-10} m) for carbon-carbon and carbon-oxygen bonds, illustrates this trend:

	C—C	C=C	C≡C	C—O	C=O	C≡O
BDE	83	144	200	86	191	256
r (in Å)	1.54	1.34	1.20	1.43	1.20	1.13

An important caveat arises because of the varying atomic radii: *bond length/BDE comparisons should only be made for <u>similar bonds</u>.* Thus, carbon-carbon bonds should be compared only to other carbon-carbon bonds; carbon-oxygen bonds should be compared only to other carbon-oxygen bonds, and so on.

Recall the shapes of unhybridized atomic orbitals: *s* orbitals are spherical about the atomic nucleus, while *p* orbitals are elongated "dumbbell"-shaped about the atomic nucleus.

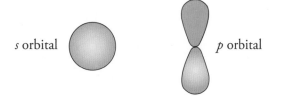

s orbital   *p* orbital

When comparing the same type of bonds, the greater the s character in the component orbitals, the shorter the bond (because *s*-orbitals are closer to the nucleus than *p*-orbitals). A greater percentage of *p* character also leads to a more directional hybrid orbital that is farther from the nucleus and thus a longer bond. In addition, when comparing the same types of bonds, *the longer the bond, the weaker it is; the shorter the bond, the stronger it is.* In the following diagram, compare all the C–C bonds and all the C–H bonds:

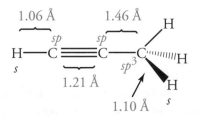

Bond	Bond length	Bond	Bond length
C—C (*sp – sp*)	1.21 Å	C–H (*sp – s*)	1.06 Å
C—C (*sp – sp³*)	1.46 Å	C–H (*sp³ – s*)	1.10 Å

3.4 ISOMERISM

3.4

Constitutional Isomerism

Constitutional (or, less precisely, *structural*) **isomers** are compounds that have the same molecular formula but whose atoms are connected together differently. Take pentane (C_5H_{12}), for example. *n*-Pentane is a fully-saturated hydrocarbon that has two additional constitutional isomers:

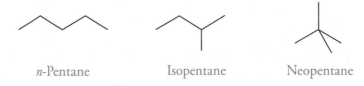

n-Pentane   Isopentane   Neopentane

Example 3-4: Draw (and name) all the constitutional isomers of hexane, C_6H_{14}. (*Hint*: There are five of them altogether.)

Solution:

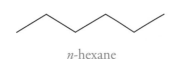
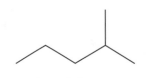
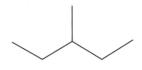

n-hexane   2-methylpentane   3-methylpentane

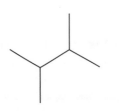

2, 3-dimethylbutane   2, 2-dimethylbutane

Conformational Isomerism

Conformational isomers are compounds that have the same molecular formula and the same atomic connectivity, but which differ from one another by rotation about a (single) σ bond. In truth, they are the exact same molecule. For saturated hydrocarbons there are two orientations of σ bonds attached to adjacent *sp³* hybridized carbons on which we will concentrate. These are the **staggered** conformation and the **eclipsed** conformation. In staggered conformations a σ bond on one carbon bisects the angle formed by two σ bonds on the adjacent carbon. In an eclipsed conformation a σ bond on one carbon directly lines up with a σ bond on an adjacent carbon. Both conformations can be visualized using either the flagged bond notation, or the Newman projection, as shown with ethane (C_2H_6) below.

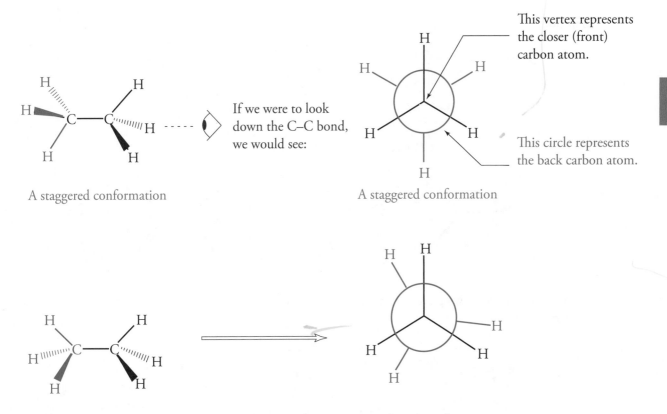

This vertex represents the closer (front) carbon atom.

This circle represents the back carbon atom.

If we were to look down the C–C bond, we would see:

A staggered conformation

A staggered conformation

An eclipsed conformation

An eclipsed conformation

Example 3-5: For (a) and (b), represent the flagged bond notation conformation as a Newman projection. For (c) and (d), represent the Newman projection using flagged bond notation, and be sure to label which bond you are looking down when translating from the Newman projection.

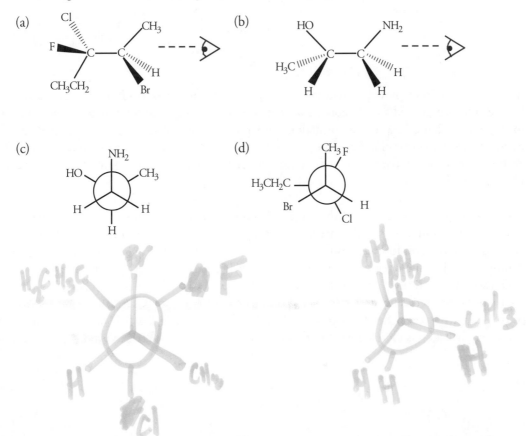

Solution:

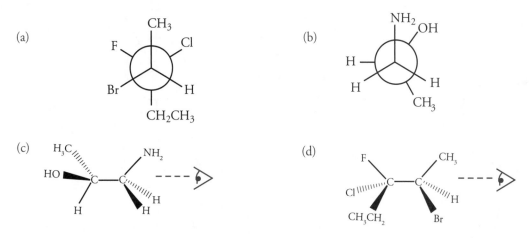

(a)

(b)

(c)

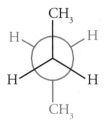

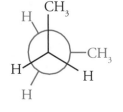

(d)

Using these notations, we turn our attention to the conformational analysis of hydrocarbons as demonstrated for *n*-butane.

staggered conformation

less crowded
more stable

eclipsed conformation

more crowded
electronic repulsion
less stable

The σ bonds should
actually directly
line up with each other.
For clarity here,
they are not
directly aligned.

It's important to note, however, that there are an infinite number of conformations for a molecule that has free rotation around a C–C bond, and that all of these other conformations are energetically related to the staggered and eclipsed conformations on which we will concentrate. For example, relative to the carbon atom in the rear of a Newman projection, the front carbon atom could be rotated *any number of degrees*. Any change in the rotation of one carbon, relative to its adjacent neighbor, is a change in molecular conformation.

What are the relative stabilities of the staggered conformations, the eclipsed conformations, and the infinite number of conformations that are in between them? A staggered conformation is more stable than an eclipsed conformation for two reasons. First, the staggered conformation is more stable than the eclipsed conformation because of electronic repulsion. Covalent bonds repel one another simply because they are composed of (negatively charged) electrons. That being the case, the staggered conformation is more stable than the eclipsed, since in the staggered conformation, the σ bonds are as far apart as possible, while in the eclipsed conformation they are directly aligned with one another. The other major reason the staggered conformation is more stable than the eclipsed conformation is steric hindrance. It is more favorable to have atoms attached to the σ bonds in the roomier staggered conformation where they are 60° apart, rather than the eclipsed conformation where they are directly aligned with one another. There are further aspects to consider in conformational analysis. Not all staggered conformations are of equal energy. Likewise, not all eclipsed conformations are of equal energy. There are particularly stable staggered conformations and particularly unstable eclipsed conformations. The following demonstrates this by examining all staggered and eclipsed conformations for *n*-butane.

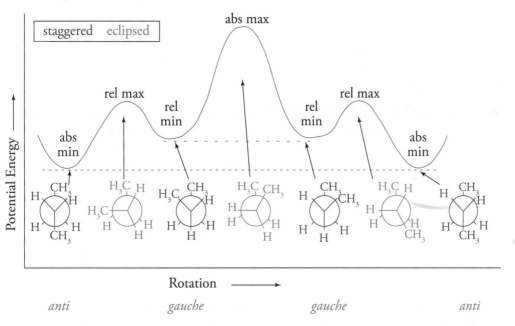

We begin our discussion with the most stable conformation of *n*-butane. This staggered conformation is referred to as the ***anti* conformation** and arises when the two largest groups attached to adjacent carbons are 180° apart. This produces the most sterically favorable, and hence the most energetically favorable (lowest energy) conformation. Now we proceed through a series of 60° rotations around the C2–C3 σ bond until we return to the initial conformation (360°). In our first rotation, we go from the *anti* staggered to an eclipsed conformation and observe the relative energy maximum that results from the alignment of the methyls and hydrogens. Next as we rotate another 60° we fall again into a staggered conformation that resides in a relative energy minimum. Notice that this energy minimum is not as low as the *anti* conformation. In this structure the methyl substituents are closer together than in the *anti* conformation. They are now 60° apart; this is referred to as a ***gauche* conformation.** A *gauche* conformation arises when the two largest groups on adjacent carbon atoms are in a staggered conformation 60° apart. In our next 60° rotation we travel to the absolute maximum on our potential energy diagram. In this eclipsed conformation, the two methyl groups are directly aligned behind one another and are therefore in the most crowded and unfavorable environment. As we continue our rotation, we fall from the absolute energy maximum and go through the corresponding staggered and eclipsed conformations encountered before.

Example 3-6: Draw a Newman projection for the most stable conformation of each of these compounds:

(a)   2,2,5,5-tetramethylhexane (about the C3–C4 bond)
(b)   2,2-dimethylpentane (about the C2–C3 bond)
(c)   1,2-ethanediol

3.4

Solution:

(a)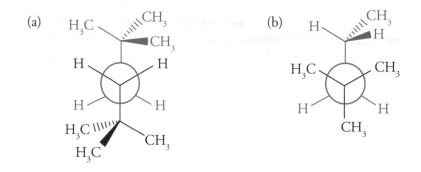

(b)

(c) In this molecule, the *gauche* conformation is more stable than the *anti* conformation, because an intramolecular hydrogen bond can be formed in the *gauche* but not in the *anti* conformation.

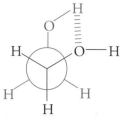

Remember that it's usually the case that the *anti* conformation is the more stable. In general, the two largest groups on adjacent carbon atoms would like to be *anti* to one another since this will minimize steric interactions. However, if the two groups are not too large and can form intramolecular hydrogen bonds with one another, then the *gauche* conformation can be more stable.

Thus far we've limited our discussion of conformational isomers to molecules with unrestricted rotation around σ bonds. Let's now consider the conformational analysis of two very common cycloalkanes, cyclopentane (C_5H_{10}) and cyclohexane (C_6H_{12}).

In cyclopentane, the pentagonal bond angle is 108° (close to normal tetrahedral of 109°), so we might expect cyclopentane to be a planar structure. If all of the carbons of cyclopentane were in a plane, however, all of the carbon-hydrogen σ bonds on adjacent carbons would eclipse each other. In order to compensate for the eclipsed C–H σ bonds, cyclopentane has one carbon out of the plane of the other carbons and so adopts a puckered conformation. This puckering allows the carbon-hydrogen σ bonds on adjacent carbons to be somewhat staggered, and thus reduces the energy of the compound. This puckered form of cyclopentane is referred to as the "envelope" form.

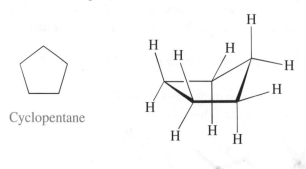

Cyclopentane

If cyclohexane were planar, it would have bond angles of 120°. This would produce considerable strain on sp^3 hybridized carbons as the ideal bond angle should be around 109°. Instead, the most stable conformation of cyclohexane is a very puckered molecule referred to as the **chair form**. In the chair conformation, four of the carbons of the ring are in a plane with one carbon above the plane and one carbon below the plane. There are two chair conformations for cyclohexane, and they easily interconvert at room temperature:

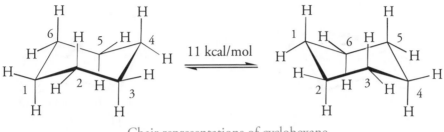

Chair representations of cyclohexane

As one chair conformation flips to the other chair conformation, it must pass through several other less stable conformations including some (referred to as *half-chair* conformations) that reside at energy maxima and one (the *twist boat* conformation) at a local energy minimum (but still of much higher energy than the chair conformations). The boat conformation represents a transition state between twist boat conformations. It is important to remember, however, that all of these conformations are much more unstable than the chair conformations and thus do not play an important role in cyclohexane chemistry.

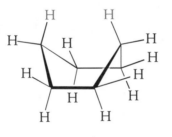

Boat conformation

Notice that there are two distinct types of hydrogens in the chair forms of cyclohexane. Six of the hydrogens lie on the equator of the ring of carbons. These hydrogens are referred to as **equatorial hydrogens**. The other six hydrogens lie above or below the ring of carbons, three above and three below; these are called **axial hydrogens**.

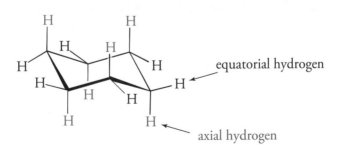

3.4

There is an energy barrier of about 11 kcal/mol between the two equivalent chair conformations of cyclohexane. At room temperature there is sufficient thermal energy to inter-convert the two chair conformations about 10,000 times per second. Note that when a hydrogen (or any substituent group) is axial in one chair conformation, it becomes equatorial when cyclohexane flips to the other chair conformation. The same is also true for an equatorial hydrogen which flips to an axial position when the chair forms inter-convert. This property is demonstrated for deuterocyclohexane:

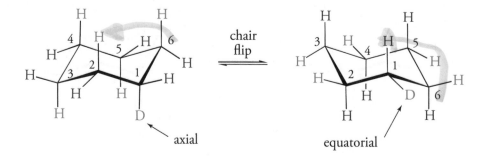

These factors become important when examining substituted cyclohexanes. Let's first consider methylcyclohexane. The methyl group can occupy either an equatorial or axial position:

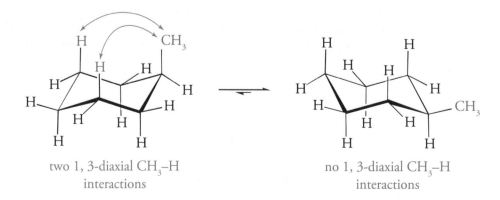

two 1,3-diaxial CH$_3$–H
interactions

no 1,3-diaxial CH$_3$–H
interactions

Is one conformation more stable than the other? *Yes.* It is more favorable for large groups to occupy the equatorial position rather than a crowded axial position. For a methyl group, the equatorial position is more stable by about 1.7 kcal/mol over the axial position. This is because in the axial position, the methyl group is crowded by the other two hydrogens that are also occupying axial positions on the same side of the ring. This is referred to as a **1,3-diaxial interaction**. It is more favorable for methyl to be in an equatorial position where it is pointing out, away from other atoms.

3.4

Example 3-7: In each of the following pairs of substituted cyclohexanes, identify the more stable isomer:

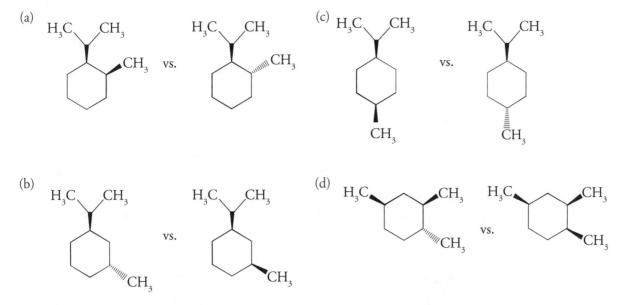

Solution: Draw chair conformations of each isomer and compare them to see which is more stable. As a good rule of thumb, it's best to first put the bulkier (i.e., the larger) substituent in a roomier equatorial position and decide if it's the more stable of the two chair conformations; it usually is. (See figures below and on the following page.)

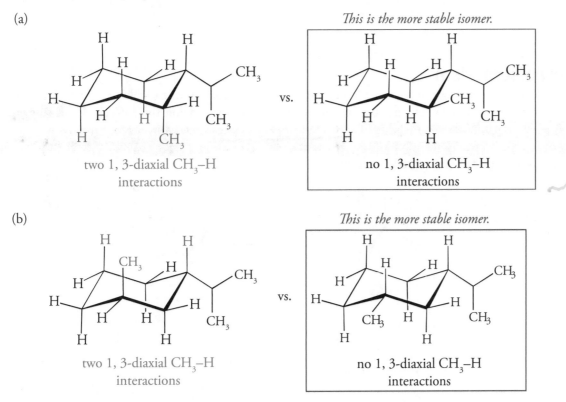

3.4

(c)

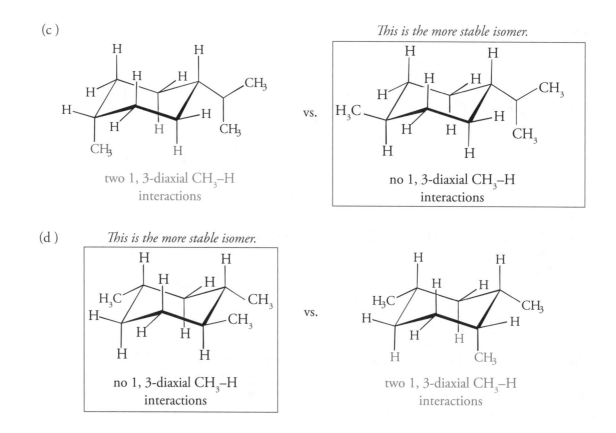

two 1, 3-diaxial CH$_3$–H
interactions

vs.

This is the more stable isomer.

no 1, 3-diaxial CH$_3$–H
interactions

(d)

This is the more stable isomer.

no 1, 3-diaxial CH$_3$–H
interactions

vs.

two 1, 3-diaxial CH$_3$–H
interactions

Stereoisomerism

Stereoisomerism is of major importance in organic chemistry, especially when looking at biological molecules, so several questions relating to stereochemistry routinely appear on the MCAT. **Stereoisomers are molecules that have the same molecular formula and connectivity but which differ from one another only in the spatial arrangement of the atoms. They cannot be interconverted by rotation of σ bonds.** For example, consider the following two molecules:

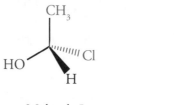

Molecule I

Molecule II

Both molecules have the same molecular formula, C_2H_5ClO, with the same atoms bonded to each other. However, if one superimposes II onto I without any rotation, the result is:

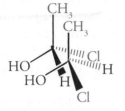

Note that while the –CH_3 and –OH groups superimpose, the –Cl and –H do not. Likewise, if we rotate Molecule II so that the –OH is pointing directly up (12 o'clock) and the –CH_3 is pointing at about 7 o'clock, and then attempt to superimpose II on I, the result is:

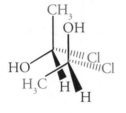

While the –Cl and the –H groups are now superimposed, the –CH_3 and the –OH are not. No matter how one rotates Molecules I and II, two of the substituent groups will be superimposed, while the other two will not. Hence they are indeed different molecules: They are stereoisomers.

Chirality

3.4

Any molecule that cannot be superimposed on its mirror image is said to be **chiral**, while a molecule that *can* be superimposed on its mirror image has a plane of symmetry and is said to be **achiral**. It's important that you be able to identify **chiral centers**. For carbon, a chiral center will have four different groups bonded to it. Note that since a carbon atom has four different groups attached to it, it must be sp^3 hybridized with (approximately) 109° bond angles and tetrahedral geometry. Such a carbon atom is also sometimes referred to as a **stereocenter**, a **stereogenic center**, or an **asymmetric center**.

Example 3-8: Identify all the chiral centers in the following molecules and determine how many possible stereoisomers each compound has by placing a star next to each chiral center. (Note: the number of possible stereoisomers equals 2^n, where n is the number of chiral centers.)

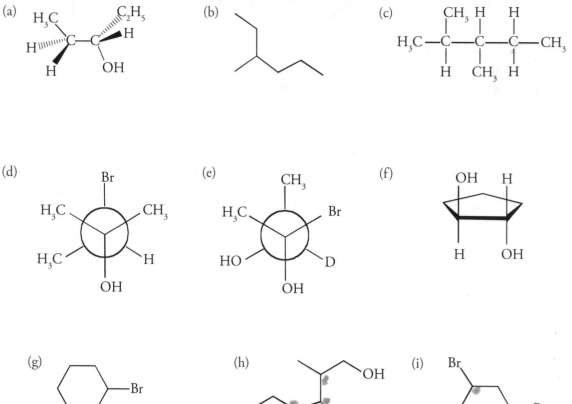

(b)

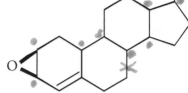

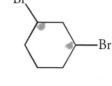

Solution:

(a)   This molecule has no chiral centers.

(b)   This molecule has 1 chiral center and, therefore, 2 possible stereoisomers:

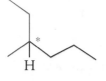

(c)   There is 1 chiral center and, therefore, 2 possible stereoisomers:

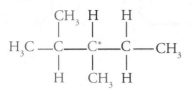

(d)   This molecule has 1 chiral center and, therefore, 2 possible stereoisomers:

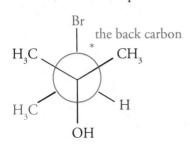

(e)   There are 2 chiral centers and, therefore, 4 possible stereoisomers:

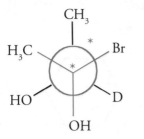

(f)   There are 2 chiral centers, which would seem to indicate 4 possible stereoisomers:

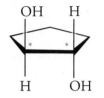

However, there are only 3, because the following "2" molecules are actually the same:

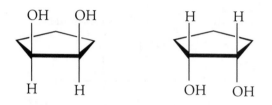

(g)   This molecule has no chiral centers.

(h)   This molecule has 9 chiral centers and, therefore, $2^9 = 512$ possible stereoisomers:

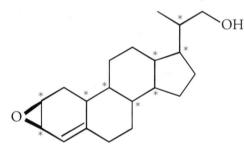

(i)   Although there are two chiral centers,

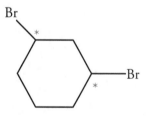

there are 3, not 4 stereoisomers, because—see (f) above—the following "two" molecules are actually the same:

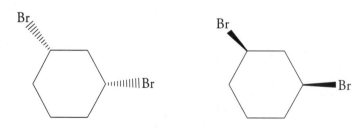

Absolute Stereocenter Configuration

Chiral centers (carbon atoms bearing four different substituents) can be assigned an **absolute configuration**. There is an arbitrary set of rules for assigning absolute configuration to a stereocenter (known as the **Cahn-Ingold-Prelog rules**), which can be illustrated using Molecule A:

Molecule A

1. Priority is assigned to the four different substituents on the chiral center according to increasing atomic number of the atoms directly attached to the chiral center. Going one atom out from the chiral center, bromine has the highest atomic number and is given highest priority, #1; oxygen is next and is therefore #2; carbon is #3, and the hydrogen is the lowest priority group, #4:

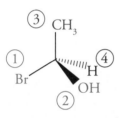

If isotopes are present, then priority among these are assigned on the basis of atomic weight with the higher priority being assigned to the heavier isotope (since they are all of the same atomic number). For example, the isotopes of hydrogen are ^1H, ^2H = D (deuterium), and ^3H = T (tritium), and for the following molecule, we'd assign priorities as shown:

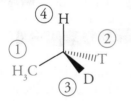

3.4

If two identical atoms are attached to a stereocenter, then the next atoms in both chains are examined until a difference is found. Once again this is done by atomic number. Note the following example:

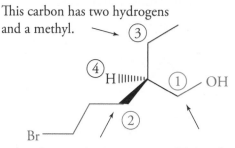

This carbon has two hydrogens and a methyl.

This carbon has two hydrogens followed by a –CH_2CH_2Br.

This carbon has two hydrogens and an –OH.

2. A multiple bond is counted as two single bonds for both of the atoms involved. For example:

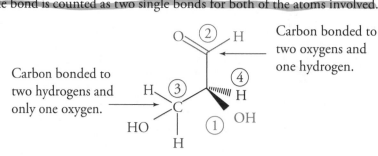

Carbon bonded to two oxygens and one hydrogen.

Carbon bonded to two hydrogens and only one oxygen.

3. Once priorities have been assigned, the molecule is rotated so that the lowest priority group points directly away from the viewer. Then simply trace a path from the highest priority group to the lowest remaining priority group. If the path traveled is *clockwise*, then the absolute configuration is *R* (from the Latin *rectus*, right). Conversely, if the path traveled is *counterclockwise*, then the absolute configuration is *S* (from the Latin *sinister*, left).

Note: The two-dimensional representation (on the left) of the following hypothetical molecule is known as the "Fischer projection," named after famous organic chemist Emil Fischer.

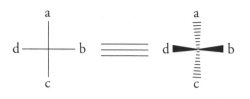

The Fischer projection is a simplification of the actual three-dimensional structure. In the Fischer projection, as shown on the right, vertical lines are assumed to go back into the page, and horizontal lines are assumed to come out of the page.

The Fischer projection will be very important in our discussion of carbohydrates and will be covered extensively in future chapters.

Example 3-9: Assign absolute configurations to the following molecules.

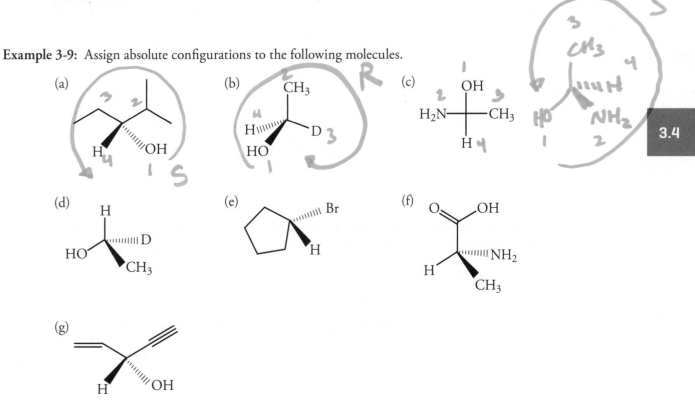

(a)

(b)

(c)

(d)

(e)

(f)

(g)

Solution:

(a) *R.* Either rotate the molecule so the lowest priority group is in the back,

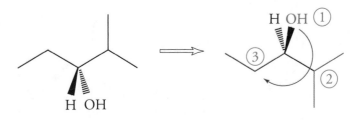

or simply trace it as it stands and invert the configuration (since the lowest priority group is coming toward you):

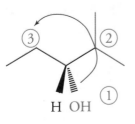

(b)   *R.* The lowest priority group is already pointing away from you and the trace is clockwise.

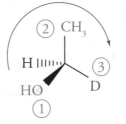

(c)   *S.* Recall Fisher notation for molecules, note that the lowest priority group is pointing away from you, and the trace is counterclockwise.

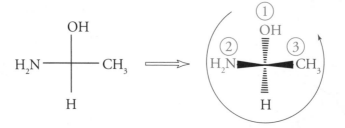

(d)   *R.* The lowest priority group is neither going into nor coming out of the plane of the page. One method is to rotate the molecule so the lowest priority group is in the back and redraw the molecule. Since the path is traveled clockwise, the configuration is *R.*

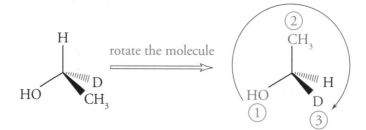

Here's a trick to help in the rotation of molecules. Exchanging two groups on a chiral center necessarily changes the absolute configuration. So in this case, it is perhaps most convenient to exchange any two groups such that the lowest priority group is going into the page:

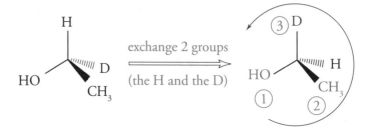

Note that this trace is going counterclockwise. Remember, however, that we exchanged two groups (the hydrogen and the deuterium), which necessarily changes the absolute configuration. Since the counterclockwise trace in the altered molecule means an *S* configuration, the true configuration is *R.*

(e)   Because this molecule is not chiral, we cannot assign it an absolute configuration.

(f)   *S*. Rotate so the lowest priority group is in back,

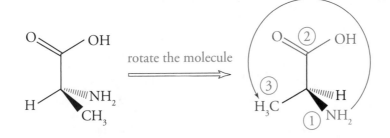

or exchange two groups, –H and –NH₂:

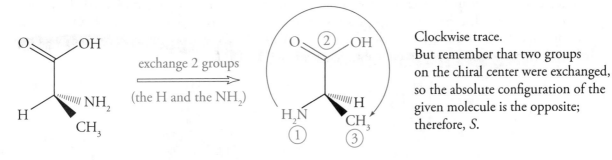

Clockwise trace.
But remember that two groups
on the chiral center were exchanged,
so the absolute configuration of the
given molecule is the opposite;
therefore, *S*.

(g)   *R*. Rotate so the lowest priority group is in the back:

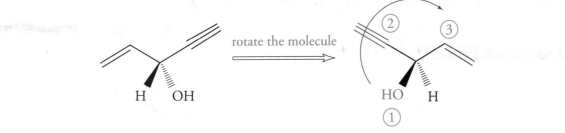

3.4

Enantiomers

It is important to be able to identify chiral centers because, as we have seen, when there are four different groups attached to a centralized carbon, there are two distinct arrangements or configurations possible for these groups in space. Consider the following two molecules:

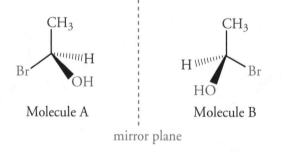

Molecule A has one chiral center with four different groups attached. Notice that Molecule B also has a chiral center and that the four groups attached to it are the same as those in Molecule A. Observe the mirror plane that has been drawn between Molecules A and B. Molecules A and B are mirror images of each other, but they are not superimposable; therefore, they are chiral.

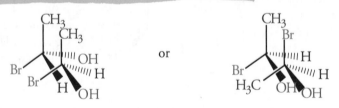

These molecules are **enantiomers**: non-superimposable mirror images.

Enantiomers can occur when chiral centers are present. Note that two molecules that are enantiomers will always have opposite absolute configurations; for example:

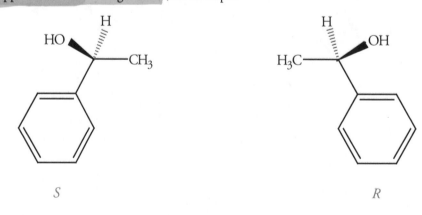

What are the properties of enantiomers? That is, how do they differ from one another? Most chemical properties such as melting point, boiling point, dipole moment, and dielectric constant are the same for both pure enantiomers of an enantiomeric pair. That is, the pure enantiomers shown above will have many identical physical properties.

Optical Activity

One important property that differs between enantiomers is the manner in which they interact with plane-polarized light. A compound that rotates the plane of polarized light is said to be **optically active**. A compound that rotates plane-polarized light clockwise is said to be **dextrorotatory** (*d*), also denoted by (+), while a compound that rotates plane-polarized light in the counterclockwise direction is said to be **levorotatory** (*l*), also denoted by (−). The magnitude of rotation of plane-polarized light for any compound is called its **specific rotation**. This property is dependent on the structure of the molecule, the concentration of the sample, and the path length through which the light must travel.

A pair of enantiomers will rotate plane-polarized light with equal magnitude, but in opposite directions. For example, pure (+)-2-bromobutanoic acid has a specific rotation of +39.5°, while (−)-2-bromobutanoic acid has a specific rotation of −39.5°.

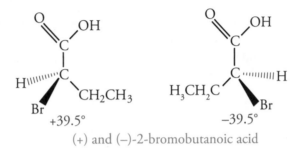

(+) and (−)-2-bromobutanoic acid

What do you think the specific rotation of an equimolar mixture of the two enantiomers above will be? Since one enantiomer will rotate plane-polarized light in one direction, while the other enantiomer will rotate light by the same magnitude in the opposite direction, the specific rotation of a 50/50 mixture of enantiomers —a **racemic mixture**—is 0°. Therefore, a racemic mixture of enantiomers, also known as a *racemate*, is not optically active.

Example 3-10: What is the specific rotation of the *R* enantiomer of 2-bromobutanoic acid? Of the *S* enantiomer?

Solution:

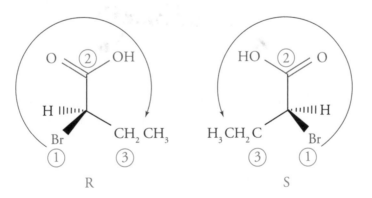

The magnitude of rotation cannot be predicted; it must be experimentally determined. It just so happens in this case that the *R* enantiomer has the (+) rotation [while the *S* enantiomer has the (−) rotation.] But be careful: *This is only coincidental. (+) and (−) say nothing about whether the absolute configuration is R or S.* There is no correlation between the sign of rotation and the absolute configuration.

3.4

Diastereomers

In the preceding discussions on stereoisomerism we have focused on molecules that have only one chiral center. What about molecules with multiple stereocenters? Remember that the number of possible stereoisomers is 2^n, where n is the number of chiral centers. If there is one chiral center, then there are two possible stereoisomers: the enantiomeric pair R and S. Two chiral centers means there are four possible stereoisomers. Consider the following molecule (3-bromobutan-2-ol), for example:

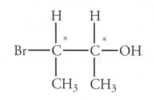

Each of the two chiral centers in 3-bromobutan-2-ol can have either R or S absolute configuration. This leads to four possible combinations of absolute configurations at the chiral centers. Both carbons could be of the S configuration or both could be of the R configuration; or, the left carbon could be R and the right carbon S, or vice versa. Here are the four possible combinations:

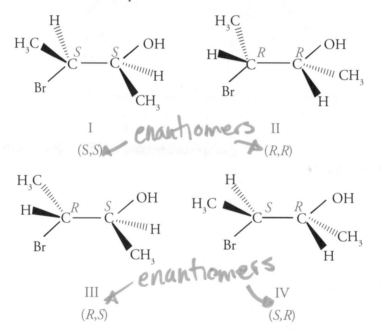

What's the relationship between Molecules I and II? Each of the two chiral centers in Molecule I is of the opposite configuration of Molecule II: S, S vs. R, R. Note that they are non-superimposable mirror images:

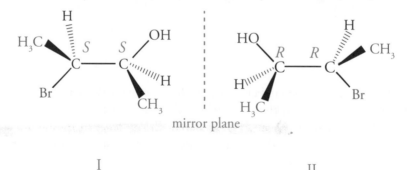

Therefore, these molecules are enantiomers. What about Molecules III and IV? Once again, each of the two chiral centers in Molecule III is of the opposite configuration of those in Molecule IV. This makes Molecules III and IV an enantiomer pair, just as we noted for Molecules I and II above. Is there a relationship between Molecules I and III?

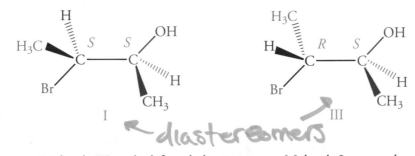

By mentally moving Molecule III to the left and aligning it over Molecule I, we see that the right chiral centers of both molecules are directly superimposable (S superimposes onto S). Also note that no matter what we do, we cannot get the left chiral centers of Molecules I and III to superimpose (S does not superimpose onto R).

Molecules I and III are diastereomers. **Diastereomers** are stereoisomers that are not enantiomers. That is, diastereomers are stereoisomers that are non-superimposable, non-mirror images. The same is true for Molecules I and IV. One of the chiral centers is of the same absolute configuration, while the other chiral center is of the opposite configuration:

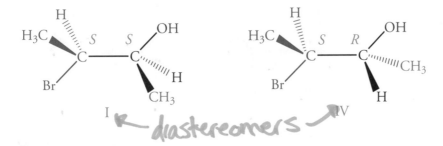

The figure below summarizes all possible stereochemical relationships between isomers containing two stereocenters. Inverting at least one, but not all, of the chiral centers within a molecule will form a diastereomer of that molecule. Enantiomers can be formed by inverting every stereocenter within the molecule.

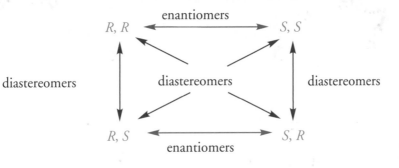

Example 3-11: For each pair of molecules below, state the relationship between them.

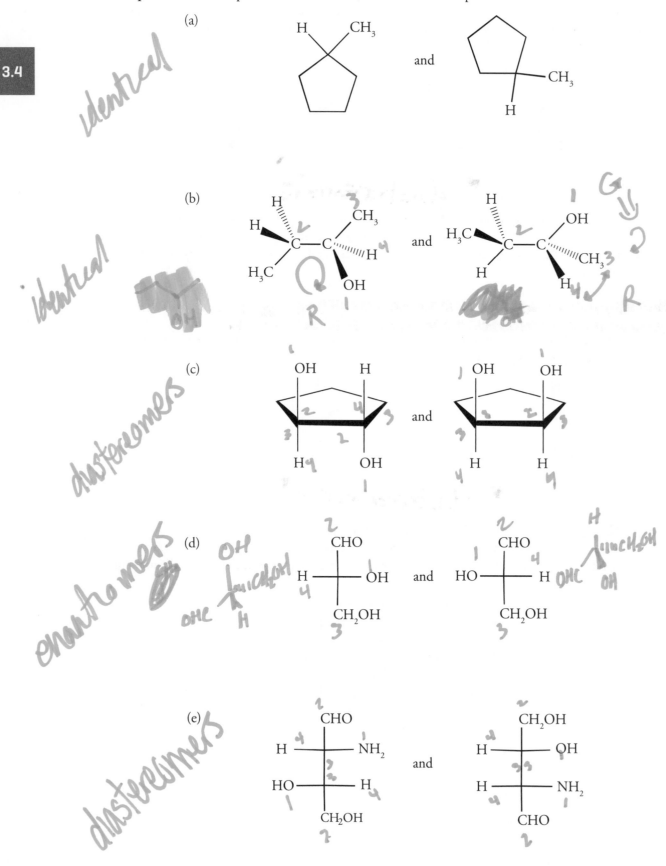

(a) *identical*

(b) *identical*

(c) *diastereomers*

(d) *enantiomers*

(e) *diastereomers*

Solution:

(a) The molecules are superimposable and therefore *identical*.

(b) The molecules are *identical*. (The left carbon is not a chiral center.)

(c) *Diastereomers*.

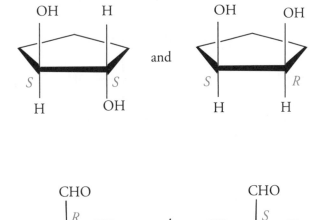

(d) *Enantiomers*.

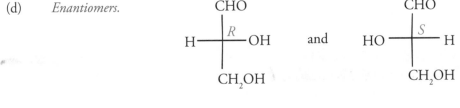

(e) *Diastereomers*.

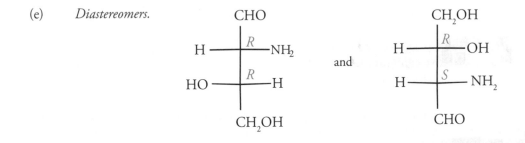

While the structures of diastereomers are similar, their physical and chemical properties can vary dramatically. They can have different melting points, boiling points, solubilities, dipole moments, specific rotations, etc. Most importantly for the MCAT, the specific rotation of diastereomers is also different, but *there is no relationship between the specific rotations of diastereomers as there is for enantiomers.* There is no way to predict the specific rotation of one diastereomer if you know the degree of rotation of another.

Epimers

Epimers are a subclass of diastereomers that differ in their absolute configuration at a single chiral center (only *one* stereocenter is inverted). To illustrate epimeric relationships, let's look at the Fischer projections of some sugars (see Chapter 8):

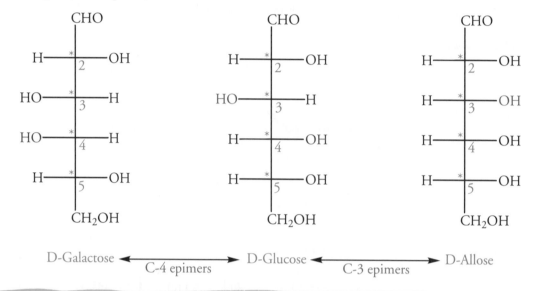

The prefix D on the name of these molecules refers to the orientation of the hydroxyl group (–OH) on the highest-numbered chiral center in a Fischer projection (C-5 in these cases). When the hydroxyl group is on the *right* of this carbon in the Fischer projection, the molecule is a D sugar. (When the hydroxyl group is on the *left*, the molecule is an L sugar.)

You must understand that D and L, like *R* and *S*, are entirely unrelated to optical activity, (+) or (–). Distinctions between D and L (or between *R* and *S*) can be made just by looking at a drawing of the molecule, but distinctions between (+) and (–) can be made only by running experiments in a polarimeter.

- *R* or *S* = absolute configuration (structure)
- D or L = relative configuration (structure)
- (+) or (–) = observed optical rotation (property)

Concerning the three sugars above, we see that D-glucose and D-galactose differ in stereochemistry at only one chiral center (C-4). Thus, D-glucose and D-galactose are said to be C-4 epimers, and C-4 is called the **epimeric carbon**. Likewise, D-glucose and D-allose differ in structure at a single chiral center (C-3). D-Glucose and D-allose are C-3 epimers, with C-3 being the epimeric carbon.

What about D-galactose and D-allose? What is the relationship between these two molecules? We can see that these two sugars differ at two chiral centers (C-3 and C-4). At least one, but not all, of the stereocenters have been inverted. Therefore they are diastereomers, but *NOT* epimers. Note that all epimers are diastereomers, but not all diastereomers are epimers.

Anomers

Epimers that form as a result of ring closure are known as **anomers**. For the MCAT, anomers will be encountered only with regard to sugar chemistry. To illustrate anomerism, consider D-glucose. Open-chain glucose exists in equilibrium with cyclic glucose, known as *glucopyranose*. Cyclization occurs when the C-5 hydroxyl group attacks the carbonyl (C=O) carbon, C-1. This converts a carbon with three substituents to a carbon with four different substituents. Thus, a new stereocenter is formed (C-1), and it can assume one of two possible forms: with the hydroxyl group *down*, it is α; with the hydroxyl group *up*, it is β. It is the orientation at C-1 that distinguishes the two anomers, and C-1 is known as the **anomeric center** (or **anomeric carbon**).

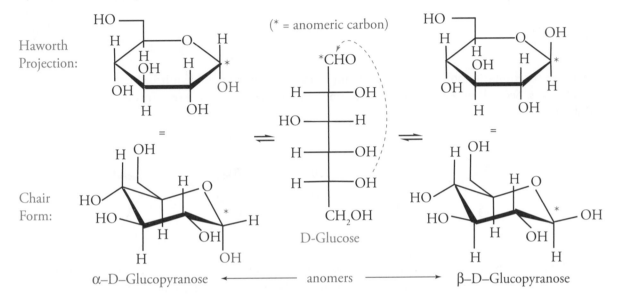

Haworth Projection:

Chair Form:

α–D–Glucopyranose   ←——— anomers ———→   β–D–Glucopyranose

Meso Compounds

Let's look at another molecule with more than one stereocenter. Consider 2,3-butanediol:

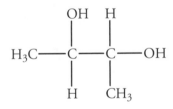

Upon inspection, we determine that there are two chiral centers and therefore four possible stereoisomers. Notice that both chiral centers have the same groups attached to them: –H, –CH₃, –OH, and –CH(OH)CH₃. When the same four groups are attached to two chiral centers, the molecule can have an internnal plane of symmetry. Let's examine this a little more closely. We first consider 2,3-butanediol's *R*, *R* stereoisomer and the *S*, *S* stereoisomer:

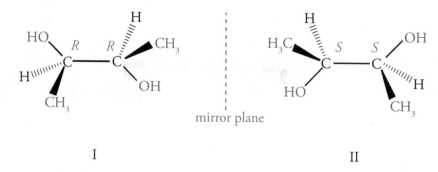

I   II

There are two things to notice here. First, I and II are non-superimposable mirror images and therefore enantiomers. Second, in both I and II there is no internal plane of symmetry. This is demonstrated for Molecule II:

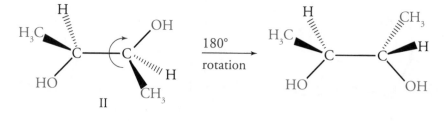

The –OH's line up on the two chiral centers, but the –CH₃'s and –H's do not. The optical rotation of a 50/50 mixture of molecules I and II would measure zero because this is a racemic mixture.

Now look at the *R*, *S* stereoisomer and its mirror image:

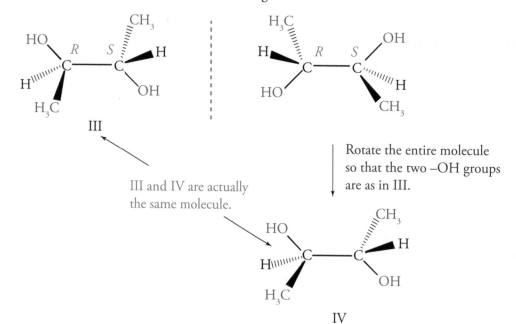

III and IV are actually the same molecule.

Rotate the entire molecule so that the two –OH groups are as in III.

It turns out that Molecules III and IV are directly superimposable and therefore identical. This is because there is an internal plane of symmetry within the molecule.

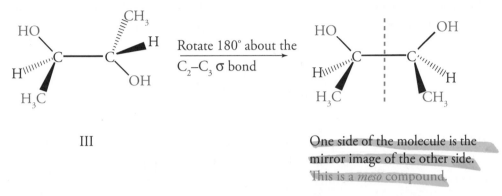

III

One side of the molecule is the mirror image of the other side. This is a *meso* compound.

When there's an internal plane of symmetry in a molecule that contains chiral centers, the compound is called a **meso** compound. Actually then, 2,3-butanediol has only *three* stereoisomers, not four. Molecules I and II are enantiomers, while III and IV are the same molecule. Molecule III (or IV) is an example of a meso compound. Meso compounds have chiral centers but are not optically active because one side of the molecule is a mirror image of the other. In a sense, the optical activity imparted by one side of the molecule is canceled by its other side.

Example 3-12: Which of the following molecules are optically active?

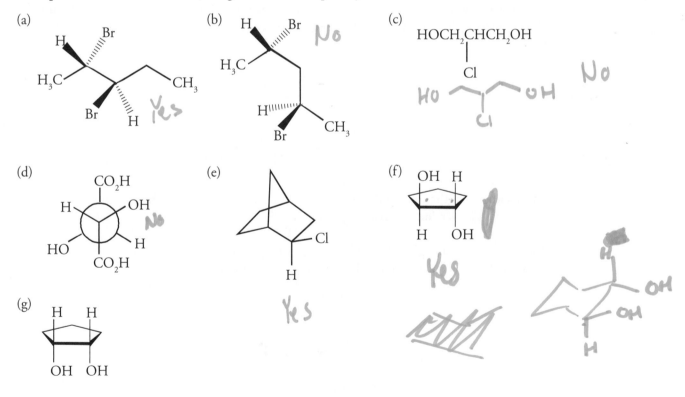

Solution:

(a) This molecule is optically active. It has two chiral centers, but no internal mirror plane. Therefore it is not a meso compound and will rotate plane-polarized light.

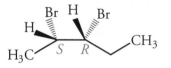

(b) This molecule is a meso compound due to its two chiral centers and internal mirror plane. It will be optically inactive. Be sure to look for rotations around σ bonds in order to find the mirror planes of some molecules.

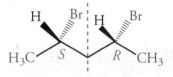

(c) This molecule has no chiral centers, so will have no optical activity.

(d) By rotating around the C-2 to C-3 bond to put the molecule into an eclipsed conformation, you can see that there is an internal mirror plane in the molecule. Since C-2 and C-3 are also chiral centers with four different substituents, this is a meso compound, and will be optically inactive.

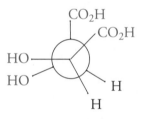

(e) This molecule has three chiral centers (the two bridgehead carbons are chiral), but no plane of symmetry. It is therefore chiral and optically active.

(f) There is no mirror image in this molecule even though it has two chiral centers (they have the same absolute configuration). It will therefore be optically active.

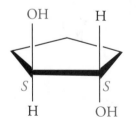

(g) This molecule does have an internal mirror plane, and its two chiral centers have opposite absolute configurations. It is therefore meso, and not optically active.

Geometric Isomers

Geometric isomers are diastereomers that differ in orientation of substituents around a ring or a double bond. Cyclic hydrocarbons and double bonds (alkenes) are constrained by their geometry, meaning they do not rotate freely about all bonds. So, there's a difference between having substituents on the same side of the ring (or double bond) and having substituents on opposite sides. For example, the following are geometric isomers of 1,2-dimethylcyclohexane:

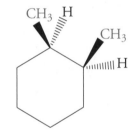

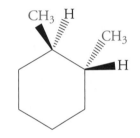

cis-1,2-Dimethylcyclohexane   *trans*-1,2-Dimethylcyclohexane

Priority of substituent groups is assigned the same way as for absolute configuration. On C-1, the methyl group is given higher priority than the H, and the same is true on C-2. The molecule in which the two higher-priority groups are on the same side is termed *cis*, and the molecule in which the two higher-priority groups are on opposite sides of the ring is termed *trans*.

The same-side/opposite-side substituent relativity also occurs with double bonds, but in this case the stereochemistry is officially designated by (Z) or (E). The (Z)/(E) notation is a completely unambiguous way to specify the appropriate stereochemistry at the double bond. In this system, a high and low priority group are assigned at each carbon of the double bond based on atomic number, just as with absolute configuration. If the two high priority groups are on the *same* side, the configuration at the double bond is Z (from the German *zusammen*, meaning *together*). On the other hand, if the two high priority groups are on opposite sides of the double bond, the configuration is referred to as E (from the German *entgegen*, meaning *opposite*). Be aware, that the MCAT may also use the terms *cis* and *trans* when referring to double bonds. However, this is usually reserved for the case when there is one H attached to each carbon of the double bond, as shown below. The geometric isomers of 2-bromo-1-chloropropene and of 1,2-dibromoethene are shown below:

Highest priority
groups (Br and Cl)
on same side, so Z.

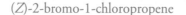

(Z)-2-bromo-1-chloropropene

Highest priority
groups (Br and Cl)
on opposite side,
so E.

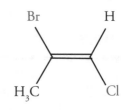

(E)-2-bromo-1-chloropropene

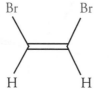

cis-1,2-dibromoethene

trans-1,2-dibromoethene

SUMMARY OF ISOMERS

3.4

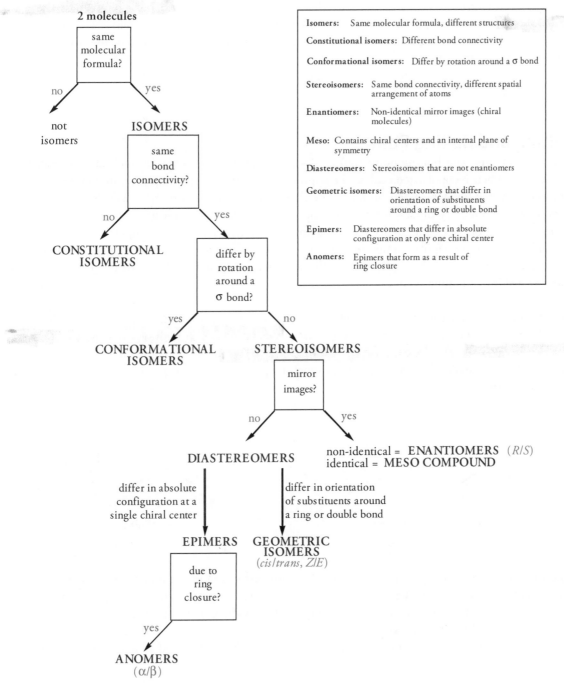

2 molecules

same molecular formula?

no → not isomers

yes → **ISOMERS**

same bond connectivity?

no → **CONSTITUTIONAL ISOMERS**

yes → differ by rotation around a σ bond?

yes → **CONFORMATIONAL ISOMERS**

no → **STEREOISOMERS**

mirror images?

no → **DIASTEREOMERS**

yes → non-identical = **ENANTIOMERS** (*R/S*)
identical = **MESO COMPOUND**

differ in absolute configuration at a single chiral center → **EPIMERS**

differ in orientation of substituents around a ring or double bond → **GEOMETRIC ISOMERS** (*cis/trans, Z/E*)

due to ring closure?

yes → **ANOMERS** (α/β)

Isomers:	Same molecular formula, different structures
Constitutional isomers:	Different bond connectivity
Conformational isomers:	Differ by rotation around a σ bond
Stereoisomers:	Same bond connectivity, different spatial arrangement of atoms
Enantiomers:	Non-identical mirror images (chiral molecules)
Meso:	Contains chiral centers and an internal plane of symmetry
Diastereomers:	Stereoisomers that are not enantiomers
Geometric isomers:	Diastereomers that differ in orientation of substituents around a ring or double bond
Epimers:	Diastereomers that differ in absolute configuration at only one chiral center
Anomers:	Epimers that form as a result of ring closure

3.5 PHYSICAL PROPERTIES OF HYDROCARBONS

The physical properties of organic molecules that you need to know are melting point, boiling point, and solubility. For melting point and boiling point, consider the interactions between identical molecules. For solubility, we'll consider interactions between the solute (the dissolved substance) and the solvent (the dissolving liquid).

Melting and Boiling Points

Melting point (mp) and boiling point (bp) are indicators of how well identical molecules interact with (attract) each other. Nonpolar molecules, like hydrocarbons, interact principally because of an attractive force known as the London dispersion force, one of the intermolecular (van der Waals) forces. This force exists between temporary dipoles formed in nonpolar molecules as a result of a temporary asymmetric electron distribution. Such intermolecular forces must be overcome to melt a nonpolar compound (solid → liquid) or to boil a nonpolar compound (liquid → gas). The greater the attractive forces between molecules, the more energy will be required to get the compound to melt or boil. The weaker these forces, the lower the melting or boiling point.

Many factors determine the degree to which molecules of a given compound will interact. For hydrocarbons, the most significant of these factors is *branching*. Branching tends to inhibit van der Waals forces by reducing the surface area available for intermolecular interaction. Thus, branching tends to reduce attractive forces between molecules and to lower both melting point and boiling point. Consider the following two constitutional isomers:

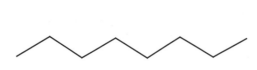

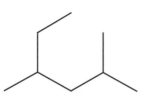

Molecule I	Molecule II
n-octane	2,4-dimethylhexane

Molecule I, *n*-octane, is unbranched. Molecule II, 2,4-dimethylhexane, is a branched isomer of *n*-octane. Although each compound has the same molecular formula, C_8H_{18}, these two constitutional isomers have dramatically different melting points and boiling points. *n*-Octane requires much more energy to melt or boil, because unbranched, it experiences greater van der Waals forces than does the branched isomer 2,4-dimethylhexane. Therefore, *n*-octane has both a higher melting point and a higher boiling point than does 2,4-dimethylhexane.

The second factor influencing melting point and boiling point for hydrocarbons is molecular weight. The greater the molecular weight of a compound, the more surface area there is to interact, the greater the number of van der Waals interactions, and the higher the melting point and boiling point. Therefore, hexane—a six-carbon alkane—has a higher mp and bp than propane, a three-carbon alkane.

The influence of molecular weight on melting point and boiling point is readily seen when considering the following trends for hydrocarbons:

- Small hydrocarbons (1 to 3 carbons) tend to be gases at room temperature.
- Intermediate hydrocarbons (4 to 16 carbons) tend to be liquids at room temperature.
- Large hydrocarbons (more than 16 carbons) tend to be (waxy) solids at room temperature.

Melting Point / Boiling Point Rules:
1. Increasing branching decreases mp and bp
2. Increasing molecular weight increases mp and bp

Example 3-13: Rank the following six hydrocarbons in order of increasing boiling point:

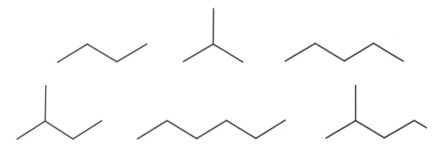

Solution: Since branching lowers the boiling point, each of the branched hydrocarbons has a lower boiling point than the unbranched hydrocarbon of the same molecular formula. Also, the larger the molecule, the greater the surface area over which van der Waals forces can act, so heavier molecules have higher boiling points. We can now put the whole sequence in order of increasing bp:

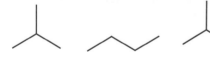

Increasing Boiling Point

Example 3-14: Rank the following three compounds in order of increasing boiling point:

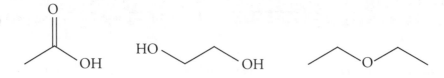

3.5

Solution: Hydrogen bonding is another intermolecular force that can affect melting and boiling points. (Remember that hydrogen bonding occurs between a hydrogen-bond *donor*—a hydrogen attached to a nitrogen, oxygen, or fluorine atom, and a hydrogen-bond *acceptor*—a lone pair of electrons on a nitrogen, oxygen, or fluorine in another molecule.) The more hydrogen-bond donors and hydrogen-bond acceptors there are in a molecule, the higher the boiling and melting points will be. This is because the hydrogen bonds, like dispersion forces, act to *hold* the molecules together, resisting the change to becoming either a liquid or a gas. The first molecule, acetic acid ($C_2H_4O_2$), has one hydrogen-bond donor and four hydrogen-bond acceptors. The second molecule, 1,2-ethanediol ($C_2H_6O_2$), has two hydrogen-bond donors and four hydrogen-bond acceptors. The third molecule, diethyl ether ($C_4H_{10}O$), has two hydrogen-bond acceptors, but no hydrogen bond donors. From this we can now correctly assign the order of their boiling points:

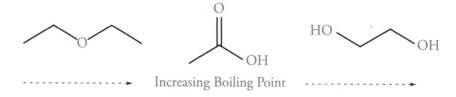

Increasing Boiling Point

Solubility

Solubility depends on two things: the polarity of the solute and the polarity of the solvent. When it comes to solubility, *like dissolves like*. Polar molecules are soluble in polar solvents, and nonpolar molecules are soluble in nonpolar solvents. Hydrocarbons have either zero or a very small dipole moment. Water, on the other hand, is a polar molecule. Since hydrocarbons are generally nonpolar molecules, they aren't very soluble in water.

3.6 THE ORGANIC CHEMIST'S TOOLBOX

In the following chapters, we will frequently discuss several fundamental principles necessary to understand the reactivity of organic molecules. These "tools" are collected here.

Reaction Intermediates

Most organic reactions proceed through one of the following three types of intermediate species:

1. carbocations (carbonium ions),
2. alkyl radicals,
3. carbanions.

Carbocations, or **carbonium ions**, are positively charged species with a full positive charge on carbon. The reactivity of these species is determined by what type of carbon bears the positive charge. On the MCAT, carbocations will always be sp^2 hybridized with an empty p orbital.

Alkyl radicals are reaction intermediates that contain one unpaired electron. The reactivity of these species is determined by what type of carbon bears the lone radical electron. Even though these species are not positively charged, they are electron deficient, like carbocations. Consequently, the reactivity trends for alkyl radicals are the same as those for carbocations. Alkyl radicals on the MCAT will be sp^2 hybridized with the unpaired electron in an unhybridized p orbital.

Carbanions are negatively charged species with a full negative charge localized on carbon. The reactivity of these species is determined by what type of carbon bears the negative charge. On the MCAT, carbanions may be sp^2 hybridized with the lone pair in an unhybridized p orbital, or they may be sp^3 hybridized with the lone pair in an sp^3-hybridized orbital.

Stability Continuum				
Carbocations	3°	2°	1°	methyl
Alkyl Radicals	3°	2°	1°	methyl
Carbanions	methyl	1°	2°	3°
	more stable	→		less stable
	less reactive	→		more reactive
	lower energy	→		higher energy

It's essential to understand the stabilities of reaction intermediates, because generally the major product of a reaction is derived from the most stable intermediate. Organic intermediates are stabilized in two major ways: **Inductive effects** stabilize charge through σ bonds, while **resonance effects** stabilize charge by delocalization through π bonds.

Inductive Effects

All substituent groups surrounding a reaction intermediate can be thought of as electron-withdrawing groups or electron-donating groups. **Electron-withdrawing** groups pull electrons toward themselves through σ bonds. **Electron-donating** groups donate (push) electron density away from themselves through σ bonds. Groups *more* electronegative than carbon tend to withdraw, while groups *less* electronegative than carbon tend to donate. On the MCAT, alkyl substituents are always electron-donating groups.

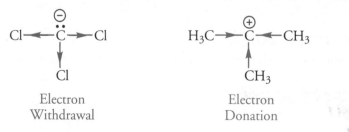

Electron
Withdrawal

Electron
Donation

Electron-donating groups tend to stabilize electron-deficient intermediates (carbocations and radicals), while electron-withdrawing groups tend to stabilize electron-rich intermediates (carbanions). The stabilization of reaction intermediates by the sharing of electrons through σ bonds is called the **inductive effect**.

Example 3-15: Inductive effects frequently alter the reactivity of molecules. Justify the fact that trichloroacetic acid (pK_a = 0.6) is a stronger acid than acetic acid (pK_a = 4.8).

Solution: The chlorine atoms in trichloroacetic acid are electron withdrawing. This decreases the amount of electron density elsewhere in the molecule, especially in the O–H bond. With less electron density, the O–H bond is weaker, making it more acidic than the O–H bond in acetic acid.

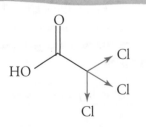

An alternative explanation would be to consider the stability of the conjugate bases of these acids.

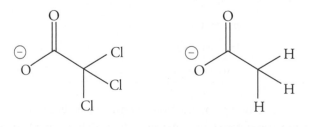

The chlorine atoms in trichloroacetate anion distribute the negative charge better, making it more stable than the acetate anion. Remember from general chemistry that the stronger the acid, the weaker (the more stable) the conjugate base. Therefore, because trichloroacetate anion is a weaker base (is more stable) than acetate anion, trichloroacetic acid is a stronger acid than acetic acid.

Resonance Stabilization

While induction works through σ bonds, resonance stabilization occurs in conjugated π systems. A conjugated system is one containing three or more atoms that each bear a p orbital. These orbitals are aligned so they are all parallel, creating the possibility of delocalized electrons.

Electrons that are confined to one orbital, either a bonding orbital between two atoms or a lone-pair orbital, are said to be **localized**. When electrons are allowed to interact with orbitals on adjacent atoms, they are no longer confined to their original "space," and so are termed **delocalized**. Consider the allyl cation:

The electrons in the π bond can interact with the empty p orbital on the carbon bearing the positive charge. This is illustrated by the following resonance structures:

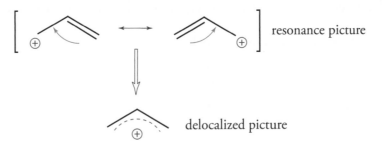

resonance picture

delocalized picture

The electron density is spread out—delocalized—over the entire 3-carbon framework in order to stabilize the carbocation. So, we might say of the allyl cation that both the electrons and the positive charge are delocalized.

As the allyl cation demonstrates, it often happens that a single Lewis structure for a molecule is not sufficient to most accurately represent the molecule's true structure. It is important to remember that resonance structures are just multiple representations of the actual structure. The molecule does not become one resonance structure or another; it exists as a combination of all resonance structures, although all may not contribute equally. All resonance structures must be drawn to give an accurate picture of the real nature of the molecule. In the case of the allyl cation, the two structures are identical and will have equivalent energy. They will also contribute equally to the delocalized picture of what the molecule really looks like. This average of all resonance contributors is called the **resonance hybrid**.

Benzene (C_6H_6) is another common molecule that exhibits resonance. Looking at a Lewis representation of benzene might lead one to believe that there are two distinct types of carbon-carbon bonds: single σ bonds (this structure of benzene has three such bonds) and double bonds (of which there are also three):

benzene

3.6

Thus one might expect two distinct carbon-carbon bond lengths: one for the single bonds, and one for the double bonds. Yet experimental data clearly demonstrate that all the C–C bond lengths are identical in benzene. All the carbons of benzene are sp^2 hybridized, so they each have an unhybridized p orbital. Two structures can be drawn for benzene, which differ only in the location of the π bonds. The true structure of benzene is best pictured as a resonance hybrid of these structures. Perhaps a better representation of benzene shows both resonance contributors, like this:

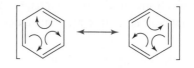

Notice that these resonance structures differ only in the arrangement of their π electrons, not in the locations of the atoms. All six unhybridized p orbitals are aligned parallel with one another. This alignment of adjacent unhybridized p orbitals allows for delocalization of π electrons over the entire ring. Whenever we have a delocalized π system (aligned p orbitals), resonance structures can be drawn.

Delocalization of electrons is also observed in thiophene:

Here the sulfur atom has two pairs of non-bonding electrons. Notice that these electrons are one atom away from two π bonds. One pair of these electrons is actually in an unhybridized p orbital, such that it can be delocalized into the cyclic π system. Here are the representative resonance structures:

The other pair of electrons, however, is in a hybrid orbital and cannot delocalize into the π system. Here the delocalization of sulfur's electrons imparts aromatic stability to the molecule (see Section 5.2). The hybridization of the sulfur is therefore most correctly represented as sp^2.

Let's consider one more example:

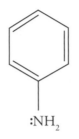

The nitrogen in aniline has an unshared electron pair that is one atom removed from a cyclic π system. Again these electrons can be delocalized by overlap of the lone pair-containing orbital with the p orbitals of the benzene ring. This can be demonstrated by the following resonance structures:

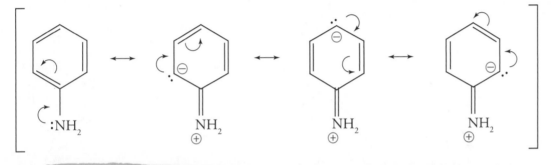

In this case, the delocalization of the nitrogen's electrons disrupts the aromaticity of the benzene ring and is therefore less favorable. Experimental determination of the nitrogen's bond angles reveals that they are actually intermediate between 120° and 109°, so the hybridization of the nitrogen can best be described not as sp^2 or sp^3, but as something intermediate between them. The important point, however, is that the electrons are at least somewhat delocalized into the π system. Therefore, the nitrogen's hybridization is not strictly sp^3.

Example 3-16: For the following molecules, indicate the hybridization and idealized bond angles for the indicated atoms.

(a)

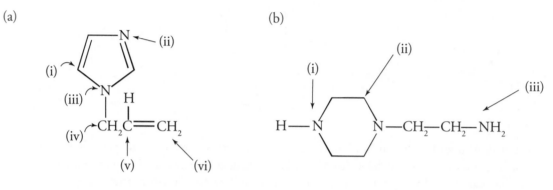

(b)

(c)

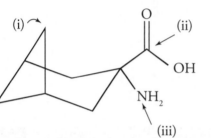

(d)

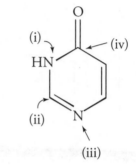

(e)

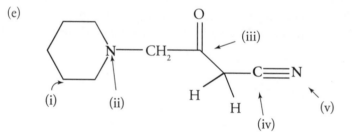

(f)

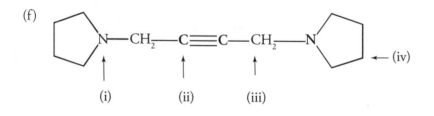

3.6

Solution: Remember to always draw the electrons on nitrogen if they are not drawn in the structure.

(a) i) sp^2, 120°   ii) sp^2, 120°   iii) sp^2, 120° (The lone pair is delocalized, so it's not counted.)
     iv) sp^3, 109°   v) sp^2, 120°   vi) sp^2, 120°

(b) i) sp^3, 109°   ii) sp^3, 109°   iii) sp^3, 109°

(c) i) sp^3, 109°   ii) sp^2, 120°   iii) sp^3, 109°

(d) i) sp^2, 120°   ii) sp^2, 120°   iii) sp^2, 120°   iv) sp^2, 120°

(e) i) sp^3, 109°   ii) sp^3, 109°   iii) sp^2, 120°   iv) sp, 180°   v) sp, 180°

(f) i) sp^3, 109°   ii) sp, 180°   iii) sp^3, 109°   iv) sp^3, 109°

So why all this focus on resonance? In general, π electrons—in alkenes and alkynes, for example—are (relatively) chemically reactive; just think of all the reactions you have studied involving π electrons (for instance, the protonation of a π bond).

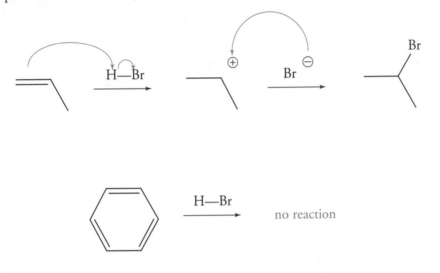

However, the π electrons of benzene do not react with the strong acid HBr. (Due to its aromaticity, benzene has a particularly stable delocalized system. For more on this see Chapter 5.) The localized π electrons of the alkene do react with HBr producing the addition product shown. Since it's important to recognize molecules that are stabilized by resonance delocalization, we'll next review the three basic principles of resonance delocalization.

1. Resonance structures usually involve electrons that are adjacent to (one atom away from) a π bond or an unhybridized *p* orbital. Here are some examples of molecules that are stabilized by resonance delocalization:

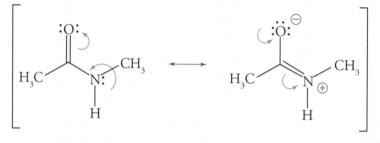

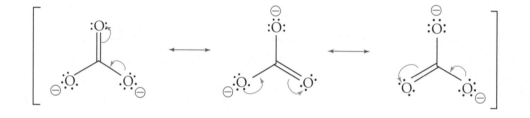

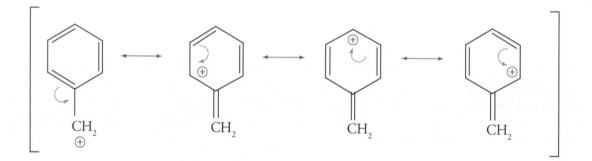

2. Resonance structures of lowest energy are the most important. Remember that the evaluation of resonance structures involves primarily three criteria:

   (i) Resonance contributors in which the octet rule is satisfied (for all the atoms it should be) are more important than ones in which it is not.

   (ii) Resonance contributors that minimize separation of charge are better than those with a large separation of charge.

   (iii) In structures that have separation of charge, the more important resonance contributor has negative charge on the more electronegative atom, and positive charge on the less electronegative atom.

3. Resonance structures can never be drawn through atoms that are truly sp^3 hybridized. Remember that an sp^3 hybridized atom is one with a total of four σ bonds and non-bonding electron pairs.

No resonance
structures possible!

No resonance structures are
possible with these electrons.

No resonance structures are
possible with these electrons.

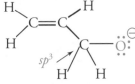

To demonstrate the applications of resonance theory, here are some examples that examine the acidity of functional groups. Subsequent chapters will examine the application of resonance theory to the properties of nucleophilicity and basicity.

What happens when a molecule acts as an acid? A Brønsted-Lowry acid is a molecule that donates a proton (H^+). Since H^+ is donated, it is usually the case that the atom which donates the proton takes on a negative charge. The extent to which that negative charge is stabilized determines the relative acidity of the compound. Consider these examples:

$CH_3CH_2CH_2$ — Ö — H $\xrightarrow{-H^+}$ $CH_3CH_2CH_2$ — Ö$^{\ominus}$

an alcohol

an alkoxide ion

H_3CH_2C — C(=O)—Ö—H $\xrightarrow{-H^+}$ H_3CH_2C — C(=O)—Ö$^{\ominus}$

a carboxylic acid

a carboxylate ion

an alkoxide ion

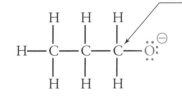

sp^3 hybridized carbon

This carbon has no unhybridized p orbital. Therefore no resonance delocalization of the adjacent lone pairs is possible.

n-Propoxide

The electrons on the oxygen in the alkoxide ion above have no adjacent empty *p* orbital or π system. Therefore, they are localized and highly reactive. This makes the alkoxide ion a very strong base (much like OH⁻).

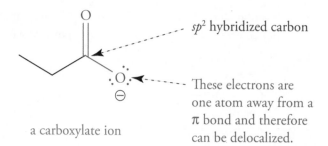

a carboxylate ion

In the carboxylate ion, the electrons on the negatively charged oxygen are adjacent to a π bond and can therefore be delocalized. This leads to greater stability of the carboxylate anion and thus to higher acidity of the conjugate acid. The following demonstrates resonance stabilization for the carboxylate ion. (*Note:* These two resonance structures are identical and therefore of equal energy.)

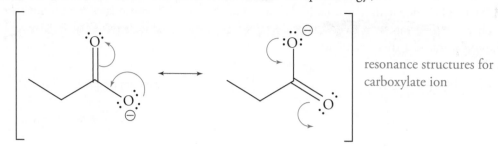

resonance structures for carboxylate ion

Example 3-17: Of the following two molecules, which one would you expect to be the stronger acid?

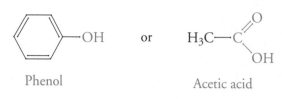

Phenol   Acetic acid

Solution: We examine the conjugate base of each acid in order to determine which one will have the more stabilized anion. Since both conjugate bases have electrons that can be delocalized, the question is: Which conjugate base is more stabilized by resonance delocalization?

Let's examine the resonance structures for the phenoxide and the acetate ions:

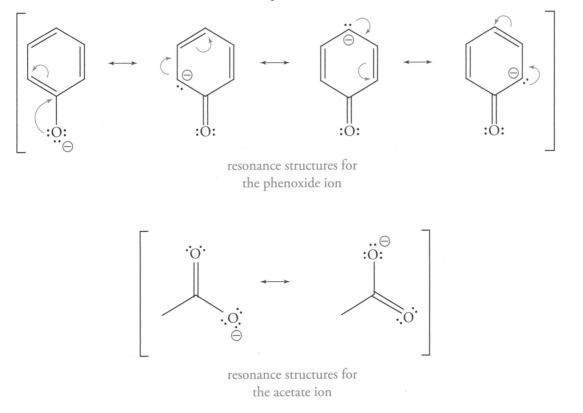

resonance structures for
the phenoxide ion

resonance structures for
the acetate ion

The resonance structures for the acetate ion are of equivalent energy with the negative charge on electronegative oxygen in both structures. In examining the resonance structures for the phenoxide ion, notice that although there are four resonance structures, three of them have the negative charge on carbon rather than on the electronegative oxygen. Also note that the three phenoxide resonance structures that have negative charge on carbon disrupt the aromaticity of the benzene ring. So, acetate ion is more resonance stabilized than phenoxide ion and hence acetic acid is a stronger acid.

Example 3-18: Use resonance structures to explain why *para*-nitrophenol (pK_a = 7.2) is a stronger acid than phenol (pK_a = 10).

Solution: The nitro group helps to distribute the negative charge in the corresponding conjugate base, making *para*-nitrophenol a stronger acid.

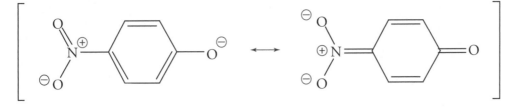

Example 3-19: Rank the following acids in order of decreasing acidity.

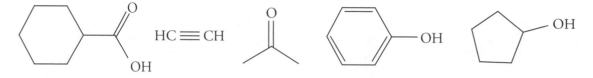

Solution:

1. For this molecule, there are two good resonance structures of equivalent energy with negative charge on the electronegative oxygen, so **rank 1ˢᵗ**.

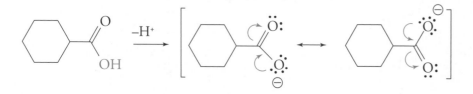

2. Four resonance structures are possible, but they are not of equivalent energy. In addition, the negative charge resides on the less electronegative C in three of these structures. Therefore, it's not as good as the resonance structures above; **rank 2ⁿᵈ**.

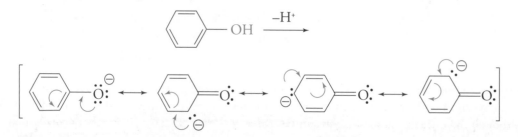

3. There are no possible resonance structures for this molecule, but the negative charge resides on an electronegative oxygen; **rank 3ʳᵈ**.

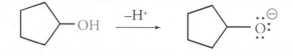

4. The hydrogens next to the carbonyl carbon are acidic because there are two resonance structures for the conjugate base of a ketone. One is stable with the negative charge on oxygen, and one is higher in energy with the negative charge on carbon. Even though it has resonance, it is less acidic than cyclopentanol because some of the charge resides on the carbon; **rank 4th.**

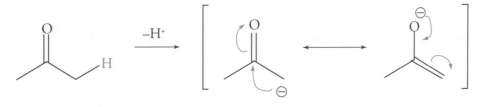

5. There are no possible resonance structures for this molecule, and the negative charge is on carbon, an atom with low electronegativity; **rank 5th.**

$$HC \equiv CH \xrightarrow{-H^+} HC \equiv C^{\ominus}$$

General Rule of Thumb for Organic Compound Acidity.

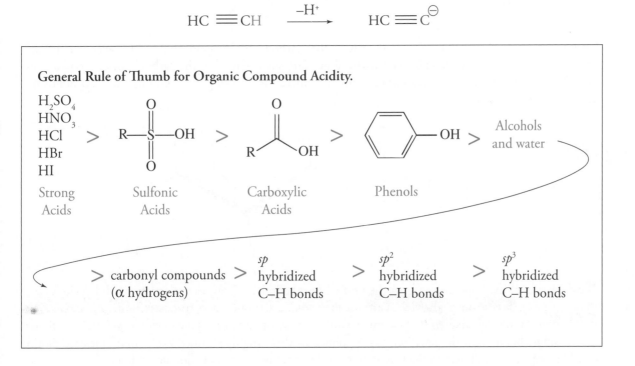

Ring Strain

The last item in our toolbox is a feature of organic molecules that, unlike inductive and resonance effects, contributes to instability in a molecule: **ring strain**. Ring strain arises when bond angles between ring atoms deviate from the ideal angle predicted by the hybridization of the atoms. Let's examine several cycloalkanes in turn.

Cyclopropane (C_3H_6) is very strained because the carbon-carbon bond angles are 60° rather than the idealized 109° for sp^3 hybridized carbons.

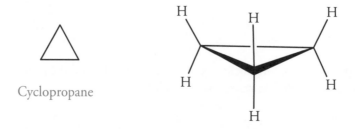

Cyclopropane

Cyclobutane (C_4H_8) might be expected to have 90° carbon-carbon bond angles. However, one of the carbons is bent out of the plane of the ring by about 20°, such that all of the carbon-carbon bond angles are 88°. The distortion of the cyclobutane ring minimizes the eclipsing of carbon-hydrogen σ bonds on adjacent carbon atoms.

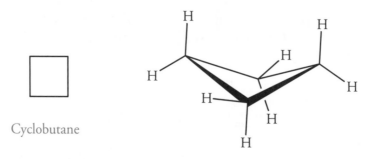

Cyclobutane

The deviation of the bond angles from the normal tetrahedral 109° causes cyclopropane and cyclobutane to be unstable. The strain weakens the carbon-carbon bonds and increases reactivity of these cycloalkanes in comparison to other alkanes. For example, while it is essentially impossible to cleave the average alkane C—C single bond via hydrogenation, C—C bonds in these highly strained cyclic molecules are significantly more reactive. However, they are still much less reactive than C=C double (π) bonds.

3.6

Hydrogenation Reactions of Cyclopropane and Cyclobutane

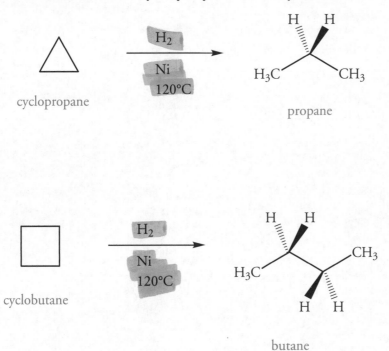

cyclopropane → propane

cyclobutane → butane

Unlike cyclopropane and cyclobutane, cyclopentane has a low degree of ring strain, and cyclohexane is strain free. Both molecules have near-tetrahedral bond angles (109°) due to the conformations they adopt. Consequently, these cycloalkanes do not undergo hydrogenation reactions under normal conditions, and react similarly to straight chain alkanes.

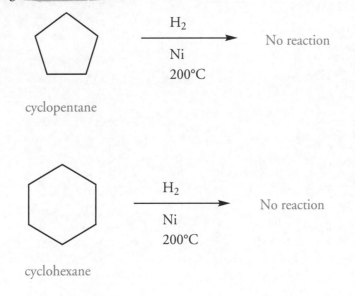

cyclopentane

cyclohexane

Chapter 3 Summary

- Sigma (σ) bonds generally form through the end-on-end overlap of hybrid orbitals; pi (π) bonds form through the side-to-side overlap of unhybridized p orbitals.

- Saturated compounds have the general formula C_nH_{2n+2}; unsaturated molecules contain rings or π bonds.

- Compounds with the same molecular formula are known as *isomers*; structural, or constitutional isomers differ by the connectivity of atoms in the molecule.

- Conformational isomers differ by rotation around a σ bond.

- Stereoisomers have the same atom connectivity, but different spatial orientation of atoms.

- Chiral molecules have chiral centers (carbon with four different substituents), are not superimposable on their mirror image, and rotate plane-polarized light.

- Enantiomers are non-superimposable mirror images and have opposite absolute configuration at all chiral centers.

- Enantiomers rotate plane-polarized light an equal magnitude, but in opposite direction, therefore a 50:50 mixture of enantiomers, or a racemic mixture, is not optically active.

- Diastereomers are stereoisomers that are not mirror images; they differ in absolute configuration for at least one, but not all carbons.

- Epimers are diastereomers that differ in absolute configuration at only one stereocenter.

- Geometric isomers are diastereomers that are *cis/trans* (or *Z/E*) pairs on a ring or double bond. When highest priority groups are on the same side of a ring or bond the molecule is *cis* (or *Z*); when they're on opposite sides, the compound is *trans* (or *E*).

- Meso compounds are achiral molecules with chiral centers and an internal mirror plane.

- As the substitution of carbocations and radicals increases, so does their stability due to the inductive effect; carbanions are more stable when they are less substituted.

- Resonance stabilization results from the ability of π electrons or charge to move and delocalize through a system of conjugated π bonds or unhybridized p orbitals.

CHAPTER 3 FREESTANDING PRACTICE QUESTIONS

1. In the molecule below, what are the hybridizations of C_1, C_2, C_3, and C_4 respectively?

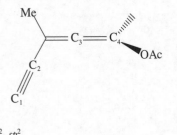

A) sp, sp, sp^2, sp^2
B) sp, sp, sp, sp^2
C) sp^2, sp^2, sp, sp
D) sp^2, sp, sp, sp

2. Which of the following structures represents the most stable possible resonance structure for acetic acid (CH_3CO_2H)?

A)

C)

B)

D)

3. Rank the conformations of 2-aminoethanol by increasing stability.

A) *anti* < *gauche* < eclipsed
B) eclipsed < *anti* < *gauche*
C) *gauche* < *anti* < eclipsed
D) eclipsed < *gauche* < *anti*

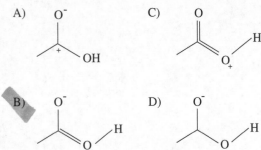

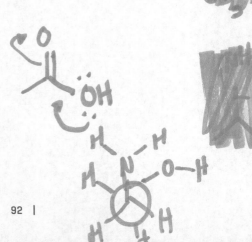

4. The most stable conformation of the following substituted cyclohexane has the methyl groups in which of the following positions?

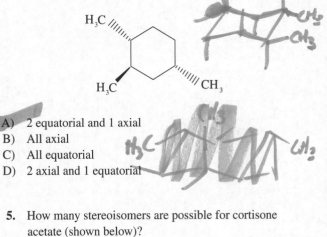

A) 2 equatorial and 1 axial
B) All axial
C) All equatorial
D) 2 axial and 1 equatorial

5. How many stereoisomers are possible for cortisone acetate (shown below)?

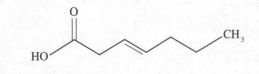

A) 32
B) 64
C) 128
D) 256

6. What is the correct IUPAC name for the following molecule?

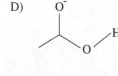

A) (*E*)-3-heptenoic acid
B) (*E*)-4-heptenoic acid
C) (*Z*)-3-heptenoic acid
D) (*Z*)-4-heptenoic acid

CHAPTER 3 PRACTICE PASSAGE

In mammalian systems, aromatic hydrocarbons are enzymatically metabolized by cytochrome P_{450} into arene oxides when ingested or inhaled. Arene oxides are compounds in which one of the double bonds of an aromatic ring has been converted into an epoxide. These molecules can rearrange to form phenols, which are harmlessly excreted. As shown in Figure 1, arene oxide rearrangement requires the formation of an intermediate carbocation and subsequent hydride shift.

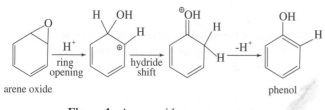

Figure 1 Arene oxide rearrangement

Benzo[a]pyrene, found in tobacco smoke and automobile exhaust, is one of the most troublesome natural arene oxides because it is a procarcinogen due to its bioconversion to a number of harmful molecules such as the 7,8-diol epoxide shown in Figure 2. The danger of the 7,8-diol epoxide lies in the unwillingness of the epoxide ring to rearrange and form a phenol. Instead, the diol epoxide intercalates in DNA and is covalently bound by 2′-deoxyguanosine nucleosides, leading to point mutations in the course of DNA replication.

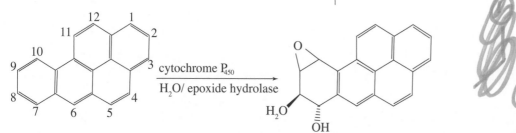

Benzo[a]pyrene   Benzo[a]pyrene7,8-dihydrodiol-9,10-epoxide

Figure 2 Oxidation of Benzo[a]pyrene

1. Determine the absolute configurations of Carbons 7 and 8 of the diol epoxide shown in Figure 2.

A) 7R, 8R
B) 7R, 8S
C) 7S, 8S
D) 7S, 8R

2. All of the following statements about epoxides are correct EXCEPT:

A) epoxides and ethers bear the same leaving groups.
B) ring strain and torsional strain increase the free energy of an epoxide.
C) epoxide hydrolysis under basic conditions produces trans-1,2-diols.
D) epoxide oxygen atoms are capable of donating hydrogen bonds.

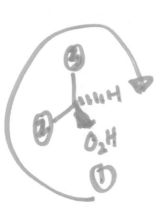

3. Rank the following four substances in order of increasing reactivity with ethylene oxide.

    I.   Hydroxide
    II. Ammonia
    III. Methide
    IV. Water

A) III < I < II < IV
B) IV < II < I < III
C) IV < II < III < I
D) II < IV < I < III

4. Which labeled atom in the molecule shown below would be the fastest site of reaction with a thiolate ($R\text{-}S^-$)?

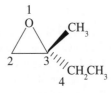

A) 1
B) 2
C) 3
D) 4

5. Which of the following arene oxides will react as in Figure 1 to form the most stable carbocation intermediate?

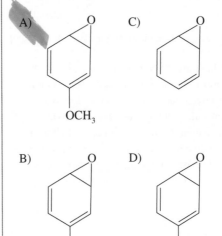

SOLUTIONS TO CHAPTER 3 FREESTANDING QUESTIONS

1. **B** Both C_1 and C_2 make up the triple bond. They are both *sp* hybridized so you can eliminate choices C and D. C_3 is part of an allene. The bonds that it forms with its neighbors are linear (180°), so it is also *sp*. You can eliminate choice A, which leaves choice B as the correct choice. C_4 has a double bond and two single bonds so it is *sp²*.

2. **B** Good resonance structures must do the following: obey the octet rule, accrue the fewest charges possible, and place negative charges on electronegative atoms and positive charges on electropositive atoms (listed in priority). Further, resonance structures don't represent oxidation or reduction of molecules, and as such the total charge of each structure must be the charge of the molecule. This eliminates choices C and D. Choices A and B are both valid resonance structures, but only choice B places a full octet on all non-H atoms.

3. **B** Since this is a ranking question, look for obvious extremes and eliminate answers. Choices A and C should be eliminated because the eclipsed conformation is always the least stable due to sterics and electron repulsions in aligned bonds. Choice D is the more enticing answer of the remaining two because the general rule of thumb is that the anti conformation is the most stable because the bulky groups are farthest apart, while they are 60° apart in a *gauche* conformation. This question is tricky, however, because in this case there is intramolecular hydrogen bonding which can occur in the *gauche* conformation, making it the most stable one (eliminate choice D).

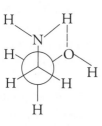

4. **A** Choice B can be eliminated before analyzing the structure since if all three substituents could be axial, then by a ring flip, all three could also be equatorial. The more stable chair conformation puts substituents in an equatorial position since they are less sterically crowded than those in axial positions. Similarly, if choice A is true of the molecule, then by ring flip, choice D must be also. Therefore choice D should be eliminated since it has more axial substituents. Between choices A and C, only choice A fits the compound shown because the relationship between the methyl groups on Carbons 1 and 2 is *trans* and the relationship between the methyl groups on Carbons 1 and 4 is *cis*. In this conformation, the methyl groups on Carbons 1 and 2 would be found in the equatorial position and the methyl group on Carbon 4 would be axial, making A the better choice.

5. **B** The maximum number of stereoisomers is given by the formula 2^n, where *n* equals the number of stereocenters. Cortisone acetate has six stereocenters and $2^6 = 64$. Five of the six ring junctures are chiral centers (all *sp³* carbons), as is the carbon with the OH substituent. Choice A would correspond to five stereocenters, choice C would require seven stereocenters, and choice D would correspond to a compound with eight stereocenters.

6.   **A**   When naming a compound, number the carbons starting at the end nearest a functional group (the carboxylic acid in this case). Based on the position of the double bond in the molecule, you can eliminate choices B and D. Since the two largest substituents on each carbon of the double bond are on opposite sides of the bond, the double bond has *E* stereochemistry; therefore, eliminate choice C.

SOLUTIONS TO CHAPTER 3 PRACTICE PASSAGE

1.   **D**

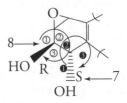

Note that the configuration for Carbon 7 reads as *R*, but because the hydroxyl group occupies an into-plane position, this assignment is incorrect. One way to get around this is to exchange the hydroxyl group's position with the hydrogen also on this carbon. Doing so will place the hydroxyl group in a correct position, which results in a clockwise trace. This reads as *R* but because two groups have been exchanged, the true configuration is *S*. Once the configuration of Carbon 7 is determined to be *S*, choices A and B can be eliminated.

2.   **D**   Epoxides and ethers all bear an OR leaving group so choice A can be eliminated. Choice B is incorrect because epoxides, due to their 3-point ring structure, possess ring strain and torsional strain, which imparts a relatively high free energy. Epoxide hydrolysis (basic or acidic) will produce *trans*-1,2-diols, also eliminating choice C. Choice D is the only answer choice consistent with the EXCEPT wording of the question because epoxides are only capable of accepting hydrogen bonds, not donating them.

3.   **B**   Each of the four substances listed will act as nucleophiles with ethylene oxide (C_2H_4O). The strongest nucleophile has a negative charge on the least electronegative atom, which is carbon. Choices B and D both list methide as the strongest nucleophile (eliminate choices A and C). The weakest nucleophile is going to be listed first. The choice is between water and ammonia. Since nitrogen is less electronegative than oxygen, NH_3 is a better nucleophile than water (eliminate choice D).

4.   **B**   Thiolate is a relatively weak base, but a great nucleophile. This means it will be attracted to the electrophilic carbons of the molecule, C-2 and C-3, and effect an epoxide ring opening (eliminate choices A and D). Because the question asks about the fastest site of reaction, the least sterically hindered carbon is the best choice. Thiolate will have easier access to the primary carbon, so eliminate choice C.

5. **A**   The nature of the substituents on each ring act to stabilize or destabilize the carbocation that forms. The methoxy substituent in choice A is an electron-donating group, which will stabilize the carbocation through resonance due to the lone electron pairs on the oxygen.

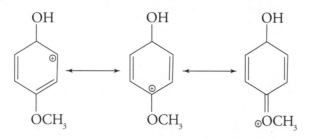

On the other hand, the nitro group in choice B will destabilize the intermediate since one resonance structure, shown below, puts two atoms with a positive charge next to each other (eliminate choice B). Choice C affords no increase or decrease in stability. Choice D will show mild stabilization due to the inductive donation offered by its methyl group (also shown below).

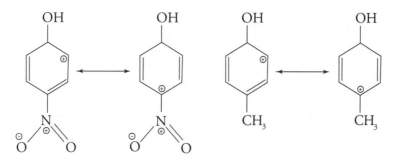

Overall, choice A shows the strongest carbocation stabilization since resonance effects are generally stronger than inductive ones.

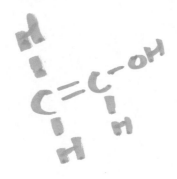

Chapter 4
Substitution and
Elimination Reactions

In Chapter 3 we explored the fundamentals of structure and stereochemistry. In this chapter we will discuss three major reaction types: free radical halogenations, nucleophilic substitutions, and elimination reactions. We will examine these reactions in the context of five functional groups: alkanes, haloalkanes, alcohols, ethers, and amines.

Substitution reactions are defined by the bonding changes that occur over the course of the reaction. In a substitution reaction, one σ bond in the starting material is converted into a new σ bond in the product. Let's take a closer look at the two most common types of substitution reactions.

4.1 FREE RADICAL HALOGENATION

We will now examine the basic principles of **free-radical halogenation**, the most important reaction of alkanes on the MCAT, by focusing on the mechanism of this reaction. Free-radical halogenation is a reaction that proceeds by a multi-step mechanism that includes **initiation**, **propagation**, and **termination** (and is often subject to **inhibition** by molecular oxygen).

Initiation

A free radical reaction can be initiated by light or heat. In a light-initiated reaction, a photon ($E = h\nu$) collides with (usually) a molecular halogen such as Cl_2 or Br_2 causing homolytic cleavage of a bond (see Section 3.3). This results in the formation of two halogen radicals.

Homolytic Cleavage: One electron goes with each atom of the bond being broken. This produces two radicals.

$$X\!\!-\!\!X \xrightarrow{\;h\nu\;} X^{\cdot} \;+\; {}^{\cdot}X$$

Propagation

For every halogen radical formed in the initiation step, about 10,000 alkyl halide molecules are formed in the propagation steps of this chain reaction. In the first step of the propagation reactions, a halogen radical collides with an alkane molecule (R—H) causing homolytic cleavage of a C—H bond with formation of a molecule of hydrogen halide (H—X) and an alkyl radical (R$^{\cdot}$).

In the next step of the propagation, the alkyl halide product is formed. This is accomplished by the collision of an alkyl radical (R$^{\cdot}$) with molecular halogen (X—X). This collision results in the homolytic cleavage of the molecular halogen so that a molecule of alkyl halide (R—X) product is formed and a halogen radical (X$^{\cdot}$) is regenerated.

$$R\!\!-\!\!H \;+\; {}^{\cdot}X \longrightarrow R^{\cdot} \;+\; H\!\!-\!\!X$$

$$R^{\cdot} \;+\; X\!\!-\!\!X \longrightarrow R\!\!-\!\!X \;+\; {}^{\cdot}X$$

The halogen radical then proceeds to collide with another alkane molecule, continuing the propagation of the chain reaction. Therefore, one halogen radical is able to lead to the production of many, many alkyl halide products since the halogen radical is always regenerated in the process.

Termination

The propagation of the chain reaction continues until one of the reactive radicals of the propagation steps combines with another radical. This can be accomplished by the combination of two halogen radicals ($X^{\bullet}$) to form a molecule of molecular halogen (X—X), or the combination of two alkyl radicals ($R^{\bullet}$) to form a molecule of alkane (R—R), or finally, by the combination of an alkyl radical ($R^{\bullet}$) with a halogen radical ($X^{\bullet}$) to form an alkyl halide (R—X). The consumption of reactive radicals stops the propagation of the chain reaction.

$$X^{\bullet} + {}^{\bullet}X \rightarrow X\text{—}X$$

$$R^{\bullet} + {}^{\bullet}R \rightarrow R\text{—}R$$

$$R^{\bullet} + {}^{\bullet}X \rightarrow R\text{—}X$$

Inhibition

Finally, as previously stated, the free-radical halogenation reaction is inhibited by molecular oxygen. This occurs when an alkyl radical reacts with a molecule of molecular oxygen to form a less reactive alkyl peroxy radical (R—O—O$^{\bullet}$). The reaction slows down because the concentration of the more reactive alkyl radical intermediate is reduced.

$$R^{\bullet} + O{=}O \rightleftharpoons R\text{—}O\text{—}O^{\bullet}$$

Summary of Free-Radical Halogenation of Alkanes Mechanism

Initiation: A step that yields a net increase in the number of radicals.

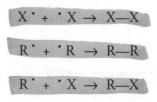

(1) $X\text{—}X \xrightarrow[\text{or heat}]{h\nu} 2\ X^{\bullet}$

Propagation: A step that yields no net change in the number of radicals.

(2) $R\text{—}H + {}^{\bullet}X \longrightarrow R^{\bullet} + H\text{—}X$

(3) $R^{\bullet} + X\text{—}X \longrightarrow R\text{—}X + X^{\bullet}$

Then (2), (3), (2), (3), . . .

Termination: A step that yields a net decrease in the number of radicals.

(4) $X^{\bullet} + X^{\bullet} \longrightarrow X\text{—}X$

(5) $R^{\bullet} + R^{\bullet} \longrightarrow R\text{—}R$

(6) $R^{\bullet} + X^{\bullet} \longrightarrow R\text{—}X$

Inhibition: *Inhibition by molecular oxygen slows down the reaction by reducing the amount of reactive radical intermediate. This is reversible.*

$$(7) \quad R^{\cdot} + O_2 \rightleftharpoons R{-}O{-}O^{\cdot}$$

Stereochemistry of Free-Radical Halogenation

When the halogen radical collides with the alkane, it abstracts a hydrogen from an sp^3 hybridized tetrahedral carbon atom in a homolytic cleavage that results in the formation of a molecule of H—X and a carbon radical intermediate. The next important point to consider is the hybridization of the intermediate alkyl carbon radical. As the hydrogen radical is abstracted, the resulting carbon radical rehybridizes to place the single electron in an unhybridized p orbital. The geometry is planar with 120° bond angles, and the lone electron resides above and below the plane of the molecule in an unhybridized p orbital.

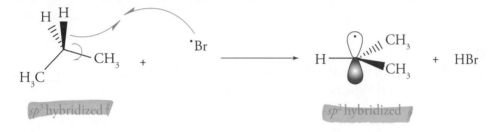

When the alkyl radical then reacts with a molecule of molecular halogen in the next step of the reaction, the carbon-halogen bond can form on either side of the plane defined by the sp^2 hybridized atom. This leads to racemization at carbon if its substitution is unsymmetrical, since bond formation can occur to an equal extent from either side of the unhybridized p orbital.

Racemization of an Unsymmetrical Alkyl Radical

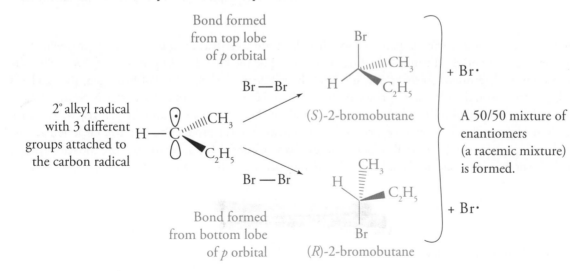

Stability of Alkyl Radicals

Next we examine the relative stability of carbon alkyl radicals. Free radicals are like carbocations in the sense that they have an unfilled p orbital (one electron for a radical vs. zero electrons for a carbocation). Also, like carbocations (see Section 3.6) alkyl substituents on carbon increase the relative stability of the radical.

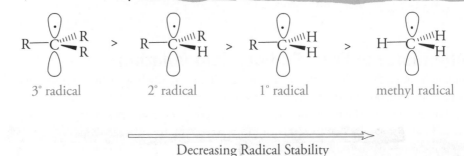

Decreasing Radical Stability

Selectivity

The varying stabilities of alkyl radicals have a profound effect on the selectivity of these reactions. First we will look at the free-radical chlorination of 2-methylpropane.

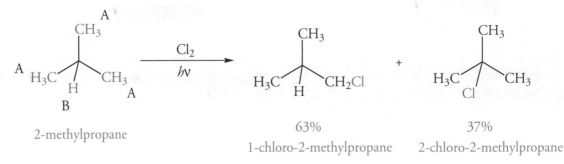

Upon inspection of 2-methylpropane we see that there are two distinct types of hydrogens, which we shall refer to as A and B. The nine A hydrogens are 1°, while the lone B hydrogen is 3°. If the product distribution were determined solely by statistics and the abundance of each type of hydrogen, the products of the reaction would be formed in the ratio 9:1 (= A:B). However, as you can see, this is clearly not the case; 63/37 is not equal to 9/1. This is because not all of the C—H bonds are of equal reactivity. Since there's much more (than we would expect based on statistics) of the product derived from reaction at position B, we can infer that position B is more reactive than position A. In order to calculate the selectivity of the different positions, one needs to factor out the number of reactive sites:

$$Selectivity = \frac{reactivity}{\#\ of\ sites\ available}$$

Therefore, in this case we have

$$\frac{selectivity\ of\ 3°}{selectivity\ of\ 1°} = \frac{(reactivity\ at\ 3°)\ /\ (\#\ of\ 3°\ sites)}{(reactivity\ at\ 1°)\ /\ (\#\ of\ 1°\ sites)} = \frac{37\,/\,1}{63\,/\,9} = \frac{37}{7} = 5.3$$

We now consider the corresponding free radical bromination of 2-methylpropane. The bromine radical is less reactive than the corresponding chlorine radical. The lower reactivity of the bromine radical results in a much higher selectivity (3° > 2° > 1°) in the bromination reaction compared to the corresponding chlorination reaction. The reason for this beyond the scope of the MCAT, but you should have a sense of the degree of selectivity, which has been quantified and is on the order of 1640:82 : 1 (see the calculations below).

Bromination of Alkanes is Much More Selective than Chlorination

Reaction Rate

	R_3CH (3°)	>	R_2CH_2 (2°)	>	RCH_3 (1°)
Bromination:	1640.0		82.0		1
Chlorination:	5.3		3.9		1

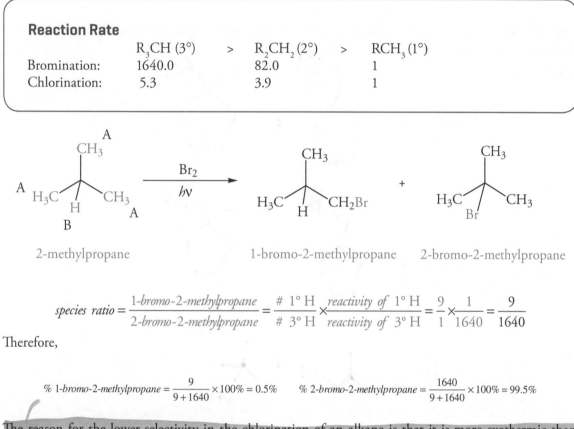

2-methylpropane   1-bromo-2-methylpropane   2-bromo-2-methylpropane

$$species\ ratio = \frac{\textit{1-bromo-2-methylpropane}}{\textit{2-bromo-2-methylpropane}} = \frac{\#\ 1°\ H}{\#\ 3°\ H} \times \frac{\textit{reactivity of }1°\ H}{\textit{reactivity of }3°\ H} = \frac{9}{1} \times \frac{1}{1640} = \frac{9}{1640}$$

Therefore,

$$\%\ \textit{1-bromo-2-methylpropane} = \frac{9}{9+1640} \times 100\% = 0.5\% \qquad \%\ \textit{2-bromo-2-methylpropane} = \frac{1640}{9+1640} \times 100\% = 99.5\%$$

The reason for the lower selectivity in the chlorination of an alkane is that it is more exothermic than the corresponding bromination reaction. In the bromine case, only one of the two propagation steps is exothermic (the other is endothermic). For this reason, bromination is slower and more selective than chlorination.

Enthalpies for Radical Halogenation of Methane

$$CH_4 + X_2 \rightarrow CH_3X + HX$$

X	$\Delta H°$ (kcal/mol)
F	−102.8
Cl	−24.7
Br	−7.3
I	+12.7

Propagation Steps of Radical Bromination of Methane

Step	ΔH° (kcal/mol)
$CH_4 + Br^{\bullet} \rightarrow CH_3^{\bullet} + HBr$	+18
$CH_3^{\bullet} + Br_2 \rightarrow CH_3Br + Br^{\bullet}$	-25

It is predicted from the enthalpy values in the table above that fluorine should be a very unselective re-agent. This is, in fact, experimentally observed.

Example 4-1: Predict the organic product(s) from the following free-radical halogenation reactions. For the brominations, determine the major and minor products.

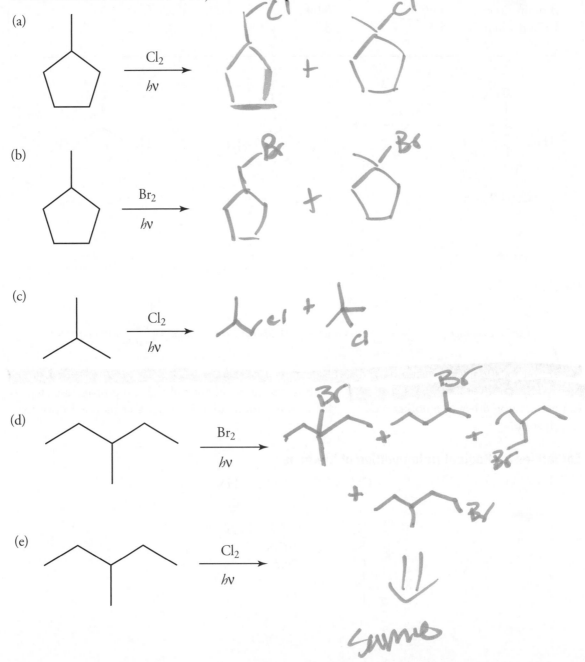

Solution:

(a)

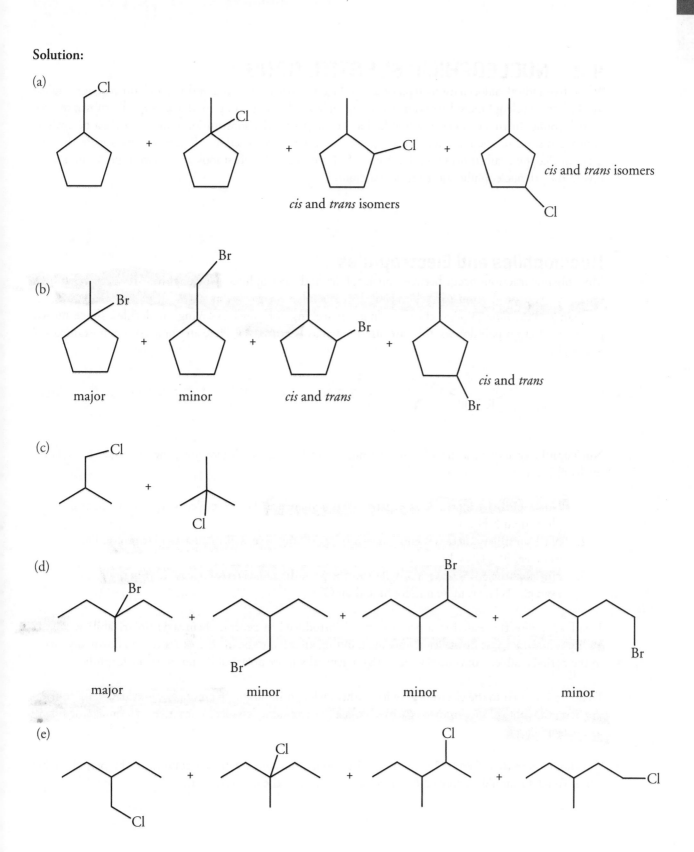

(b)

major   minor   *cis* and *trans*

(c)

(d)

major   minor   minor   minor

(e)

4.2 NUCLEOPHILIC SUBSTITUTIONS

While free-radical halogenations replace a C—H bond with a C—X bond via a chain reaction radical mechanism, nucleophilic substitution reactions replace a leaving group in an electrophilic substrate with a nucleophile. In this context, the bonds that break during the substitution will do so via a heterolytic cleavage instead of the homolytic cleavage we saw for radical reactions. Before we investigate the two main nucleophilic substitution mechanisms—S_N1 and S_N2—let's first look at the two types of molecules involved in all nucleophilic substitution reactions.

Nucleophiles and Electrophiles

Most organic reactions occur between nucleophiles and electrophiles. Nucleophiles are species that have unshared pairs of electrons or π bonds and, frequently, a negative (or partial negative, δ^-) charge. As the name *nucleophile* implies, they are "nucleus-seeking" or "nucleus-loving" molecules. Since nucleophiles are electron pair donors, they are also known as Lewis bases. Here are some common examples of nucleophiles:

Nucleophilicity is a measure of how "strong" a nucleophile is. There are general trends for relative nucleophilicities:

1. Nucleophilicity increases as negative charge increases. For example, NH_2^- is more nucleophilic than NH_3.
2. Nucleophilicity increases going down the periodic table within a particular group. For example, $F^- < Cl^- < Br^- < I^-$.
3. Nucleophilicity increases going left in the periodic table across a particular period. For example, NH_2^- is more nucleophilic than OH^-.

Trend #2 is directly related to a periodic trend introduced in general chemistry: polarizability. Polarizability is how easy it is for the electrons surrounding an atom to be distorted. As you go down any group in the periodic table, atoms become larger and generally more polarizable and more nucleophilic.

Trend #3 is related to the electronegativity of the nucleophilic atom. The more electronegative the atom is, the better it is able to support its negative charge. Therefore, the less electronegative an atom is, the higher its nucleophilicity.

You should note that Trend #2 should only be applied for atoms within a column of the periodic table, while Trend #3 should be applied for atoms across a row of the periodic table.

Example 4-2: In each of the following pairs of molecules, identify the one that is more nucleophilic.

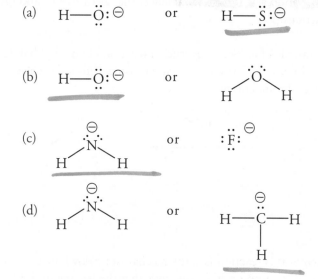

Solution:

(a) SH^-, since by Trend #2 above, S is more nucleophilic than O.
(b) OH^-, because OH^- carries a negative charge, while H_2O does not (Trend #1, previous page).
(c) NH_2^-, since F is more electronegative than N.
(d) CH_3^-, because N is more electronegative than C.

Electrophiles are electron-deficient species. They have a full or partial positive (δ^+) charge and "love electrons." Frequently, they have an incomplete octet. **Electrophilicity** is a measure of how strong an electrophile is. Since electrophiles are electron pair acceptors, they are also known as **Lewis acids**. Here are some common examples of electrophiles:

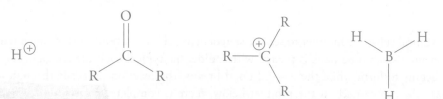

In all organic reactions (except free-radical and pericyclic reactions), nucleophiles are attracted—and donate a pair of electrons—to electrophiles. When the electrophile accepts the electron pair (a Lewis acid/Lewis base reaction), a new covalent bond forms between the two species, which we can represent symbolically like this:

The S$_N$2 Mechanism

The first nucleophilic mechanism we'll examine is the S$_N$2 mechanism. Typical electrophiles (also known as the substrates) for this type of reaction are alkyl halides. Alkyl halides are alkanes that contain at least

4.2

one halogen (fluorine, chlorine, bromine or iodine). Since halogen atoms are very electronegative, most halides (Cl⁻, Br⁻, I⁻) make good leaving groups. Hence, the chemistry of alkyl halides involves substitution and elimination reactions.

Let us first consider an example of an S_N2 substitution reaction of an alkyl halide. When 1-iodobutane is treated with a Br⁻ nucleophile, an S_N2 reaction occurs in which bromide replaces the I⁻ group (known as the leaving group) to yield 1-bromobutane.

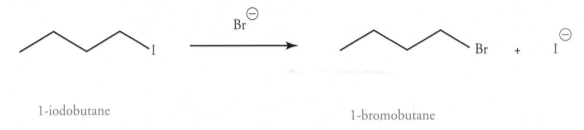

1-iodobutane   1-bromobutane

In the first (and only) step of this reaction (see the mechanism below), because the nucleophilic bromide anion attacks the electrophilic carbon at the *same time* that the leaving group leaves, the attack must occur *from the backside* of the substrate. The bromine-carbon bond forms as the iodine-carbon bond is broken, *in a single step*, to yield bromobutane.

The Mechanism

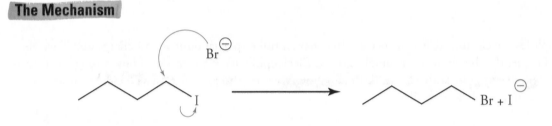

Let's look at a chiral substrate in order to see the stereochemical implications of this concerted mechanism. When (*R*)-1-deutero-1-chloroethane is treated with iodide, the typical backside attack occurs. As the new C—I bond begins to form while the C—Cl bond breaks, the reaction proceeds through a *pentavalent transition state*. As you can see in the product below, there is complete *inversion of configuration* at the carbon being attacked by the nucleophile. This is always the case in an S_N2 reaction on a chiral substrate.

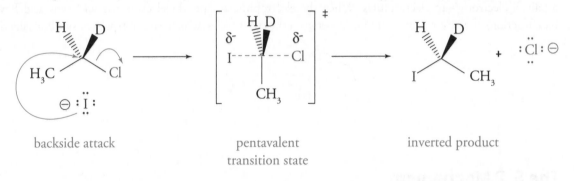

backside attack   pentavalent   inverted product
                           transition state

Furthermore, the rate of the reaction is a function of two variables—that is, **bimolecular**. The rate of the reaction depends on the concentrations of both the nucleophile and the electrophile, and is equal to the product of the rate constant (k), the concentration of the nucleophile ($[I^-]$), and the concentration of the electrophile ($[R\text{-}Cl]$).

$$\text{reaction rate} = k[\text{nucleophile}][\text{electrophile}]$$

We can now explain what we mean when we say that this reaction proceeds by an "S_N2" mechanism. The "S" indicates that it is a <u>s</u>ubstitution reaction mechanism, the subscript "N" indicates that it is <u>nu</u>cleophilic, and the "2" indicates that it is <u>b</u>imolecular. The rate of the reaction depends not only on the concentration of the electrophile, but also on the degree of substitution of the electrophilic carbon. Since the transition state is sterically crowded with five groups attached, the more bulky those groups are, the harder it is for the nucleophile to gain access to the reactive site. Therefore, less substituted substrates react faster than more substituted ones.

The last factor to consider in substitution reactions is the solvent. To favor an S_N2 mechanism, protic solvents such as water and alcohols should be avoided. Since these hydrogen bonding solvents are able to strongly solvate the nucleophile, they hinder the backside attack necessary for the concerted reaction. To prevent this interference, polar, *aprotic* solvents such as acetone, DMF (dimethylformamide), or DMSO (dimethylsulfoxide) should be used. Their polar nature allows the charged nucleophiles and leaving groups to remain dissolved, but they are not as efficient at completely solvating the nucleophile.

Key Features of an S_N2 Reaction

Reactivity of substrate:	$CH_3 > 1° > 2° \gg 3°$ (Because of steric hindrance)
Stereochemistry:	Complete stereochemical inversion of the carbon that is attacked by the nucleophile.
Kinetics:	reaction rate = $k[\text{nucleophile}][\text{electrophile}]$
Solvent:	S_N2 reactions are favored by polar, aprotic (non-hydrogen bonding) solvents.
Rearrangements:	Not possible due to concerted mechanism. No carbocations are present in solution.
Favoring Conditions:	Strong, non-bulky nucleophile will favor S_N2 reactions over S_N1 (see next section).

4.2

The S$_N$1 Mechanism

Over the course of S$_N$1 substitution reactions, a carbocation (carbonium ion) forms. So let's take a moment to review the relative stability of carbocations. Remember that the formation of charged species from neutral ones is generally an energetically disfavorable process; that is, it is energetically *uphill*. But some ions are more stable than others. For alkyl cations, the relative stabilities are given below.

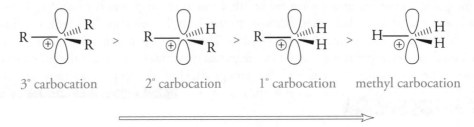

3° carbocation   2° carbocation   1° carbocation   methyl carbocation

Decreasing carbocation stability

The order of stabilities for carbocations is thought to be the result of the electron-donating ability of alkyl groups. (The mechanism of this interaction is beyond the scope of the MCAT.)

Now that we have reviewed the basics of carbocation stability, let's consider an example where a chiral halide undergoes an S$_N$1 substitution reaction. When (*R*)-3-bromo-3-methylhexane is treated with H$_2$O, a racemic mixture of 3-methylhexan-3-ol is formed:

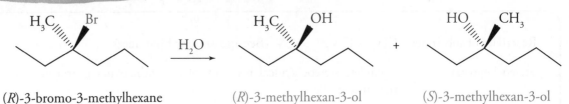

(*R*)-3-bromo-3-methylhexane   (*R*)-3-methylhexan-3-ol   (*S*)-3-methylhexan-3-ol

S$_N$1 substitution occurs in *two distinct steps*, unlike S$_N$2 reactions that occur in one step. In the first step of the S$_N$1 reaction, a *planar carbocation* with 120° bond angles forms (see mechanism below). This occurs when the leaving group falls off (dissociates). This is the slow step of the mechanism, or the rate limiting step. In the final step of this reaction, *racemization* occurs as the nucleophile attacks equally *on either side* of the carbocation. The result is a racemic mixture.

The Mechanism

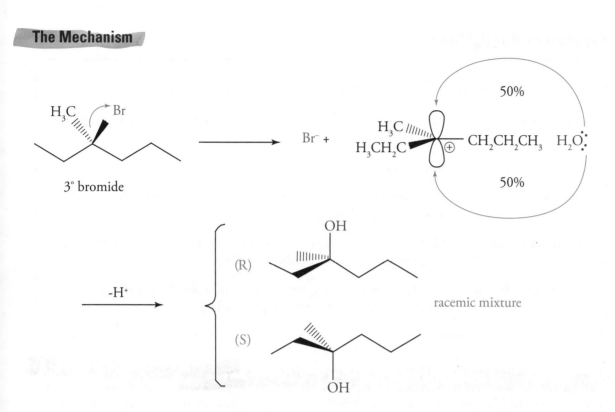

3° bromide

racemic mixture

Unlike the S_N2 reaction explained above where the rate of the reaction was a function of two variables, the S_N1 reaction rate is a function of only one variable, that is, **unimolecular**. The rate of the S_N1 reaction depends only upon the concentration of the electrophile (the species that loses the leaving group over the course of the reaction). The rate of the reaction is equal to the product of the rate constant (k), and the electrophile concentration ([R-Br]):

$$\text{reaction rate} = k[\text{electrophile}]$$

As before, we can now explain what we mean when we say that this reaction proceeds by an "S_N1" mechanism. The "S" indicates that it is a <u>s</u>ubstitution reaction mechanism, the subscript "N" indicates that it is <u>n</u>ucleophic, and the "1" indicates that it is <u>uni</u>molecular.

The rate of the reaction depends not only on the concentration of the electrophile, but also on the degree of substitution of the electrophilic carbon. Since the dissociation of the leaving group is the slow step of the mechanism, anything that makes that step more favorable will speed up the reaction. As was just discussed, the more substituted the carbocation intermediate, the more stable it is. Therefore, more substituted substrates will dissociate to make more stable intermediates faster, speeding up the rate of the entire reaction.

To favor an S_N1 mechanism, protic solvents such as water and alcohols should be used. The role of the solvent is twofold. The protic solvent helps to stabilize the forming carbocation and solvate the leaving group, thereby facilitating the first, or slow step of the mechanism. Secondly, the solvent then behaves as the nucleophile in a **solvolysis** reaction, attacking the carbocation intermediate. This produces an alcohol product if water is used as the solvent and an ether if the reaction is run in an alcoholic solvent.

Key Features of an S_N1 Reaction

Reactivity of substrate:	$3° > 2° \gg 1°$ (Due to stabilization of the carbocation.)
Stereochemistry:	Almost complete racemization due to nucleophilic attack on either side of p orbital.
Kinetics:	reaction rate $= k[\text{electrophile}]$
Solvent:	S_N1 reactions are favored by protic (hydrogen bonding) solvents. (This stabilizes the carbocation.)
Rearrangements:	Carbocation rearrangement is possible; if the carbocation can rearrange to one that is more stable, it will.
Favoring conditions:	Non-basic, weaker nucleophiles favor unimolecular substitutions. Often the solvent acts as the nucleophile (solvolysis).

Alcohols undergo substitution reactions just as alkyl halides do. They can undergo either S_N1 or S_N2 substitution reactions depending upon the degree of substitution of the alcohol. Alcohols are treated with strong mineral acids to make their bad –OH leaving group into a good one (H_2O). In S_N2 reactions, the conjugate base of the mineral acid will attack while the leaving group leaves. In S_N1 reactions, the water will first dissociate, followed by nucleophilic attack of the halide ion on the carbocation intermediate.

While this chapter focuses on substitution and elimination reactions, since alcohols are an important class of compounds for the MCAT because of their distinctive properties, we will discuss them in more detail in Section 4.4.

Example 4-3: Predict whether the following substitution reactions will proceed via an S_N1 or an S_N2 mechanism.

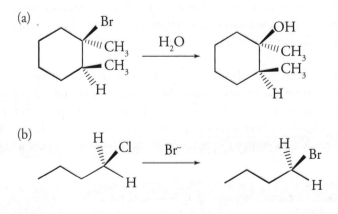

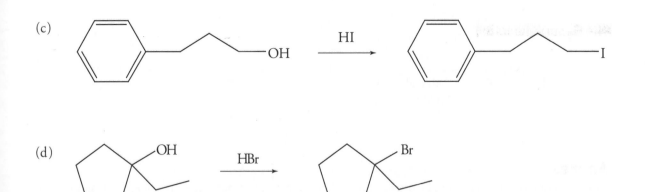

Solution:

(a)   3° bromide, S_N1
(b)   1° chloride, S_N2
(c)   1° alcohol, S_N2
(d)   3° alcohol, S_N1

Substitution Reactions with Other Functional Groups

Ethers

Ethers are weak bases that are generally quite chemically unreactive in the absence of strong acids. The chemical reactions that ethers participate in are due to the weak basicity of the ether oxygen. Let's consider a reaction in which an ether is cleaved in the presence of strong acid. The acid protonates the oxygen of the ether, converting a poor leaving group into a good leaving group.

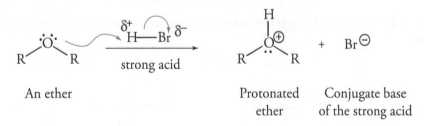

| An ether | | Protonated ether | Conjugate base of the strong acid |

At this point, the reaction can proceed by either an S_N1 or S_N2 mechanism depending on the structure of the protonated ether intermediate. In the subsequent substitution reaction, the halide (X^-) from the acid acts as the nucleophile. The ether cleavage reaction ultimately yields two molecules of haloalkane.

The General Reaction

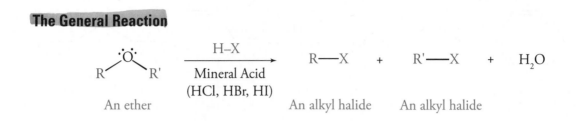

An ether   An alkyl halide   An alkyl halide

Amines

Organic compounds that contain nitrogen are of fundamental importance in biological systems. The most common class of nitrogen-containing compounds are referred to as **amines** and have the general structure of $R-NH_2$. Amines can be further classified as either **alkyl amines** or **aryl amines**. *Alkyl* amines are compounds in which nitrogen is bound to sp^3-hybridized carbon, while *aryl* amines are compounds in which nitrogen is bonded to an sp^2-hybridized carbon of an aromatic ring.

Below are a few examples of common amines.

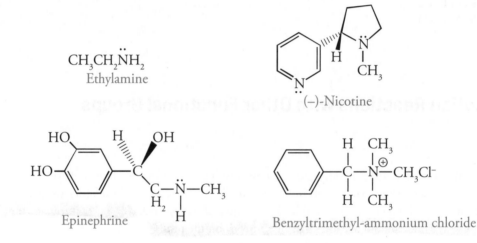

$CH_3CH_2\overset{..}{N}H_2$
Ethylamine

(–)-Nicotine

Epinephrine   Benzyltrimethyl-ammonium chloride

Amines can be further categorized as primary amines, secondary amines, tertiary amines, and quaternary ammonium ions.

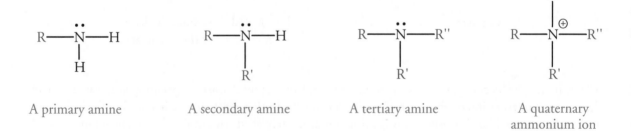

A primary amine   A secondary amine   A tertiary amine   A quaternary ammonium ion

Next, we'll examine the structure and bonding of alkyl amines. As an example we will look at the simple alkyl amine, methyl amine, CH_3NH_2. Notice that the nitrogen has three σ bonds and one lone electron pair. Its hybridization is therefore sp^3 with approximately 109° bond angles. The molecular geometry of an alkyl amine is pyramidal.

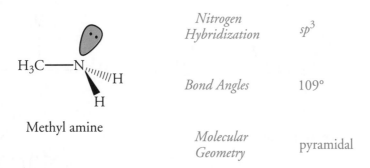

	Nitrogen Hybridization	sp^3
	Bond Angles	109°
	Molecular Geometry	pyramidal

Methyl amine

An interesting phenomenon of alkyl amines is that they undergo rapid pyramidal inversion at the sp^3-hybridized nitrogen. This rapid process has a low energy barrier (energy of activation) of only 6 to 7 kcal/mol, so that at room temperature the two pyramidal forms of the alkyl amine readily interconvert between one another. Because of this rapid interconversion, amines are not chiral.

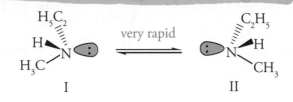

Methylethylamine
(Energy of activation for inversion only about 6-7 kcal/mol)

Alkylation

We now examine an important reaction of amines: alkylation. Alkyl amines can participate in S_N2 type substitution reactions because of their lone electron pairs. We now consider an example of an exhaustive alkylation of methylamine with methyl iodide.

In this S_N2 substitution reaction, the lone pair of electrons on the nitrogen of the alkyl amine serves as the nucleophile by attacking the electrophilic, sterically-unhindered carbon atom of methyl iodide. The primary amine, methylamine, first reacts with methyl iodide, to form a 2° amine. The 2° amine then reacts with another molecule of methyl iodide to form a 3° amine. Finally, the 3° amine reacts with yet another molecule of methyl iodide to yield a quaternary ammonium ion.

Notice that the quaternary ammonium ion no longer has a lone electron pair and can no longer act as a nucleophile.

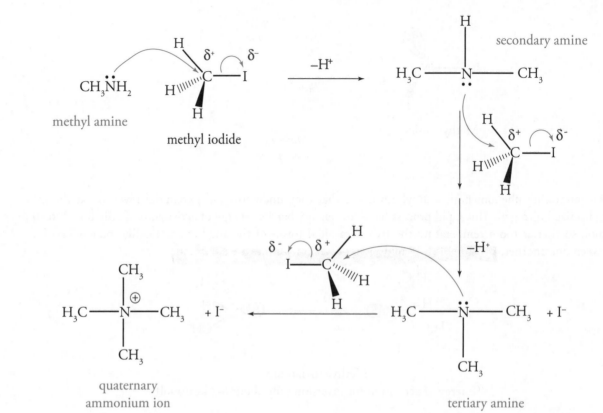

4.3 ELIMINATION REACTIONS

Elimination reactions are defined by the bonding changes that occur over the course of reaction. In an elimination reaction, two σ bonds in the starting material are converted into a π bond in the product. You should note that this is the reverse pathway of an addition reaction (see Section 5.1).

In the example above, the two σ bonds in the starting material that are broken are the C—Cl and the adjacent C—H bond. The π bond that forms in the product is the C=C double bond.

The E1 Mechanism

Like substitution, elimination can be either a unimolecular (E1) or a bimolecular (E2) process. E1 elimination, like S_N1 substitution, occurs via a 2-step mechanism.

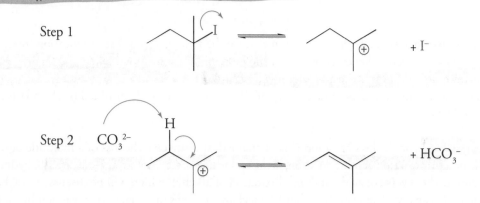

The iodide anion ionizes by falling off the carbon to which it was attached (Step 1), leaving behind a carbocation. A weak base then removes a proton on the carbon next to the carbon formerly attached to iodine (Step 2), leaving behind its electrons to form a C=C double bond.

E1 works best with 3° substrates, because they best support the positive charge after the leaving group leaves (remember, 3° > 2° > 1° for carbocation stability). Furthermore, in the E1 mechanism, the overall rate of the reaction is proportional only to the concentration of the substrate: rate = k[R-LG]. It's important to note that the base must remove a proton that is adjacent to the leaving group for elimination to proceed.

4.3

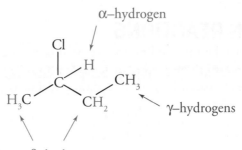

If no adjacent protons exist, elimination cannot occur directly.

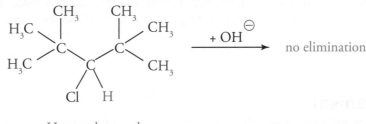

Here we have only
α and γ-protons

If there is more than one type of adjacent proton that can be removed from the carbocation intermediate by the base to give different alkenes as products, the more highly substituted alkene is usually formed in the greatest amount because it is thermodynamically favored. *Trans* isomers are generally favored over *cis* isomers. The regioselectivity and stereoselectivity of E1 reactions is thus determined by the relative stabilities of the products.

Dehydration reactions of alcohols are appropriately named; they involve the loss of a molecule of water to form an alkene. This reaction requires a strong acid and is favored by high temperatures. Dehydration of alcohols is simply the reverse of acid-catalyzed hydration of alkenes, which will be discussed in Chapter 5 This reaction is also an excellent example of an E1 mechanism. Let's investigate this reaction by looking at the dehydration of *tert*-butanol under anhydrous conditions.

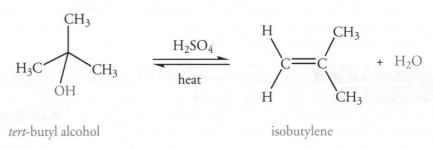

tert-butyl alcohol   isobutylene

In the first step of this reaction, protonation of the oxygen converts a poor leaving group (–OH) into a good leaving group (H_2O). Next, the oxygen departs with its electrons as a neutral water molecule and leaves behind a carbocation—this is the first step of the E1 mechanism. The mechanism is completed when the conjugate base of the acid removes a proton from a carbon atom adjacent to the carbon bearing the positive charge. The electrons from the C—H bond are used to satisfy the positively-charged carbon by forming a carbon-carbon π bond.

The Mechanism

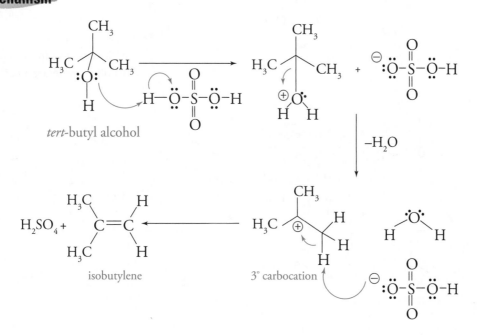

Remember that any proton on a carbon *adjacent* to a carbocation may be removed to form an alkene, but the *major* organic product will be the most substituted alkene since it is thermodynamically most stable. The following example, the dehydration of 3-methylpentan-2-ol, will clarify this point.

4.3

The Mechanism

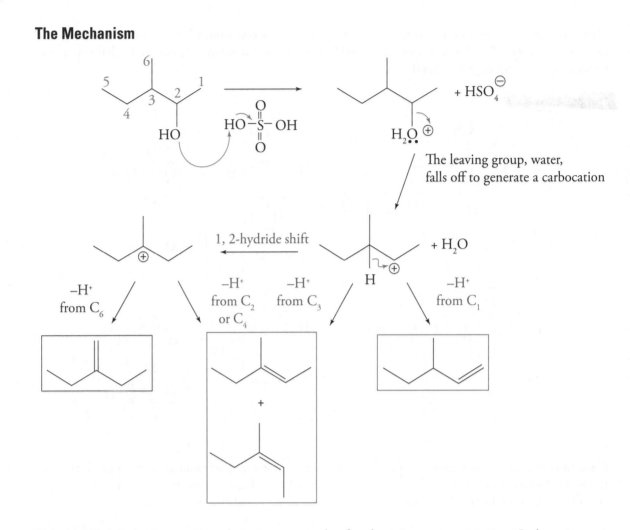

The alcohol dehydration reaction above is an example of **carbocation rearrangement**. Carbocations are thermodynamically unstable due to the electron deficiency (no octet of electrons) on the carbon with the positive charge. The high degree of thermodynamic instability of the carbocation makes it quite difficult to form, and once formed, it is very reactive. Once the intermediate carbocation is formed, it will quickly rearrange to a more stable carbocation if possible. Remember that the order of stability of carbocations is: 3° carbocation > 2° carbocation > 1° carbocation > methyl carbocation.

Carbocation rearrangements occur most commonly by either 1,2-hydride (H^-) shifts or by 1,2-methide (CH_3^-) shifts. The following demonstrates both types of carbocation rearrangements.

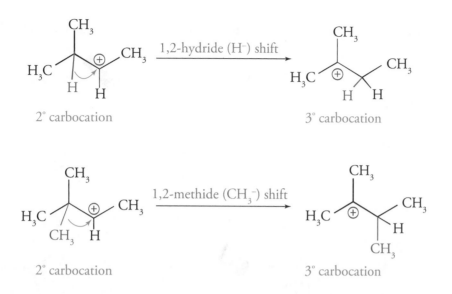

2° carbocation   3° carbocation

2° carbocation   3° carbocation

Notice that in both a 1,2-hydride shift and a 1,2-methide shift, rearrangement leads to a more stable carbocation. A carbocation will never rearrange to form a less stable carbocation.

The E1 mechanism is also favored by a protic solvent since it shares the same rate limiting step as the S_N1 reaction. After the carbocation has formed, the solvent may then act as a base if no other weak base is present in solution. Since this reaction generally occurs under conditions identical to the S_N1 reaction, these two mechanisms often compete with each other. It is rare to see 100% of either the S_N1 product or the E1 product for a given reaction. Instead, you will usually see mixtures of both products.

Key Features of an E1 Reaction

Reactivity of substrate:	3° > 2° >> 1° (Because of carbocation stability)
Stereochemistry:	Most substituted double bond forms—*trans* is favored over *cis*
Kinetics:	reaction rate = k[haloalkane]
Solvent:	E1 reactions are favored by protic (hydrogen bonding) solvents. (This stabilizes the carbocation.)
Rearrangements:	Carbocation rearrangement is possible; if the carbocation can rearrange to one that is more stable, it will.
Favoring Conditions:	Elimination reactions are favored over substitution reactions by the use of weak bases and high temperatures.

Example 4-4: Determine the major organic product (A, B, C, or D) from each of the following dehydration reactions:

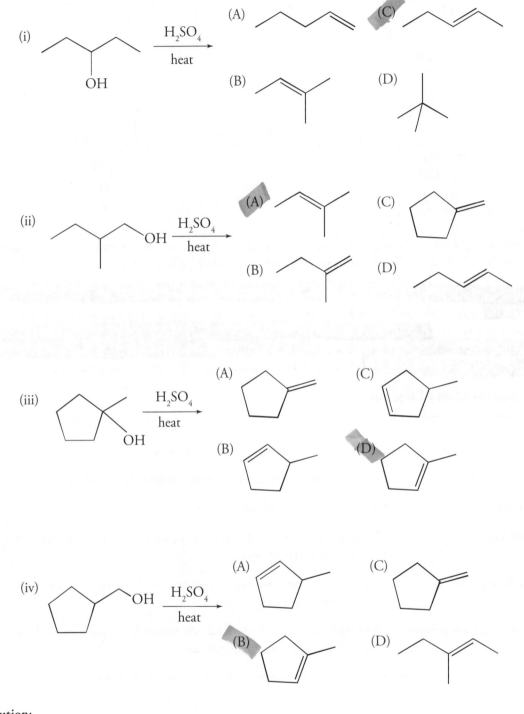

Solution:

(i)   C

(ii)   A (Note that carbocation rearrangement would occur.)

(iii)   D

(iv)   B, carbocation rearrangement.

The E2 Mechanism

E2 elimination, just as S_N2 substitution, proceeds via a 1-step mechanism. A strong base (generally hydroxide or an alkoxide ion) removes the β-hydrogen while the leaving group leaves. The carbon-carbon double bond forms at the same time. (All three changes happen in a concerted fashion.)

While all other reactions we've examined thus far work with both alkyl halides and alcohols as substrates, only alkyl halides may act as the substrate for E2 reactions. The E2 mechanism works best if the proton to be removed is *anti* to the leaving group, similar to the way the nucleophile must approach from the backside in an S_N2 reaction. Since the reaction occurs in a single step and with the β-proton *anti* to the leaving group, the stereochemistry of the double bond is predetermined by the reaction transition state. Expectedly, the reaction rate is proportional to both the concentration of the haloalkane and the concentration of the base (thus a bimolecular reaction): rate = $k[RX][HO^-]$.

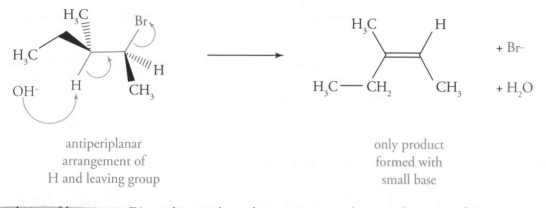

antiperiplanar
arrangement of
H and leaving group

only product
formed with
small base

The choice of base in an E2 mechanism has a large impact on the regiochemistry of the reaction. As shown above, small bases will remove the proton from the most substituted carbon, thereby yielding the most substituted, most stable alkene as the major product. However, if a bulky base is used (usually *tert*-butoxide or LDA), steric hindrance prevents the thermodynamic product from being formed. Instead, the base will remove the most accessible β-proton, yielding the least substituted alkene as the major product.

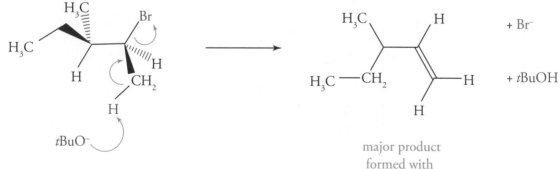

major product
formed with
bulky base

4.3

The elimination pathway in many instances may compete with the substitution pathway. This is because a base can also act as a nucleophile. Generally speaking, strong bases such as OH⁻ or OR⁻ yield exclusively the elimination product(s) unless the substrate is primary.

Key Features of an E2 Reaction

Reactivity of substrate: 3° > 2° > 1° (more substituted substrates are more likely to eliminate –1° ones substitute)

Stereochemistry: Alkene stereochemistry is determined by the antiperiplanar conformation of the substrate. Small bases yield the most substituted alkene; bulky bases favor the least substituted one.

Kinetics: reaction rate = k[base][substrate]

Solvent: E2 reactions are favored by polar, aprotic (non-hydrogen bonding) solvents.

Rearrangements: Not possible due to concerted mechanism. No carbocations are present in solution.

Favoring Conditions: E2 reactions are favored over E1 reactions by the use of strong bases. High temperatures favor eliminations over substitutions, but primary substrates will substitute.

Example 4-5: Predict the major product of the following reaction:

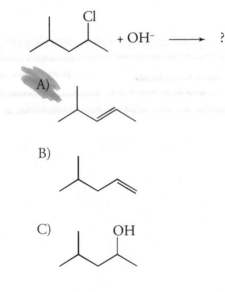

A)

B)

C) OH

D) No reaction because there are no β-protons.

Solution: Choice B would be a minor product of elimination in which OH⁻ would remove a β-proton from the right side of the molecule, as drawn. Remember that the most highly substituted alkene is the most stable. The answer is A.

Example 4-6: A chemist has a compound, C_4H_9Cl, which she believes to be either *n*-butyl chloride or *t*-butyl chloride.

n-butyl chloride    t-butyl chloride

She reacts the compound with a base and gets an alkene, C_4H_8. She determines that the rate of reaction is independent of the concentration of base used. Therefore, her original compound was:

A)   *n*-butyl chloride because the reaction is E1, and 1° alkyl halides undergo E1 elimination.
B)   *n*-butyl chloride because the reaction is E2, and 1° alkyl halides undergo E2 elimination.
C)   *t*-butyl chloride because the reaction is E1, and 3° alkyl halides undergo E1 elimination.
D)   *t*-butyl chloride because the reaction is E2, and 3° alkyl halides undergo E2 elimination.

Solution: Because the rate of the reaction is independent of the hydroxide concentration, it is only dependent on the concentration of the alkyl chloride and hence E1. E1 works best with 3° halides, so C_4H_9Cl must be *t*-butyl chloride. The answer is C.

Summary of Substitutions and Eliminations

Reaction dominance with increasing electrophile substitution →

↑ Reaction dominance with increasing nucleophile strength

$S_N 2$
- rate = $k[E^+][Nu^-]$
- one step
- backside attack
- requires strong Nu^-
- inversion of configuration
- methyl > 1° > 2° >> 3°

$S_N 1$
- rate = $k[E^+]$
- two steps
- carbocation intermediate
- requires good Nu^-
- results in racemization
- 3° > 2° >> 1° > methyl

E2
- rate = $k[E^+][B^-]$
- one step
- antiperiplanar geometry
- requires strong base (B^-)
- small base gives most substituted alkene; bulky base gives least substituted
- 3° > 2° > 1°

E1
- rate = $k[E^+]$
- two steps
- carbocation intermediate
- requires weak base (B^-)
- major product is most substituted alkene; *trans > cis*
- 3° > 2° >> 1°

4.4 PROPERTIES OF ALCOHOLS

We've seen that alcohols are a very useful class of chemicals because of their diverse reactivity. Let's review a few other properties of this important functional group, such as their intermolecular interactions and acidity.

Hydrogen Bonding

In order to examine the effect of hydrogen bonding in alcohols, let's examine two molecules that are isomers of one another, *n*-butanol and diethyl ether. Both have the same molecular formula ($C_4H_{10}O$), yet there is a dramatic difference in their boiling points (117°C for *n*-butanol vs. 34.6°C for diethyl ether). This difference arises from the ability of *n*-butanol to form intermolecular hydrogen bonds, while diethyl ether *cannot*. Alcohols form intermolecular hydrogen bonds because they have hydroxyl (–OH) groups. This results from a strong dipole in which the hydroxyl group's proton acquires a substantial partial positive charge (δ^+) and the oxygen acquires a substantial partial negative charge (δ^-). The partial positive hydrogen can interact electrostatically with a non-bonding pair of electrons on a nearby oxygen, resulting in a hydrogen bond. On the other hand, diethyl ether has an oxygen atom with non-bonding electrons but all hydrogen atoms are bound to carbons. Since carbon and hydrogen have similar electronegativity values, the bond is not very polarized, and these hydrogens cannot participate in hydrogen bonding. It's important to remember that a hydrogen bond is *not* a covalent bond; in this case it's an intermolecular interaction.

Intermolecular hydrogen bonding between molecules of *n*-butanol.

molecular weight = 74
b.p. = 117°C

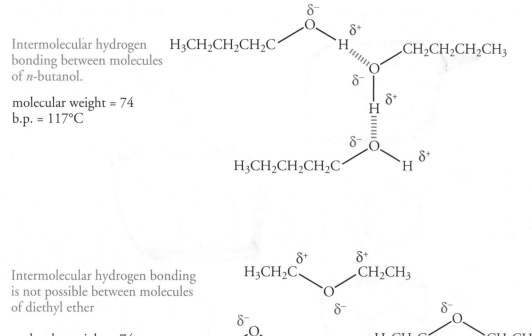

4.4

Intermolecular hydrogen bonding is not possible between molecules of diethyl ether

molecular weight = 74
b.p. = 34.6°C

Example 4-7: For each of the following pairs of compounds, predict which molecule will have the higher boiling point.

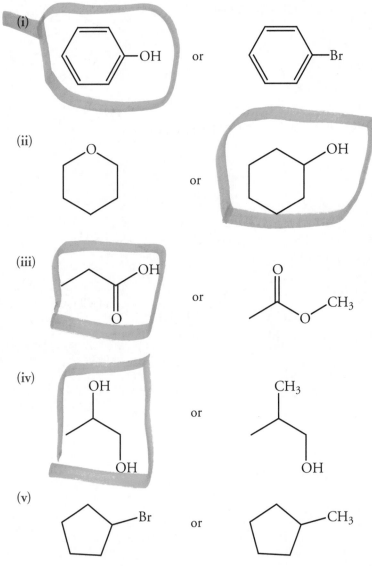

Solution:

(i)

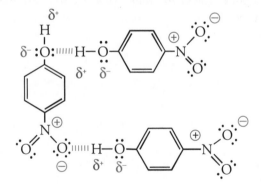

(ii) [cyclohexanol with OH group]

(iii) [propanoic acid, OH and O]

4.4

(iv) [propane-1,2-diol, two OH groups]

(v) [bromocyclopentane, Br]

(primarily because of its greater mass)

The hydrogen bonding pattern in phenols provides insight into *inter*molecular vs. *intra*molecular hydrogen bonding. Let's consider the two isomers, *para*-nitrophenol (also called 4-nitrophenol) and *ortho*-nitrophenol (also called 2-nitrophenol). (For more on the nomenclature of aromatic compounds, see Section 5.2.) First, examine the hydrogen bonding pattern in *para*-nitrophenol. Notice that hydrogen bonding can occur with both the nitro and the hydroxyl groups in this molecule and that the bonding is exclusively intermolecular. That is, all hydrogen bonding takes place between individual molecules of *para*-nitrophenol. These hydrogen bonding interactions hold molecules of *para*-nitrophenol together and increase their boiling and melting points. Now, examine the hydrogen bonding pattern in *ortho*-nitrophenol. Notice that for this molecule, the nitro group and the hydroxyl group are in close proximity so that intramolecular hydrogen bonding can occur between the hydrogen of the hydroxyl group and a lone pair of electrons on the nitro group *on the same molecule*. These intramolecular hydrogen bonding interactions decrease the amount of intermolecular hydrogen bonding interactions that can occur between molecules thereby decreasing the melting and boiling points of *ortho*-nitrophenol relative to *para*-nitrophenol.

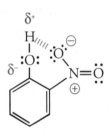

para-nitrophenol
Intermolecular hydrogen bonding

ortho-nitrophenol
Intramolecular hydrogen bonding

Acidity

The acidity of a compound is determined by the ease with which it can lose a proton (H⁺). Alcohols are a relatively acidic functional group for the same reason that they engage in hydrogen bonding: the large difference in electronegativity between oxygen and hydrogen. If an alcohol like methanol is deprotonated, an alkoxide ion is formed. The alkoxide is a relatively stable species, compared to a carbanion for example, since the negative charge that results from this reaction is located on the very electronegative oxygen atom.

$$\text{H}_3\text{C}\ddot{\text{O}}\text{H} \rightleftharpoons \text{H}_3\text{C}\ddot{\ddot{\text{O}}}{:}^{\ominus} + \text{H}^{\oplus}$$

Methanol   Methoxide   Proton
ion

Phenols are considerably more acidic than alcohols, but are not as acidic as carboxylic acids. The increased acidity of phenols relative to alcohols is due to the fact that the phenoxide ion can be stabilized by resonance, while alkoxide ions cannot. This is demonstrated by the following:

Resonance Structures for the Phenoxide Ion

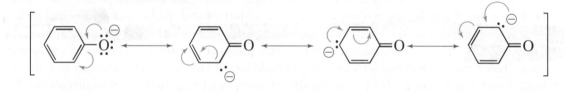

Electron-withdrawing substituents on phenols increase their acidity. As an example, consider *para*-nitrophenol. The nitro group is strongly electron withdrawing and greatly stabilizes the phenoxide ion through resonance stabilization. Once the *para*-nitrophenol is deprotonated, it's easy to see how the nitro group can withdraw electrons through the delocalized π system such that the negative charge on the phenoxide oxygen can be delocalized all the way to an oxygen atom of the nitro group. This electron-withdrawing resonance stabilization of the nitro group increases the acidity of *para*-nitrophenol as compared to a phenol that does not have electron-withdrawing substituents.

Effects of Substituents on Acidity

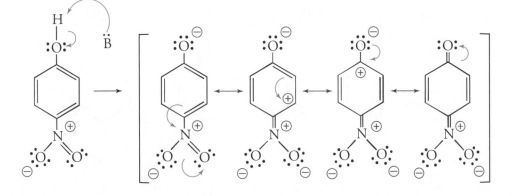

On the other hand, consider a substituted phenol that has an electron-*donating* group rather than an electron-*withdrawing* group. A good example of this is *para*-methoxyphenol. Here, it is easy to see how once *para*-methoxyphenol is deprotonated, the negative charge on the oxygen can be destabilized by the donation of a lone pair of electrons from the methoxy oxygen so a negative charge is placed on a carbon that's adjacent to the negatively charged phenoxide oxygen. Electron-donating groups tend to destabilize a phenoxide ion and decrease the acidity of substituted phenols.

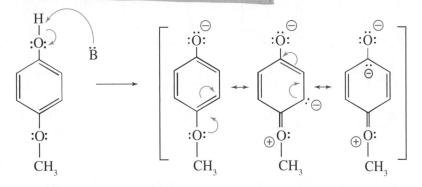

Example 4-8: For each of the following groups of four phenols, rank them in order of decreasing acidity.

(i)

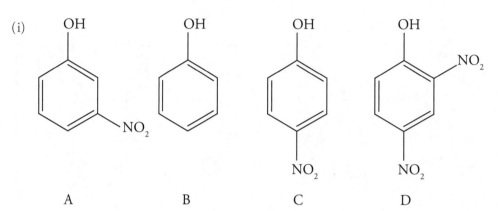

A   B   C   D

(ii)

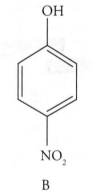
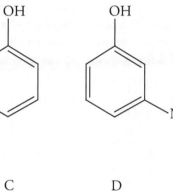

A   B   C   D

(iii)

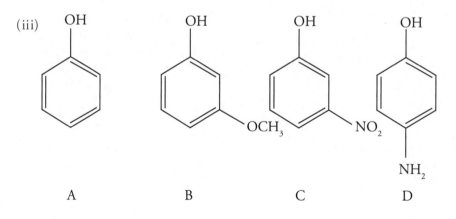

A   B   C   D

Solution:

(i)   D > C > A > B. Compound D is the most acidic because of the two electron-withdrawing nitro groups. They delocalize the charge of the conjugate base, making D a stronger acid. Although both A and C have one nitro group, the *para*-nitro group in C can also delocalize the charge by resonance, while the *meta*-nitro group in A cannot. Therefore, C is more acidic than A. Finally, B is the least acidic, since it has no electron-withdrawing groups to stabilize the charge.

Similar arguments can be made to explain the rankings for the four phenols in (ii) and (iii). See if you can construct them.

4.5

(ii)   B > D > C > A
(iii)   C > A > B > D

4.5   FORMATION OF ALKYL HALIDES—A SUMMARY

In Section 4.1, we learned that alkanes can be converted into haloalkanes by the free-radical halogenation reaction. This is the first method of haloalkane synthesis. We've also seen how halides can be interconverted via substitution of other halides, or by treating alcohols with mineral acids. Two other methods presented here involve alkyl halide preparation from the corresponding alcohol.

Reactions of Alcohols with Phosphorus Halides

One common reagent used to produce alkyl bromides and alkyl chlorides is the corresponding phosphorus trihalide compound (PBr_3 or PCl_3). For example, they can be used to convert isobutyl alcohol into isobutyl bromide or isobutyl chloride.

Reactions of Alcohols with Thionyl Chloride

Another common method for alkyl chloride synthesis is thionyl chloride (SOCl$_2$). This reaction is very convenient since the sulfur containing by-product (SO$_2$) is a gas and bubbles out of the reaction flask.

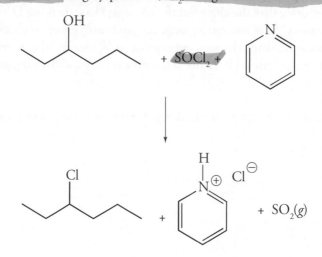

Chapter 4 Summary

- Radical brominations are regioselective for tertiary bromides, while chlorinations yield mixtures of substitution products.

- All free radical halogenations are non-stereoselective, giving racemic mixtures of products when one new stereocenter is formed.

- Radical selectivity = product distribution/# of identical hydrogens.

- Nucleophiles are Lewis bases and are electron rich, while electrophiles are Lewis acids and are electron deficient.

- Nucleophiles are stronger when negatively charged, less electronegative, or larger in size.

- Leaving groups are more likely to leave as their stability in solution increases (uncharged and/or larger groups are usually better LGs).

- More substituted substrates and protic solvents favor S_N1 over S_N2.

- Carbocation intermediates formed in either S_N1 or E1 reactions will rearrange if possible to form a more stable carbocation.

- Second order reactions (S_N2 or E2) require specific spatial orientations of the reacting species (S_N2 = backside attack of Nuc⁻; E2 = antiperiplanar conformation of H and LG).

- First order reactions (S_N1 or E1) do not depend on the concentration of the Nuc⁻ or base.

- Eliminations break two σ bonds and form one π bond.

- Non-nucleophilic bases and heat favor eliminations over substitutions, and strong bases favor E2 over E1.

- Zaitsev's rule favors the formation of the more substituted bond in elimination reactions (E2 reactions must use small bases), and *trans* double bonds are favored over *cis*.

CHAPTER 4 FREESTANDING PRACTICE QUESTIONS

1. Which of the following is the strongest nucleophile?

A) CN⁻
B) OH⁻
C) CH_3OH
D) NH_3

2. Which reaction proceeds the fastest?

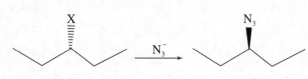

A) When X = Br
B) When X = F
C) When X = Cl
D) When X = I

3. Which of the following is associated with an S_N2 reaction?

A) sp^2 hybridized intermediate
B) A unimolecular rate law
C) An antiperiplanar conformation
D) Inversion of configuration

4. Which step of the radical process does the following reaction represent?

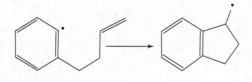

A) Initiation
B) Propagation
C) Termination
D) Elimination

5. The acid catalyzed dehydration of 3-methyl-2-butanol yields two products. What is the relationship between them?

A) Enantiomers
B) Diastereomers
C) Conformational isomers
D) Constitutional isomers

6. Which of the following compounds undergoes S_N1-type substitution most *slowly*?

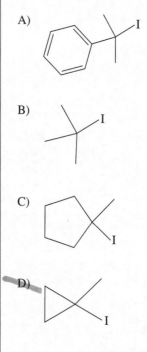

7. Which of the following alkyl halides forms the same product in both an S_N1 and S_N2 reaction?

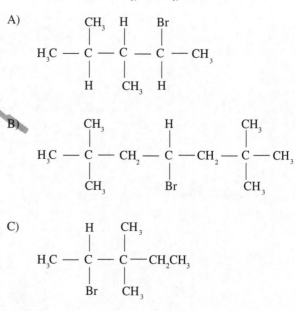

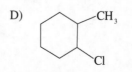

CHAPTER 4 PRACTICE PASSAGE

Radical reactions are generally chain reactions consisting of three steps: initiation, propagation, and termination. Ideally, radicals must have a sufficient lifetime to react, but not live so long that unwanted side-reactions, such as autoxidation, take place. Autoxidation occurs when the forming product reacts with molecular oxygen present in the system. In order to protect the system from autoxidation, compounds called antioxidants can be employed.

In industrial settings, benzofuranones such as Compound 1 have been used as antioxidants. Studies show their effectiveness lies in their ability to donate a hydrogen atom to oxidized products. This process terminates the autoxidation pathway because the benzofuranone radical will not react with oxygen (Scheme 1).

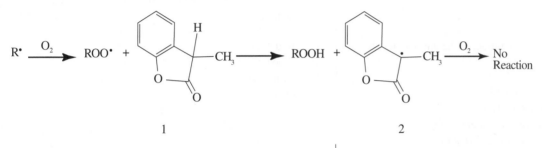

Scheme 1 Compound 1 behaves as an effective antioxidant

Studies were also performed on isobenzofuranones to determine their abilities as antioxidants. Scientists compared the reaction rates of Compounds 3–5 with oxygen (Scheme 2) to determine the effect of a nitro group at different positions on the aromatic ring. The reaction rate of Compound 5 was slower than that of Compound 3; no difference in reaction rate was observed between Compounds 3 and 4.

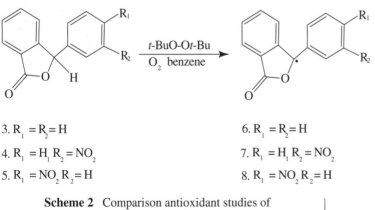

3. $R_1 = R_2 = H$

4. $R_1 = H, R_2 = NO_2$

5. $R_1 = NO_2, R_2 = H$

6. $R_1 = R_2 = H$

7. $R_1 = H, R_2 = NO_2$

8. $R_1 = NO_2, R_2 = H$

Scheme 2 Comparison antioxidant studies of isobenzofuranones

1. In what step of the reaction in Scheme 2 does *t*-BuO-O*t*-Bu play a role?

   A) Initiation
   B) Solvation
   C) Propagation
   D) Termination

2. Which of the following statements are true about the radical in Compound 2?

   I.   It is destabilized by conjugation to the carbonyl.
   II. It is stabilized by its benzylic position.
   III. It is stabilized because it is tertiary.

   A) III only
   B) I and II only
   C) II and III only
   D) I, II, and III

3. How does the nitro group influence the antioxidant ability of Compound 5?

   A) It makes it a weaker antioxidant.
   B) It makes it a better antioxidant.
   C) It doesn't influence the antioxidant ability.
   D) Cannot predict based on the information given.

4. What is the hybridization of the carbon bearing the radical in Compound 2?

   A) p
   B) sp
   C) sp^2
   D) sp^3

5. In Scheme 1, when radical R˙ reacts with oxygen it is called autoxidation. What is another term for this process?

   A) Termination
   B) Propagation
   C) Initiation
   D) Inhibition

6. What step of the radical chain does an antioxidant facilitate?

   A) Initiation
   B) Propagation
   C) Termination
   D) Oxidation

SOLUTIONS TO CHAPTER 4 FREESTANDING QUESTIONS

1. **A**   Nucleophiles are electron dense. While neutral compounds that have lone pairs can be nucleophilic, negatively charged nucleophiles tend to be stronger (eliminate choices C and D). The stronger nucleophile is the more reactive nucleophile; more reactive corresponds to less stable. Therefore, the nucleophile that is less able to stabilize a negative charge will be the stronger nucleophile. For choices A and B, the negative charge resides on the C and O, respectively. Since carbon is less electronegative than oxygen, it is therefore less able to stabilize a negative charge, making cyanide the best nucleophile (eliminate choice B).

2. **D**   This is an S_N2 reaction, since it occurs with inversion of stereochemistry. Therefore the rate of the reaction is determined by both the nucleophile and the haloalkane. The halogen that can best stabilize a negative charge will be the best leaving group and give the fastest reaction. Acidity of HX acids increases going down the periodic table because the larger halogens can spread the negative charge over a larger surface area to stabilize it. Because iodine is the largest of the halogens, it is also the best leaving group.

3. **D**   In an S_N2 reaction, the starting substrate undergoes a backside attack where the nucleophile attacks opposite the leaving group, causing a complete stereochemical inversion. Choice A can be eliminated because the there is no intermediate in this reaction. Choice B can be eliminated because S_N2 is a bimolecular process, as the name implies. Choice C can be eliminated because the conformation of the groups is not an important factor for the S_N2 reaction.

4. **B**   In a propagation step of a radical mechanism, there is no net change in the number of radicals in the reaction, as shown in this example. An initiation step results in a net increase in the number of radicals in the reaction (eliminate choice A). A termination results in a net decrease in the number of radicals in the reaction (eliminate choice C). An elimination is not part of a typical radical reaction; it results in the formation of a new pi bond. Lastly, eliminate choice D since in this reaction a pi bond is broken.

5. **D**   The first step of the reaction involves protonation of the hydroxyl group followed by elimination of water leading to a secondary carbocation intermediate. This intermediate undergoes a hydride shift to form a more stable tertiary carbocation. Loss of a β-hydrogen from the tertiary carbocation leads to formation of two products. The major product is 2-methyl-2-butene; the minor product is 2-methyl-1-butene. These are constitutional or structural isomers since the double bond is in a different position along the chain. Choice A can be eliminated because the products do not have stereocenters. Choice B can be eliminated since the products are not *cis/trans* isomers. The two products do not differ by rotation about a sigma bond, so choice C can be eliminated.

6. **D**   An S_N1 reaction must pass through a planar, sp^2 hybridized intermediate. If this intermediate is very high in energy, then the reaction will proceed slowly, since the transition state to this intermediate is, by definition, even higher in energy. For sp^2 hybridization, the optimum bond angles are 120°, but the cyclopropane ring in choice D holds two of the legs at a 60° angle. This imparts a lot of strain in the intermediate state, making it very high in energy. Choice C would have some strain in the transition state, but nowhere near the strain in choice D. Choice B has no such constraints. Not only does choice A have no ring-strain constraints, but the intermediate would be stabilized by the phenyl ring.

7. **B** All answer choices except choice B feature a halogen atom (potential leaving group) attached to a carbon atom that will allow rearrangement either via a hydride shift or a methyl shift when an S_N1 carbocation forms. Choice B shows a bromine atom attached to a secondary carbon adjacent to two other secondary carbons. Rearrangement will therefore not occur when bromine leaves, allowing both S_N1 and S_N2 products to be the same.

SOLUTIONS TO CHAPTER 4 PRACTICE PASSAGE

1. **A** Di-*tert*-butyl peroxide is a radical initiator, as many peroxides are (look for O—O bonds). When it is irradiated, it forms two *tert*-butoxy radicals that initiate the radical chain reaction, so choices C and D can be eliminated. Solvation is not a step in any radical chain reaction, so choice B can be eliminated.

2. **C** Conjugation to the carbonyl group would stabilize the radical, not destabilize it, so you can eliminate choices B and D. The remaining answer choices suggest that as a tertiary radical it is stable since Item III is in both choices (remember that more substitution inductively stabilizes radicals). To make the final distinction, note that Item II is also true since the radical is adjacent to a benzene ring, making it benzylic and resonance stabilized (eliminate answer choice A).

3. **B** The reaction rate of Compound 5 with oxygen is slowed due to the presence of the nitro group, so eliminate choices C and D. As stated in the passage, an effective antioxidant does not react with molecular oxygen in the system after hydrogen atom abstraction. Therefore, the presence of the nitro group on Compound 5 helps make it a better antioxidant since it reacts more slowly than Compound 3 with no nitro group (eliminate answer A).

4. **C** A *p*-orbital is not hybridized, so choice A can be eliminated. The carbon has three substituents, which indicates sp^2 hybridization, so choices B and D can be eliminated.

5. **D** When a radical reacts with oxygen it can also be called inhibition because it stops the radical chain reaction that leads to the desired product. Choices A, B and C are all steps in any radical reaction regardless of the presence of oxygen as the first line of the passage suggests, so they can be eliminated.

6. **C** Oxidation is not a step in the reaction chain, so eliminate choice D. As shown in Scheme 1 of the passage, an antioxidant donates a hydrogen atom to an already formed, unwanted oxidized radical. By doing so, it prevents that oxygen radical from further reacting and continuing down unwanted side reaction pathways. Therefore, it facilitates the termination of the radical reaction since the radical form of the antioxidant itself is highly *un*reactive (eliminate choices A and B).

Chapter 5
Electrophilic Addition Reactions

5.1 REACTIONS OF ALKENES AND ALKYNES

Electrophilic Addition Reactions

Addition reactions are defined by the bonding changes that occur over the course of a reaction. In an addition reaction, a π bond in the starting material is broken, and two σ bonds in the product result. You should note that this is the reverse pathway of elimination reactions (see Section 4.3).

Recall that a carbon-carbon π bond is formed by the proper alignment of two adjacent unhybridized *p* orbitals. The electrons are localized in a region that lies above and below the plane defined by the central carbons and immediately adjacent atoms.

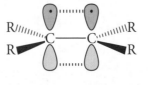

R = any alkyl group (or hydrogen)

These π electrons are more loosely held than σ electrons and can be nucleophilic. It is this property of π bonds that allows electrophilic additions to occur.

Before we turn to the specific electrophilic addition reactions that are important to be familiar with for the MCAT, be aware that trying to memorize the nitty-gritty details of each reaction is not the best use of your time. For many of the reactions below mechanisms are shown to highlight the similarities or differences between reactions. You will not need to memorize the details of all mechanisms. You should, however, pay particular attention to the general addition mechanism and the regio- and stereochemistry of all reactions.

Markovnikov Additions

H—X (H—Cl, H—Br, and H—I) Addition Across a Bond   The first reaction we will examine is the addition of a strong mineral acid (H—Cl, H—Br, or H—I) to a carbon-carbon π bond. Consider the reaction between 3-methyl-1-butene and H—Br.

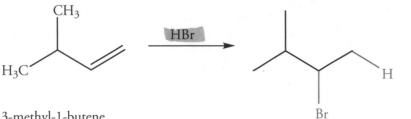
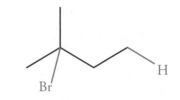

3-methyl-1-butene

(*R*),(*S*)-2-bromo-3-methylbutane
(Both enantiomers formed in equal amounts.)

2-bromo-2-methylbutane

In the first step of this reaction (shown below) the π electrons are protonated to form a new C—H σ bond, a carbocation, and bromide ion. Notice that the more substituted carbon receives the positive charge and the less substituted carbon (more hydrogens) receives the new C—H σ bond. The formation of the most stable carbocation intermediate corresponds to **Markovnikov's rule**. That is, given a choice, **the most stable carbocation intermediate is always formed.** Once the carbocation intermediate is formed, it can have two fates. The carbocation may undergo nucleophilic attack by the bromide ion, in a fashion similar to the fast step in an S_N1 reaction. As in the S_N1 reaction, the planarity of the carbocation intermediate results in a racemic mixture of products, in this case both (*R*) and (*S*)-2-bromo-3-methylbutane. Alternatively, this carbocation can rearrange to a more stable 3° carbocation by means of a 1,2-hydride (H⁻) shift, which is subsequently attacked by bromide yielding the achiral molecule 2-bromo-2-methylbutane.

The Mechanism

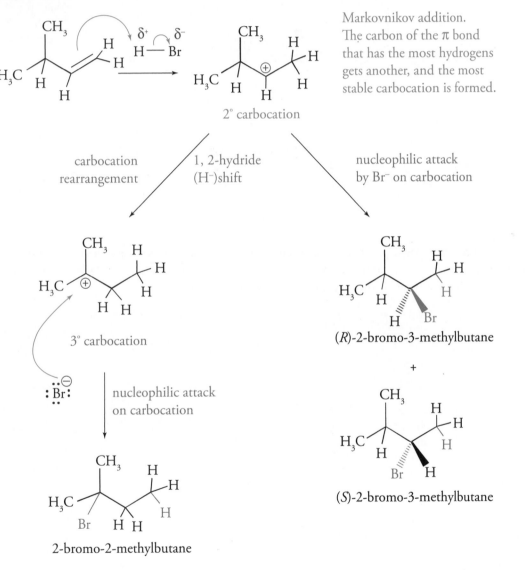

Markovnikov addition. The carbon of the π bond that has the most hydrogens gets another, and the most stable carbocation is formed.

2° carbocation

carbocation rearrangement

1, 2-hydride (H⁻)shift

nucleophilic attack by Br⁻ on carbocation

3° carbocation

(*R*)-2-bromo-3-methylbutane

+

nucleophilic attack on carbocation

(*S*)-2-bromo-3-methylbutane

2-bromo-2-methylbutane

Acid-Catalyzed Hydration of Alkenes

In acid-catalyzed hydration of alkenes, the alkene is added to an acid-water solution (a 50/50 mixture of sulfuric acid and water is typical) and allowed to react until the alcohol product is formed. Sulfuric acid is the ideal strong acid in this reaction, because, unlike Cl^- or Br^- its conjugate base, HSO_4^-, is non-nucleophilic. As such, there should be no nucleophile to compete with water for the carbocation. Note that this is a reversible reaction. (For a description of alcohol dehydration [an elimination reaction] see Section 4.3.) The following represents some typical examples of acid catalyzed alkene hydration reactions.

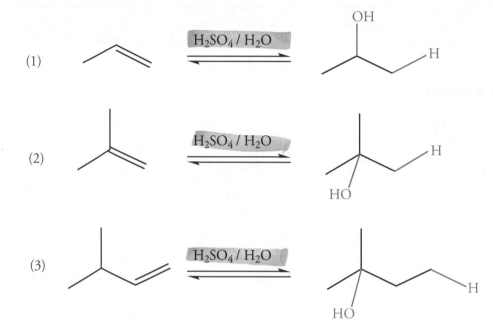

There are a few important points to note about the above hydration reactions. First, notice that all of the alcohols that are formed correspond to the Markovnikov addition product; this is because of the reaction mechanism. Shown below is the mechanism for Reaction 1 above.

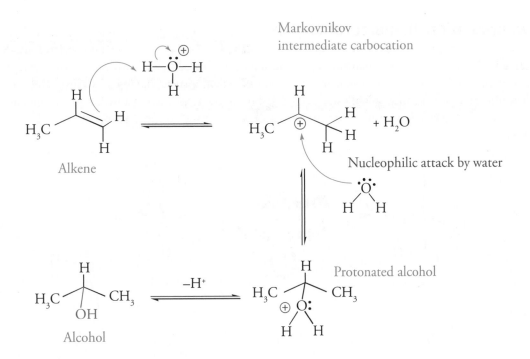

In the first step of this reaction, the π bond of the alkene is protonated to form the Markovnikov carbocation intermediate—the carbon of the π bond that has the most hydrogens to begin with receives the C—H σ bond, and the most substituted carbon is the recipient of the positive charge. Next, the carbocation is attacked by a nucleophilic water molecule to form the protonated alcohol. The protonated alcohol then quickly looses a proton to form the product. The following mechanism for reaction 3 above depicts how acid-catalyzed hydration reactions are prone to carbon skeleton rearrangements.

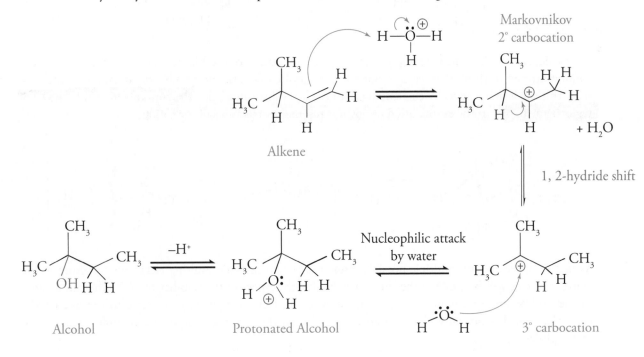

As you can see, if the original Markovnikov carbocation can rearrange to a more stable carbocation, it will.

Oxymercuration-Demercuration

The Markovnikov alcohol is also formed in the **oxymercuration-demercuration reaction**, but in this reaction there is no possibility of carbon skeleton rearrangement. As shown in the mechanism below, the alkene is allowed to react with mercuric acetate to form a three-membered, cationic, cyclic intermediate. Water then opens the highly strained ring through nucleophilic attack at the most highly substituted carbon in the ring, leaving a hydroxyalkyl mercuric acetate species. This is reduced with sodium borohydride, under basic conditions, to yield the Markovnikov alcohol.

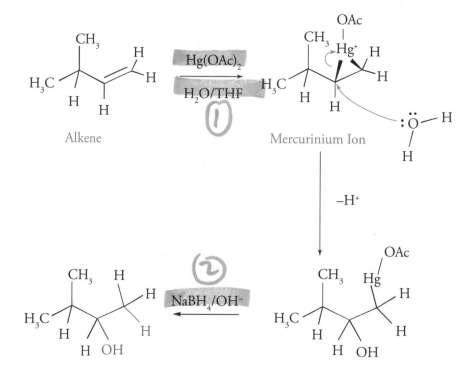

The cyclic, cationic intermediate is key in the selective formation of the Markovnikov alcohol. It may seem counterintuitive to think that water, a nucleophile, would attack the more substituted carbon of the ring, since this site is more sterically challenging than the less substituted side. The reason behind this choice of regiochemistry lies in the examination of possible resonance structures of the cation.

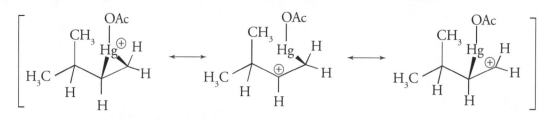

As in any molecule with multiple possible resonance structures, the resulting electronic structure of the above molecule will be a mix of the three, weighted with respect to the stability of each. The carbocation in the middle structure is more highly substituted, and thus energetically favorable to the one on the right. As such this carbon will bear a greater portion of the cationic charge, and be more attractive to nucleophiles.

This type of 3-membered cyclic intermediate plays a role in many reactions, a few of which will be mentioned shortly. In each case, so long at the species is cationic, the attack which opens the ring, and subsequent substitution, takes place at the more highly substituted of the ring carbons.

Anti-Markovnikov Addition

Hydroboration   Alcohols can be synthesized in an anti-Markovnikov fashion, with the hydroxyl occupying the least substituted of the two carbons of the double bond, through a process known as **hydroboration**. In this reaction the alkene is treated with BH_3 (either in solution as in BH_3–THF, or neat in the dimeric form, B_2H_6) to form an intermediate organoborane compound. The organoborane intermediate is then oxidized with hydrogen peroxide (H_2O_2) under basic conditions to form the anti-Markovnikov alcohol. These properties are demonstrated by the following two reactions.

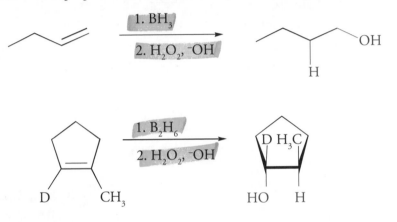

Notice that the –OH ends up on the less substituted carbon instead of the more substituted carbon. Furthermore, the stereochemistry of the addition to the π bond is *syn*. Both the hydrogen that is added and the –OH end up on the same side of the former C=C double bond.

HBr Addition in the Presence of Peroxides   Chemists have also developed tools to produce halogenated alkanes in anti-Markovnikov fashion. When an alkene is treated with H—Br in the presence of peroxides (R—O—O—R), H and Br are added to the π bond with the opposite regiochemistry than is seen in the addition of HX without peroxides. The less substituted carbon of the π bond ends up with a bond to bromine; the more substituted carbon of the π bond receives a new carbon-hydrogen σ bond. In order to understand how this occurs, we must look at the reaction mechanism.

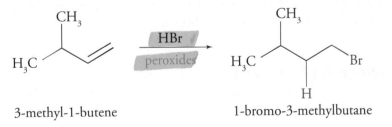

3-methyl-1-butene   1-bromo-3-methylbutane

Homolytic bond cleavage of the O—O bond of the peroxide molecule occurs in the first step of this reaction, generating two R—O• radicals. One R—O• radical then abstracts a hydrogen atom from HBr in another homolytic bond cleavage, to form a molecule of alcohol and a bromine radical. The lone electron of the bromine radical forms a σ bond with the less substituted carbon of the π bond such that the other electron of the π bond resides on the more substituted carbon. The order of stability for radicals is 3° > 2° > 1°, just as it is for carbocations. The alkyl radical then collides with a molecule of H—Br and abstracts a hydrogen atom in a homolytic bond cleavage resulting in the formation of the alkyl halide product and another bromine radical. Note that this peroxide effect only works for H—Br; it is not observed with H—Cl or H—I.

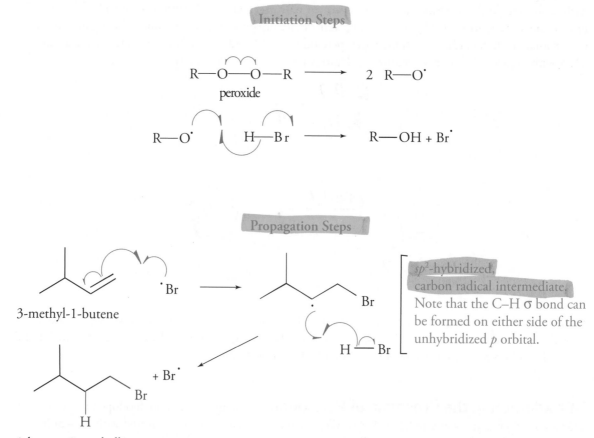

Remember, the most important features to focus on for the MCAT for all of the reactions described above are the regiochemistry differences. Therefore, be sure you know which reactions follow Markovnikov addition rules, and which follow anti-Markovnikov addition.

Addition of Halogens (X$_2$) to a π Bond
Whereas the addition of HX is an effective technique to monohalogenate double bonds, dihalogenation is known to occur through treatment of alkenes with diatomic halogens.

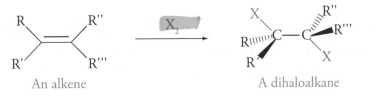

An alkene → A dihaloalkane

Consider the reaction that occurs when cyclopentene is treated with bromine (Br_2). In the first step of this reaction, the nucleophilic π electrons attack molecular bromine to yield a bromonium ion and a bromide anion in an S_N2 reaction. At first glance it would not appear that molecular bromine would be very electrophilic. However, when an electron-rich π bond comes close to a molecule of Br_2, it induces a dipole in the Br_2 molecule so that one side of the molecule becomes slightly negatively charged while the other side becomes slightly positively charged. This provides the initial driving force for the reaction.

Mechanism of Dihaloalkane Formation

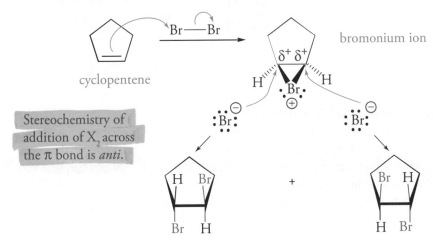

Stereochemistry of addition of X_2 across the π bond is *anti*.

enantiomeric *trans*-1,2-dibromocyclopentane

As is the case with the previously mentioned mercurinium ion, the positive charge on this bridged bromine pulls electrons away from the two carbons to which it is attached, causing them to become slightly positive and electrophilic. These electrophilic carbon atoms are susceptible to nucleophilic attack by bromide ions from the opposite side of the bridged structure. As the nucleophilic bromide ion attacks the bridged structure, it forms a bromine-carbon σ bond. Simultaneously, one of the carbon-bromine bonds of the bridged structure breaks; this reaction is essentially an S_N2 substitution. It is important to be aware of the stereochemistry of addition of the two bromines to the π bond. Notice that two chiral centers are formed in this particular reaction, and the two products that are formed (depending upon whether the bromide ion attacks the right or left carbon of the bridged bromonium ion) are nonsuperimposable mirror images of each other—that is, enantiomers. Since attack at either carbon of the bridged intermediate is equally likely, equal amounts of enantiomers are formed giving a racemic mixture. Also, it is important to note that the two bromine atoms are added across the double bond in anti-fashion. This is a result of the S_N2-like backside attack by the second bromine atom on the carbon of the bromonium ion.

If an alkene is treated with Br_2 in water, an intermediate bromonium ion is formed, which subsequently undergoes nucleophilic attack by water. This yields a halohydrin, a molecule in which a bromine atom and an –OH from water have been added across the carbon-carbon π bond. If the bromonium ion is unsymmetrical, the nucleophile will prefer to attack the more substituted carbon atom of the bridged structure for the same reason we saw water attack the more substituted carbon in the oxymercuration reaction. Again, this phenomenon can be explained by the possible resonance structures of the cation.

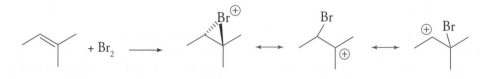

The more substituted carbon bears the greater partial positive charge, thanks to its greater inductive stabilization of this charge. As such, the ring opening attack by water occurs at the more substituted carbon, in anti-fashion.

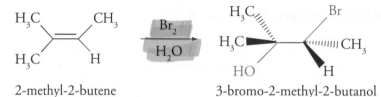

2-methyl-2-butene   3-bromo-2-methyl-2-butanol

Epoxide Formation and Hydrolysis

The next reaction we examine is **epoxide formation** and subsequent formation of *trans*-diols. In this type of reaction, a π bond in an alkene reacts with a peroxy acid to form an epoxide and a carboxylic acid. The π bond of the alkene, again, acts as the nucleophile, and the peroxy oxygen furthest from the carbonyl oxygen acts as the electrophile. We will not look at this reaction in any further mechanistic detail. The key point is that when an alkene reacts with a peroxy acid, an epoxide is formed.

Epoxide Formation: The General Reaction

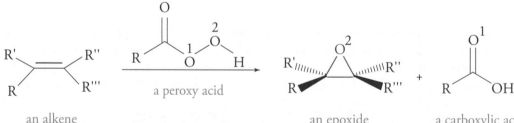

an alkene   a peroxy acid   an epoxide   a carboxylic acid

A Specific Example of an Epoxidation Followed by Acidic or Basic Hydrolysis

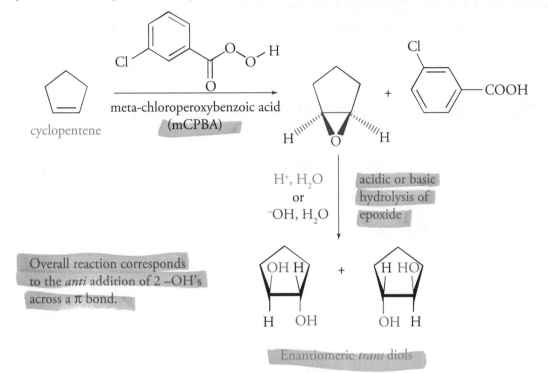

cyclopentene

meta-chloroperoxybenzoic acid
(mCPBA)

H^+, H_2O
or
$^-OH, H_2O$

acidic or basic
hydrolysis of
epoxide

Overall reaction corresponds
to the *anti* addition of 2 –OH's
across a π bond.

Enantiomeric *trans* diols

It is also important to note that when an epoxide is hydrolyzed under acidic or basic conditions, a *trans*-1,2-diol is formed.

Oxidation of π Bonds with Dilute KMnO$_4$

When alkenes are treated with dilute KMnO$_4$ (potassium permanganate) or OsO$_4$ (osmium tetraoxide), *cis*-diols are formed. The stereochemistry of this reaction requires *syn*-addition of two –OH's across the π bond.

cis-Diol Formation (*syn*-Addition of -OH Across a π Bond)

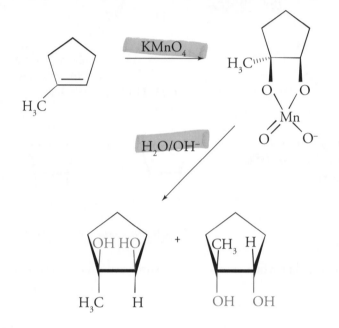

The organometallic intermediate in the above mechanism (similarly valid for OsO$_4$) is the reason only *cis*-diols are formed through the use of these reagents. The geometry of the metal complex forces both oxygen atoms to bond to the same side of the alkene. When they are replaced by OH⁻, these remain on the same side, *cis* to one another.

Hydrogenation

Another common reaction of π bonds is the hydrogenation reaction. Unsaturated hydrocarbons can be reduced by molecular hydrogen (H$_2$) in the presence of a metal catalyst. The first hydrogenation reaction we will consider is the simple reduction of an alkene to a fully saturated alkane. Methylcyclopentene is reduced by molecular hydrogen in the presence of a metal catalyst to methylcyclopentane. The stereochemistry of this reduction reaction is *syn* with the two hydrogens added to the same side of the π bond. Although this example uses nickel (Ni), palladium (Pd), or platinum (Pt) metal as the catalyst, a variety of metals (mostly from the right half of transition metal series) and metal-containing compounds can act as catalysts for this type of reaction. Don't allow a strange-looking metal catalyst to fool you on the MCAT; alkenes react with H$_2$ in the presence of any one of a variety of catalysts to make saturated alkanes.

Hydrogenation of π Bonds (*syn*-Addition of H—H)

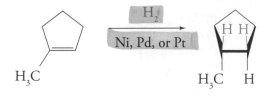

Next, we will explore hydrogenations of alkynes, compounds that have carbon-carbon triple bonds. If an alkyne is reduced by molecular hydrogen (H_2) in the presence of a metal catalyst, it will be reduced all the way to the alkane. This is demonstrated by the reduction of 2-pentyne all the way to the fully saturated pentane.

Hydrogenation of the π Bonds of Alkynes

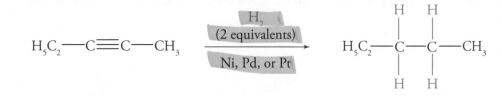

It is possible to stop the reduction of an alkyne at the alkene stage. Two distinct stereo-chemistries of addition are possible depending upon the reagent employed to carry out the reduction. If calcium carbonate ($CaCO_3$) or barium sulfate ($BaSO_4$) is used in conjunction with palladium (Pd) metal, the addition of the two hydrogens across the π bond is of a *syn* stereo-chemistry such that the two hydrogens are added to the same side of the π bond, and the resulting alkene is of the *cis* or (*Z*) variety. The reagent used to carry out this stereospecific reduction is referred to as the *Lindlar* catalyst. Note that this reduction stops at the alkene stage:

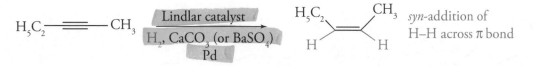

Poisoned catalyst—stops the hydrogen
reduction of alkyne at the alkene stage.

On the other hand, it is also possible to stop the reduction of an alkyne at the alkene stage with the resulting alkene being of the *trans* or (*E*) stereochemistry. This is accomplished with a reagent that consists of sodium metal in the presence of liquid ammonia. In this reaction, two hydrogens are added across a π bond of the alkyne with an anti stereochemistry such that the two hydrogens are added on opposite sides of the π bond. As with the Lindlar catalyst, the reduction stops at the alkene stage.

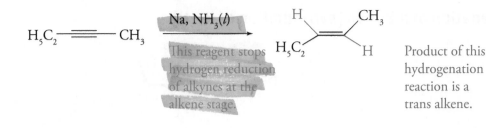

This reagent stops hydrogen reduction of alkynes at the alkene stage.

Product of this hydrogenation reaction is a trans alkene.

Ozonolysis

In the first step of this reaction, ozone (O_3) reacts with a π bond to form a cyclic intermediate called an ozonide. This intermediate is then hydrolyzed in a reductive workup step, resulting in the cleavage of the double bond to yield aldehyde or ketone products. It is quite simple to predict the products of an ozonolysis reaction. Whatever is attached to the π bond of the alkene (an alkyl group or a hydrogen) remains attached in the aldehyde or ketone product, and there is an additional carbonyl group.

Ozonolysis

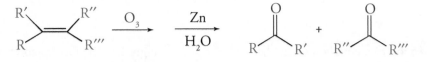

Here are two examples:

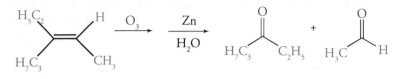

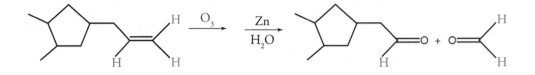

Example 5-1: Predict the products of ozonolysis for the following reactions:

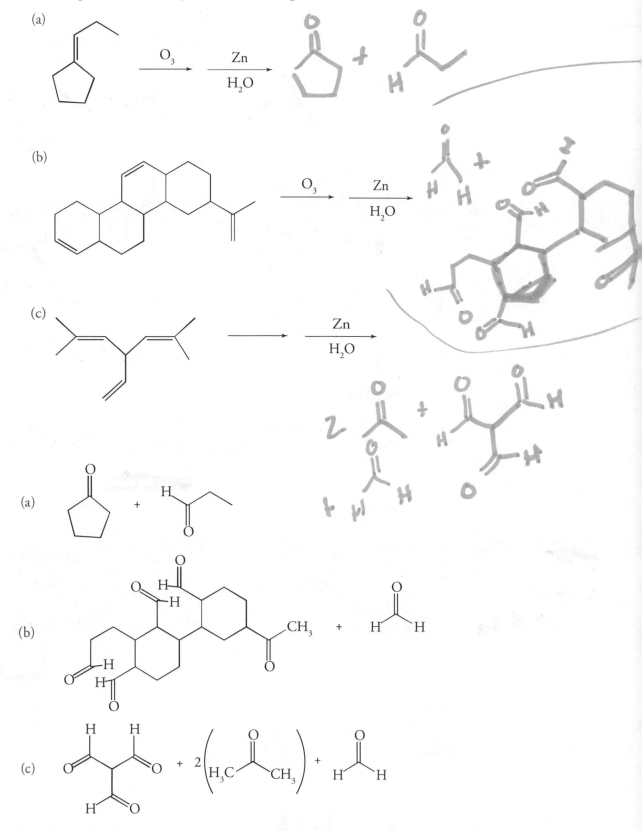

Solution:

(a)

(b)

(c)

Example 5-2: Predict the principal organic product for each of the following reactions:

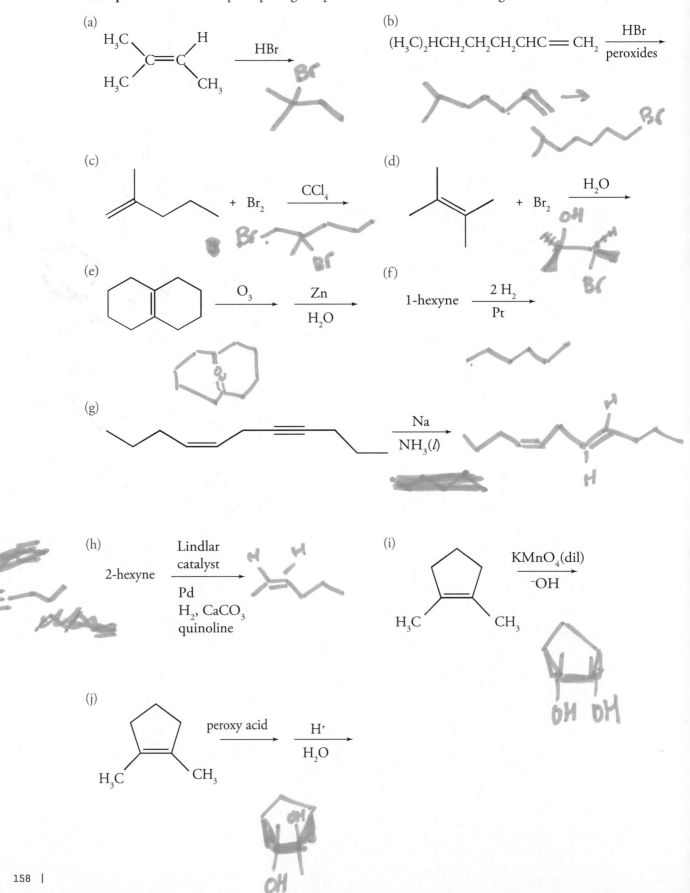

(a)

H₃C, H₃C C=C H, CH₃   HBr

(b)

$(H_3C)_2HCH_2CH_2CH_2CHC{=}CH_2$ $\xrightarrow[\text{peroxides}]{\text{HBr}}$

(c)

+ Br₂ $\xrightarrow{CCl_4}$

(d)

+ Br₂ $\xrightarrow{H_2O}$

(e)

$\xrightarrow{O_3}$ $\xrightarrow[H_2O]{Zn}$

(f)

1-hexyne $\xrightarrow[Pt]{2\ H_2}$

(g)

$\xrightarrow[NH_3(l)]{Na}$

(h)

2-hexyne   Lindlar catalyst Pd H₂, CaCO₃ quinoline

(i)

$\xrightarrow[{}^-OH]{KMnO_4(dil)}$

H₃C   CH₃

(j)

peroxy acid $\xrightarrow[H_2O]{H^+}$

H₃C   CH₃

Solution:

(a)

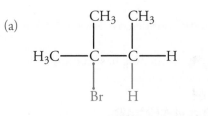

(b)

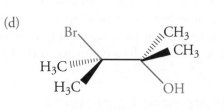

(c)

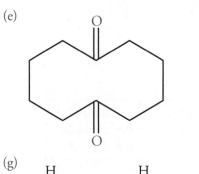

(d)

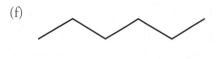

(e)

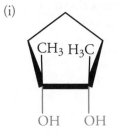

(f)

(g)

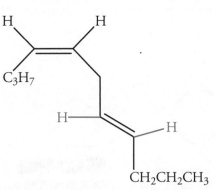

(h)

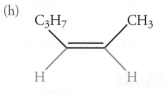

(i)

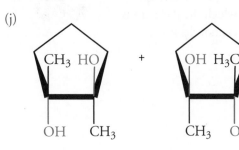

(j)

5.2 AROMATIC COMPOUNDS

Here are the criteria that must be satisfied in order for a compound to be considered *aromatic*:

1. The compound must possess a **cyclic system** in which *every atom* of the ring has an unhybridized p orbital such that the π electrons of the ring can delocalize through them.
2. The cyclic delocalized p orbital system must be flat and *planar.*
3. The delocalized p orbital system must possess a **Hückel number** of π electrons.

Hückel numbers are of the form $4n + 2$, where $n = 0, 1, 2, 3, \ldots$. When $n = 0$, we have 2 π electrons; when $n = 1$, we have 6 π electrons; when $n = 2$, we have 10 π electrons; and so on. This Hückel number of π electrons imparts an aromatic stability to delocalized, flat, planar systems of p orbitals because it corresponds to a closed-shell configuration with all bonding orbitals filled.

Some Aromatic Compounds

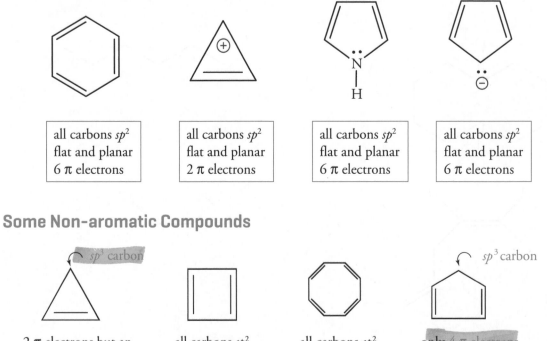

all carbons sp^2	all carbons sp^2	all carbons sp^2	all carbons sp^2
flat and planar	flat and planar	flat and planar	flat and planar
6 π electrons	2 π electrons	6 π electrons	6 π electrons

Some Non-aromatic Compounds

sp^3 carbon

2 π electrons but an sp^3 carbon through which the π electrons cannot delocalize

all carbons sp^2 but only 4 π electrons

all carbons sp^2 but 8 π electrons

sp^3 carbon

only 4 π electrons and a sp^3 carbon through which the π electrons cannot delocalize

Example 5-3: Which of the following molecules are aromatic?

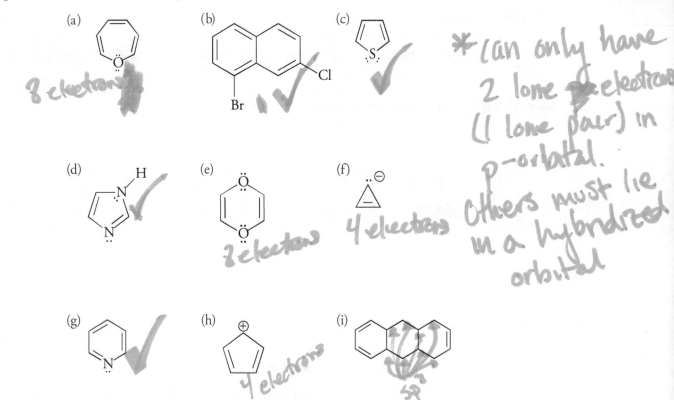

(handwritten annotations)
(a) 8 electrons
(b) ✓
(c) ✓
(d) ✓
(e) 8 electrons
(f) 4 electrons
(g) ✓
(h) 4 electrons
(i) sp

* can only have 2 lone electrons (1 lone pair) in p-orbital. Others must lie in a hybridized orbital

Solution: Only (b), (c), (d) and (g) are aromatic; the rest are not.

Nomenclature of Substituted Benzenes

Benzene with a carboxylic acid functional group is called **benzoic acid**. A second substituent on benzoic acid can be in one of three different positions relative to the carboxylic acid group. These three positions are called the *ortho* (abbreviated *o*-), *meta* (abbreviated *m*-), and *para* (abbreviated *p*-) positions. These are illustrated in the compounds below.

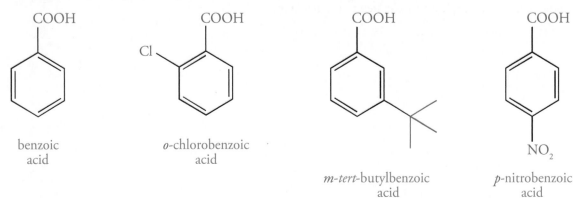

benzoic
acid

o-chlorobenzoic
acid

m-tert-butylbenzoic
acid

p-nitrobenzoic
acid

Reactivity of Aromatic Compounds: Electrophilic Aromatic Substitution

Even though aromatic compounds like benzene have π bonds, they are unusually stable and unreactive. For example, benzene does not react as alkenes do under ordinary electrophilic addition reaction conditions. Aromatic compounds will react, however, with *very* electrophilic reagents to undergo an overall substitution reaction for a hydrogen atom on the ring. These reactions are called **electrophilic aromatic substitution** reactions. Some examples are given below.

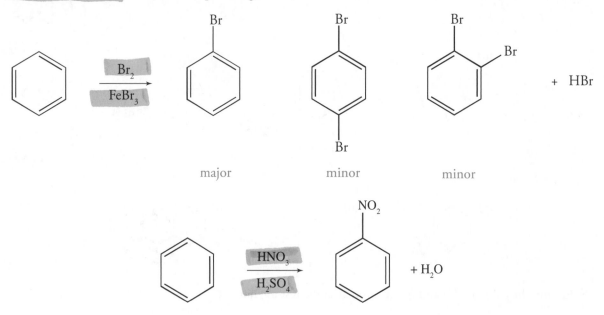

Let's now examine the mechanism of the electrophilic aromatic substitution reaction between benzene and bromine (Br_2) in the presence of catalytic $FeBr_3$. In the first step of the reaction, a very reactive adduct between bromine and the catalyst forms. As is common in all types of electrophilic aromatic substitution reactions, this initial step provides the source of the electrophile (Br^+ in this example). In the second step, benzene acts as the nucleophile and attacks the electrophile in a substitution reaction. The resulting species is a cation and is no longer aromatic since it has an sp^3 hybridized carbon in the ring. Aromaticity can be restored to the intermediate by a simple deprotonation. Either bromide ion (Br^-) or $FeBr_4^-$ is a strong enough base to accomplish this last step in the reaction.

The Mechanism

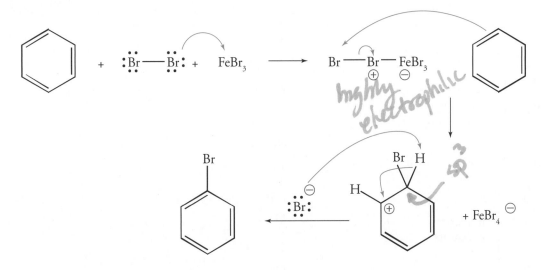

When a group is already present on the aromatic ring, it can affect the electrophilic aromatic substitution reaction in two important ways:

- First, the group already on the ring will affect the ease with which the reaction will take place (relative to the same reaction with an aromatic substrate that does not already have another group present). Groups that make it easier to introduce a new group to the aromatic compound are termed ring-activating. Groups that make it more difficult to introduce a new group to the aromatic compound are called ring-deactivating. Since the important step of the reaction involves the aromatic electrons acting as a nucleophile attacking the electrophile, ring-activating groups are groups that are electron-donating. Conversely, ring-deactivating groups are electron-withdrawing groups that remove electron density from the ring, thus making it less nucleophilic.

- The second way that groups already present on the aromatic ring affect reactivity in electrophilic aromatic substitution reactions is by influencing the position of attachment of the incoming group. Some groups only allow incoming groups to react at the meta position; they are called meta-directing. Other groups direct the incoming substituent to the ortho and para positions; they are called ortho/para-directing. Examples of ortho/para-directors and meta-directors are arranged in the table below, and their activating/deactivating natures are also indicated.

5.2

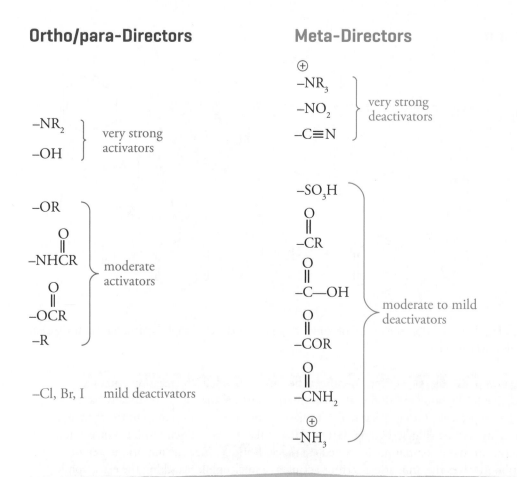

Ortho/para-Directors

−NR₂
−OH
} very strong activators

−OR
−NHCR (with O double bonded to C)
−OCR (with O double bonded to C)
−R
} moderate activators

−Cl, Br, I   mild deactivators

Meta-Directors

−NR₃ (⊕)
−NO₂
−C≡N
} very strong deactivators

−SO₃H
−CR (with O double bonded to C)
−C—OH (with O double bonded to C)
−COR (with O double bonded to C)
−CNH₂ (with O double bonded to C)
−NH₃ (⊕)
} moderate to mild deactivators

Note that all of the substituents that have lone pairs of electrons on the atom of attachment to the aromatic ring are ortho/para-directing groups, and the substituents that do not have lone pairs of electrons on the atom of attachment to the aromatic ring are meta-directing groups, with a single exception; alkyl groups do not have a lone pair of electrons on the atom of attachment, but are ortho/para-directors. This should make sense, however, since alkyl groups are known to be electron-donating groups (this is why 3° carbocations are more stable than 1° carbocations).

Example 5-4: Predict the major product of each of the following reactions:

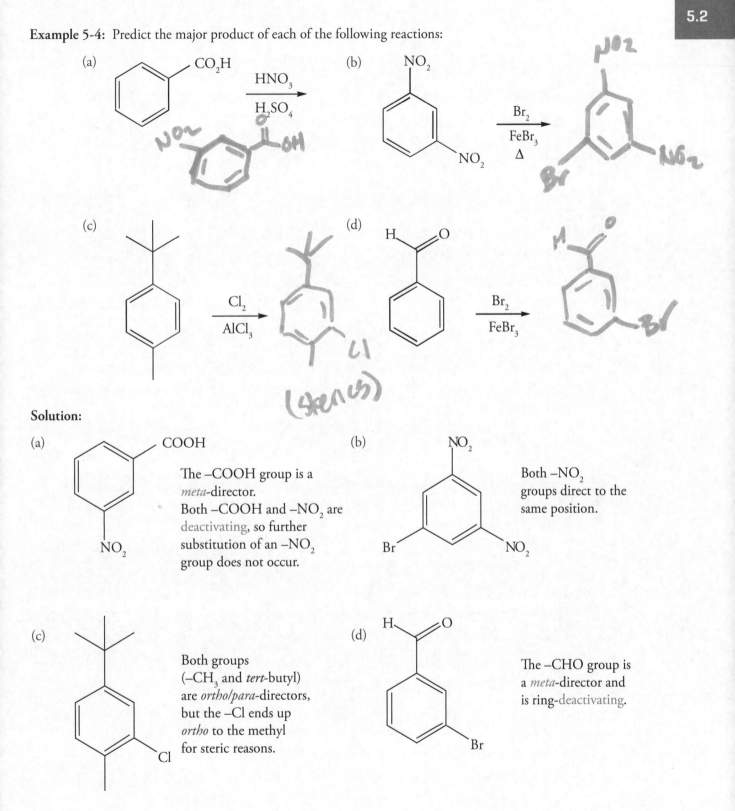

Solution:

(a)

The –COOH group is a *meta*-director. Both –COOH and –NO$_2$ are deactivating, so further substitution of an –NO$_2$ group does not occur.

(b)

Both –NO$_2$ groups direct to the same position.

(c)

Both groups (–CH$_3$ and *tert*-butyl) are *ortho/para*-directors, but the –Cl ends up *ortho* to the methyl for steric reasons.

(d)

The –CHO group is a *meta*-director and is ring-deactivating.

Chapter 5 Summary

- The loosely held electrons in C=C π bonds can act as nucleophiles in addition reactions, which replace one π bond with two σ bonds.

- When π electrons attack electrophiles, the resulting carbocation will be on the more substituted carbon and yield the Markovnikov (more substituted) product.

- Addition reactions that put the new, non-hydrogen group on the less substituted carbon are termed anti-Markovnikov additions.

- *Anti*-addition puts two new substituents on opposite sides of the planar double bond, while *syn*-addition puts two new substituents on the same side of the planar double bond.

- Addition reactions are usually not stereospecific since the alkene is planar. Electrophiles will add with equal frequency to both faces of the bond, giving mixtures of enantiomers.

- Double bonds are split by ozonolysis, yielding two carbonyl-bearing compounds.

- Alkenes and alkynes can be hydrogenated by use of H_2 and metal catalysts.

- Aromatic compounds are cyclic, planar, conjugated (all sp^2 hybridized atoms), have $4n+2$ π electrons, and are exceptionally stable.

- Under the influence of very strong electrophiles, aromatic electrons can be nucleophilic, resulting in aromatic substitution.

- Substituents that add electron density to a benzene ring are activating for substitution chemistry, and favor reaction at *ortho* and *para* positions.

- Substituents that withdraw electron density from benzene are ring deactivating, and all but the halogens favor substitution at *meta* positions.

CHAPTER 5 FREESTANDING PRACTICE QUESTIONS

1. If an alkyne is treated with two equivalents of hydrogen in the presence of platinum, what is the net change in bonds?

   A) – 1 pi bond, + 4 sigma bonds
   B) – 2 pi bonds, + 2 sigma bonds
   C) – 2 pi bonds, + 4 sigma bonds
   D) – 2 pi bonds, + 6 sigma bonds

2. Electrophilic addition reactions often go through carbocation intermediates. If possible, carbocations will rearrange to form more stable carbocations. Which of the following carbocations could potentially undergo rearrangement?

   I.

   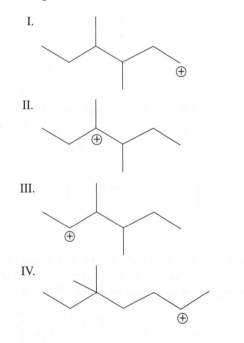

   II.

   III.

   IV.

   A) III only
   B) I and III only
   C) I, II, and IV
   D) I, III, and IV

3. If benzene is treated with two equivalents of bromine in the presence of a $FeBr_3$ catalyst and elevated temperatures, what is the maximum number of disubstituted isomeric products that could be produced?

   A) 1
   B) 2
   C) 3
   D) 4

4. The acid-catalyzed Markovnikov addition of H_2O to 1-butene should give a:

   A) primary alcohol.
   B) secondary alcohol.
   C) tertiary alcohol.
   D) *cis*-diol.

5. Phenanthrene (below) is an aromatic molecule composed of three 3 fused benzene rings. How many π electrons does phenanthrene have?

   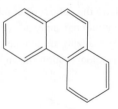

   A) 7
   B) 14
   C) 18
   D) 24

CHAPTER 5 PRACTICE PASSAGE

Aromaticity is a special property displayed by a number of organic molecules such as benzene and xylene (shown below in Figure 1). Rather than being a collection of discrete, conjoined double bonds, aromatic molecules are able to delocalize π–electrons in a continuous, conjugated, annular system. Aside from being annular, and continuously conjugated, in order to display aromaticity a molecule must have $4n + 2$ ($n = 0, 1, 2....$) electrons in its π–system.

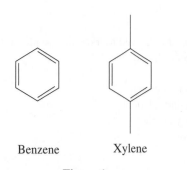

Benzene   Xylene

Figure 1

Annular, continuously conjugated molecules which have $4n$ ($n = 1, 2, 3….$) in their π systems are termed anti-aromatic. These compounds do not have the same type of resonance, and the electrons in their π system remain localized in discrete double bonds, rather than delocalizing around the molecule. Examples include the cyclopentadienyl cation shown below.

Aromatic molecules are particularly low in energy, as compared to their non- and anti-aromatic counterparts. Reactions which form aromatic products tend to be very exothermic, and similarly aromatic molecules are far less reactive than other unsaturated systems.

1. Cyclooctatetraene, shown below, exhibits one ^{1}H NMR resonance.

   In what range of ppm might this resonance be expected to fall?

   A) 3.0–4.2 ppm
   B) 4.9–6.8 ppm
   C) 7.2–8.3 ppm
   D) 8.5–13.6 ppm

2. The addition of Br_2 across simple double-bonds is a well known reaction making two C—Br σ bonds out of one C=C double bond. Which of the following molecules, if treated with Br_2, would we NOT expect to undergo bromine addition?

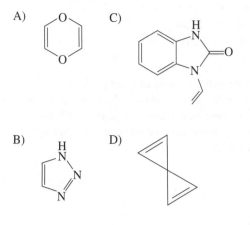

3. Cyclobutadiene is anti-aromatic and extremely unstable. The reason for this instability is that once formed it undergoes the following Diels-Alder dimerization above 35 K.

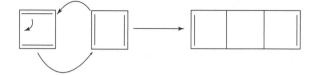

   If cyclobutadiene were produced below 35 K and slowly warmed in the presence of excess acetylene, which of the following would most likely be detected?

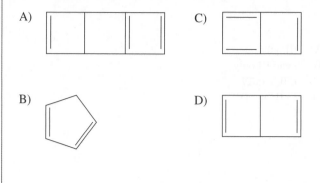

4. In the presence of a metal catalyst, concentrated acetylene can undergo cyclization reactions giving a number of cyclic compounds with alternating double bonds. Which of the following formulas represents the major product of this reaction?

A) C_6H_6
B) C_8H_8
C) C_6H_{12}
D) C_8H_{10}

5. Electrons in an aromatic ring can attack a strong Lewis acid, and as a result a substitution reaction can occur. The aromaticity of the system is transiently broken, but is regained when the hydrogen being substituted is removed. Which of the following compounds will undergo such a reaction most readily?

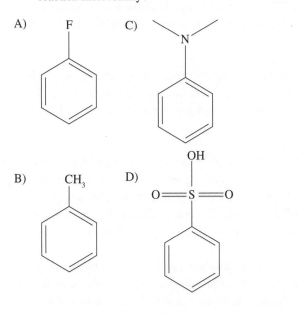

A) F

C) N

B) CH₃

D) OH, O=S=O

6. The following reaction is utilized to substitute aromatic compounds with other organic entities. It relies on the idea that non-aromatic double bonds will more readily accept protons from strong acids and form carbocations.

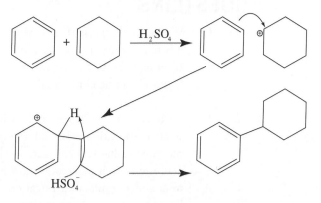

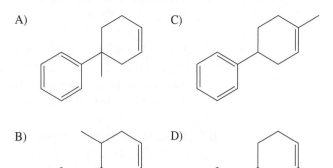

If benzene reacts with 1-methyl-1,4-cyclohexadiene in this fashion, which compound will be the major product?

A)

C)

B)

D)

SOLUTIONS TO CHAPTER 5 FREESTANDING PRACTICE QUESTIONS

1. **C**   When an alkyne is treated with two equivalents of hydrogen in the presence of platinum, it is reduced to an alkane. This results in the loss of both pi bonds from the triple bond, so eliminate choice A. The two pi bonds are converted to four C—H sigma bonds, so choices B and D can be eliminated.

2. **B**   Carbocations rearrange via hydride or alkyl shifts when the opportunity to create a more stable carbocation exists on a neighboring carbon. Item II is already a tertiary carbocation, the most stable you can get, so choice C can be eliminated. Since Item III is in all the remaining answer choices, it must be correct. This carbocation would undergo rearrangement from the secondary carbocation shown to a tertiary carbocation via a hydride shift. Item I could rearrange from the primary carbocation to a secondary carbocation via a hydride shift, so choice A can be eliminated. Item IV cannot rearrange because it is a secondary carbocation and does not have the ability to rearrange to a tertiary carbocation. Therefore, choice B is the best.

3. **B**   Although a minor product, given enough catalyst, heat, and time, the disubstituted products can form. In this reaction, two atoms of bromine will replace two hydrogens previously attached to the benzene ring. The bromine atoms can have either an *ortho* or *para* relationship to each other. This makes two possible isomers.

4. **B**   Addition of water to 1-butene will only add one OH group, so cannot form a diol (eliminate choice D). Since there are no tertiary carbons on the starting material, a tertiary alcohol cannot be formed (eliminate choice C). Markovnikov addition results in the addition of the hydroxyl group to the most substituted carbon of a double bond. Choice A can be eliminated because it represents addition of the hydroxyl group to the least substituted carbon.

5. **B**   To determine the number of π electrons in this system, you must add up all double bonds to get a total of seven. Since each double bond is composed of two electrons, the molecule has 14 π electrons. Another way to view the problem is to realize that each carbon in the molecule uses three of its four electrons in σ bonding to its three neighbors. The last electron is delocalized, so 14 carbons means 14 π electrons.

SOLUTIONS TO CHAPTER 5 PRACTICE PASSAGE

1. **B** Cyclooctatetraene is an anti-aromatic molecule, as it has eight ($4n$, $n = 2$) π electrons. As such we would expect its ^{1}H NMR resonances to fall more in the alkene region than in the aromatic region. Choice C indicates the aromatic region, so it can be eliminated. Choice D represents the upper end of the aromatic region and the region where aldehydic and very acidic protons resonate. Choice A is too upfield for an alkene-type proton. Choice B, however, is where we would expect to find protons on non-aromatic double bonds.

2. **B** The molecule in choice B is aromatic. There are two double bonds, accounting for four π electrons, and an electron pair on the top nitrogen that is delocalized into the π system. The fact that one can draw resonance structures using these electrons means that they must be in an unhybridized p orbital. The pendant double bond in choice C is not part of an aromatic system, and hence could be expected to add Br_2. Choice D contains an sp^3 center in each ring, so the π system is not continuous, and the double bonds are discrete. The molecule in choice A is anti-aromatic since each oxygen donates two electrons to the π system, and hence will add Br_2.

3. **D**

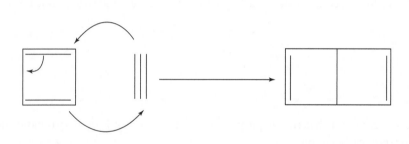

   As shown above, the Diels-Alder mechanism shown in the question would lead to the product shown in choice D. Both choices A and B have the wrong number of carbons to fit the mechanism. Choice C maintains too many π electrons to be the correct product.

4. **A** A cyclization reaction utilizing only acetylene must preserve C_xH_x stoichiometry; this eliminates choices C and D. The remaining two choices are both possible products, but of the two, C_6H_6 is aromatic, and thus lower in energy than C_8H_8. Therefore it will be the favored product.

5. **C**   The aromatic molecule most prone to act as a Lewis base will be the ring that is most electron-rich. Electron withdrawing groups will remove electron density from the ring and hinder basic properties. The sulfonic acid entity on choice D is extremely electron withdrawing
and hence will strongly deactivate the ring. Fluorine, likewise, is extremely withdrawing,
eliminating choice A. The methyl group in toluene (choice B) is very mildly donating, but
only in a sigma fashion and can give no density to the π system which must act as a Lewis
base. The figure below shows how the tertiary nitrogen on dimethyl aniline (choice C) can
donate electrons to the ring, making it more electron dense, and hence slightly more basic.

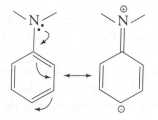

6. **A**   The initial formation of the carbocation in the reaction mechanism will favor placing it on
the most substituted carbon. As can be seen on the molecule below, there are three possible
positions for a secondary carbocation, and only one for a tertiary carbocation.

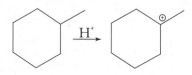

Chances are good that the major product will be the result of an aromatic substitution on
the tertiary carbocation.

Chapter 6
Nucleophilic Addition and Cycloaddition Reactions

We'll next examine two broad classes of reactions: first, the reactions of carbonyl containing compounds and second, cycloaddition reactions. Simple carbonyl-containing organic compounds display two types of reactivity. The first is deprotonation of the α-carbon atom. The second is nucleophilic addition to the C=O double bond. We will see in this chapter how these two reactivity modes interrelate. We'll then look at the reactivity of α,β-unsaturated carbonyl containing compounds and carboxylic acids and their derivatives. Lastly, we will discuss the Diels–Alder reaction as a typical cycloaddition reaction.

6.1   ALDEHYDES AND KETONES

Two very important classes of oxygen-containing organic compounds are aldehydes and ketones. We begin the discussion of these functional groups by looking at a common way carbonyls are formed—the oxidation of an alcohol:

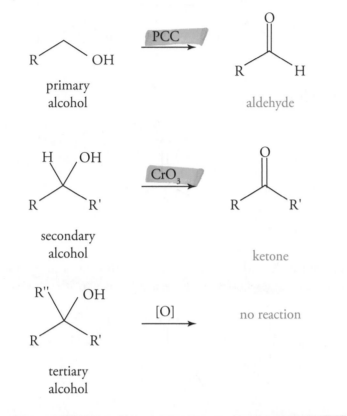

Note: Since the oxidizing agent removes a hydrogen from the carbon, tertiary alcohols are not able to react to form carbonyls since they have no hydrogen at the reactive site.

Oxidizing agents are able to absorb electrons (and be reduced). Below are some common oxidizing agents that appear on the MCAT.

Aqueous Oxidants	Anhydrous Oxidant
Chromic Acid (H_2CrO_4)	Pyridinium Chlorochromate (PCC)
Chromate Salts (CrO_4^{2-})	
Dichromate Salts ($Cr_2O_7^{2-}$)	
Permanganate (MnO_4^-)	
Chromium Trioxide (CrO_3)	

Now that we understand how aldehydes and ketones are formed, let's look at their reactivities. The key to understanding the chemistry of aldehydes and ketones is to understand the electronic structure and properties of the carbonyl group. The C=O double bond is very polarized because oxygen is much more electronegative than carbon, and so it is able to pull the π electrons of the C=O double bond toward itself and away from carbon. This is illustrated by the following resonance structures:

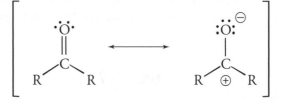

So overall, carbonyls react like

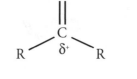

This bond polarization renders the carbon atom electrophilic (δ^+) and accounts for two kinds of reactions of aldehydes and ketones. First, these molecules have *acidic protons α to (i.e., next to) the carbonyl group*.

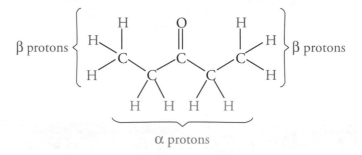

An α-proton is acidic because the electrons left behind upon deprotonation can delocalize into the π system of the carbonyl. Second, the electrophilic carbon of the carbonyl group makes aldehydes and ketones *susceptible to nucleophilic attack*. In the aldol condensation, which we will study in some detail, both of these types of reactivity are involved in a single reaction.

Acidity and Enolization

The first type of reaction that is commonly observed with aldehydes and ketones is the result of the relative acidity of protons that are α to the carbonyl group. These α-protons are sufficiently acidic that they can be removed by a strong base [such as hydroxide ion (OH^-) or an alkoxide ion (OR^-)] to yield a resonance stabilized carbanion. This carbanion can be easily formed because the electrons that are left behind on the carbon can be delocalized into the carbonyl π system. In this way, the negative charge can be delocalized onto the electronegative oxygen atom. A resonance-stabilized carbanion of this type is referred to as an enolate ion. *An enolate ion is negatively charged and nucleophilic*. The nucleophilic character of an enolate ion lies predominately at the carbon at which the proton was abstracted, *not* the oxygen atom of the carbonyl. This is why the α-carbon atom of enolates is the nucleophile in most common enolate reactions.

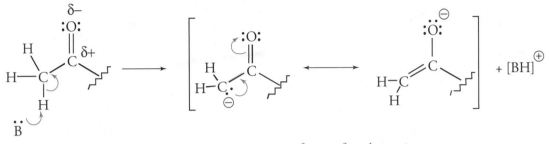

resonance forms of enolate anion

An example that demonstrates the acidity of α-protons is the exchange reaction that occurs between the α-proton of Compound I (below) and deuterium from D_2O. Compound I has a single α-proton that is α to *two* carbonyl groups in comparison to the six other α-protons in the molecule that are α to only *one* carbonyl group. It is this lone α-proton that exchanges with a deuterium of D_2O over the course of a couple of days, even in the absence of base. Being next to two carbonyl groups greatly enhances the acidity of this α-proton and allows it to exchange (although slowly) with a deuterium from D_2O. The mechanism of this exchange, which essentially consists of protonation of the intermediate enolate ion, is shown in the following figure:

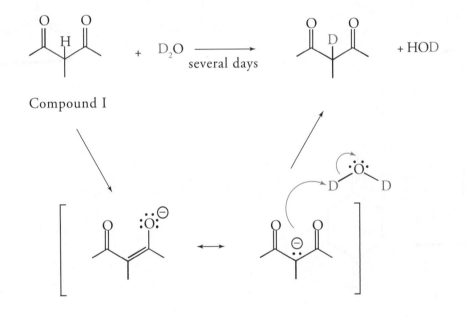

Compound I

Example 6-1: For each of the following pairs of compounds, identify the one with the more acidic proton.

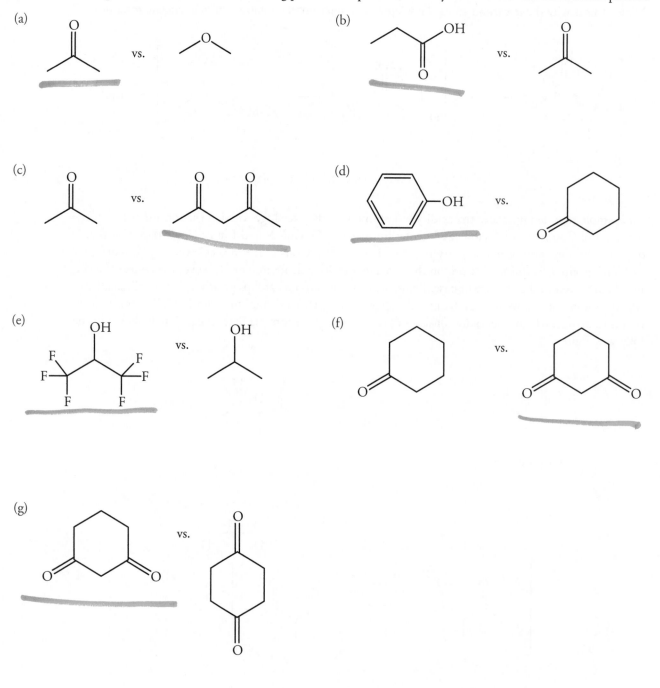

Solution:

(a)

(b)

(c)

(d)

(e)

(f)

(g)

Since fluorine is the most electronegative atom, it will have a very strong inductive effect.

Keto-Enol Tautomerism

A ketone is converted into an enol by deprotonation of an α-carbon atom and subsequent protonation of the carbonyl oxygen. These two forms are very similar to one another and differ only by the position of a proton and a double bond. This is referred to as **keto-enol tautomerism**. Two molecules are **tautomers** if they are readily interconvertible constitutional isomers in equilibrium with one another.

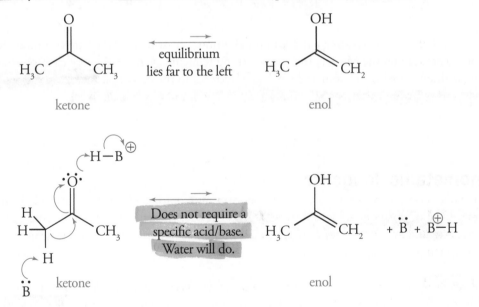

Does not require a specific acid/base. Water will do.

Nucleophilic Addition Reactions to Aldehydes and Ketones

Because of the polarized nature of the C=O double bond in aldehydes and ketones, the carbon of the carbonyl group is very electrophilic. This means that it will attract nucleophiles and can readily be reduced. The attack of a nucleophile upon the carbon of a carbonyl group, called a nucleophilic addition reaction, is shown below with a generic nucleophile (Nu:).

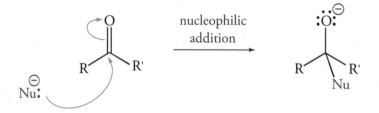

Nucleophilic addition reactions are defined by the bonding changes that occur over the course of the reaction, just as in electrophilic additions. In these reactions, a π bond in the starting material is broken, and two σ bonds in the product result. This very general reaction allows for the conversion of aldehydes or ketones into a variety of other functional groups such as alcohols via hydride reduction:

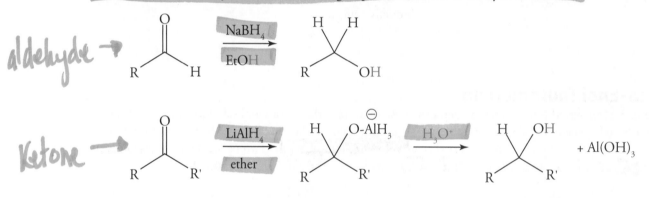

Note: Sodium borohydride (NaBH$_4$) and lithium aluminum hydride (LiAlH$_4$) are common reducing agents seen on the MCAT. In general, strong reducing agents easily lose electrons by adding hydride (a hydrogen atom and a pair of electrons) to the carbonyl. Reducing agents often have many hydrogens attached to other elements with low electronegativity.

Organometallic Reagents

Organometallic reagents are commonly used to perform nucleophilic addition to a carbonyl carbon. The basic structure of an organometallic reagent is R$^-$ M$^+$. They act as electron rich, or anionic carbon atoms and therefore function as either strong bases or nucleophiles. Grignard and lithium reagents are the most common organometallic reagents.

Grignard reagents are generally made via the action of an alkyl or acyl halide on magnesium metal, as depicted below. To avoid unwanted protonation of the very basic Grignard reagent, the reaction is carried out in an aprotic solvent such as diethyl ether.

The carbonyl containing compounds are then added to the Grignard reagents in order to yield alcohol products. In the reaction below, the methyl magnesium bromide acts as a nucleophile and adds to the electrophilic carbonyl carbon. An intermediate alkoxide ion is formed that is rapidly protonated to produce the alcohol during an aqueous acidic workup step.

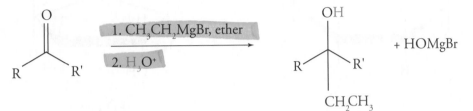

Organolithium reagents are generally made by the reduction of alkyl halides with Li metal as depicted below. The reagents are prepared by reacting alkyl halide and lithium in a 1:2 molar ratio. Organolithium reagents react as bases or nucleophiles in the same manner as Grignard reagents.

Wittig Reaction

While the *mechanism* of the Wittig reaction is not important for the MCAT and is fairly different from the standard nucleophilic addition reaction mentioned above, it is important to be able to *recognize* this reaction. Wittig reagents are also known as phosphonium ylides (pronounced *ill'-ids*), and react with aldehydes and ketones to form alkenes, as seen in the reaction below. Since the reaction involves both an addition and an elimination step in its mechanism, there is still a π bond in the product.

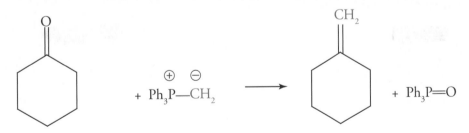

Acetals and Hemiacetals

Acetals and hemiacetals, which are of fundamental importance in biochemical reactions that occur in living organisms, can be synthesized from nucleophilic addition reactions to aldehydes or ketones. There are many examples of these molecules in common biochemical pathways. Here are two:

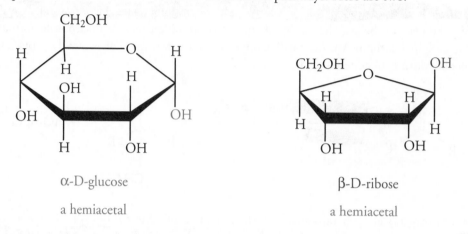

α-D-glucose

a hemiacetal

β-D-ribose

a hemiacetal

Before we learn the chemistry of these groups, we must be able to identify acetals and hemiacetals.

Note: The terms *ketal* and *hemiketal* once referred to acetals and hemiacetals made from *ketones*, but this nomenclature has been abandoned by IUPAC.

General Formulas

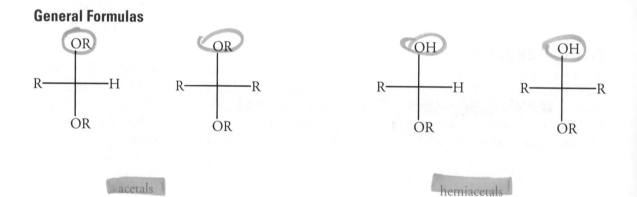

acetals

hemiacetals

Some Specific Examples

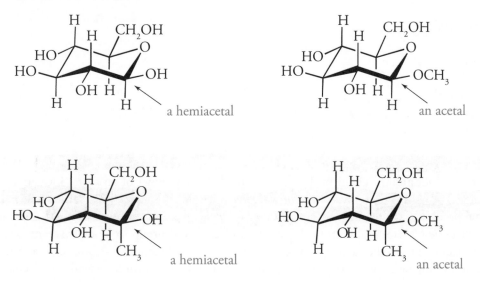

a hemiacetal

an acetal

a hemiacetal

an acetal

Example 6-2: For each of the following compounds, identify whether it's an acetal, hemiacetal, or neither:

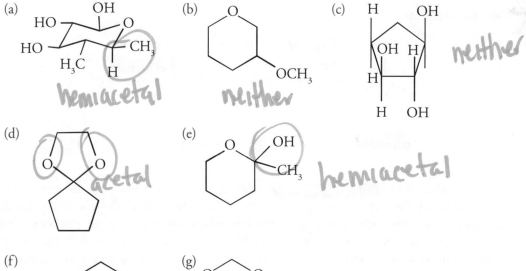

(a) hemiacetal

(b) neither

(c) neither

(d) acetal

(e) hemiacetal

(f) 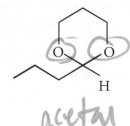 acetal

(g) acetal

Solution:

(a) hemiacetal
(b) neither
(c) neither
(d) acetal
(e) hemiacetal
(f) acetal
(g) acetal

Acetals are formed when aldehydes or ketones react with alcohols in the presence of acid. This occurs by a nucleophilic addition mechanism. It is easy to predict the product of an acetal formation reaction. Notice that *hydrogens or carbons attached to the carbonyl carbon* of the aldehyde or ketone *remain attached* in the acetal product with the subsequent addition of two –OR groups from the alcohol. Also, note that an intermediate hemiacetal results from the addition of one –OR group to an aldehyde or ketone with subsequent protonation of the carbonyl oxygen. The aldehyde or ketone, the hemiacetal, and the acetal are all in equilibrium with one another. In order for the hemiacetal to form the acetal, a molecule of water must be lost.

Acetal Formation

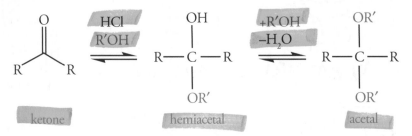

The mechanism of this important reaction is shown below. In the first step, the carbonyl oxygen is protonated, making the carbonyl carbon even more susceptible to nucleophilic attack by the oxygen of the attacking alcohol molecule. Following nucleophilic attack, the oxygen of the alcohol nucleophile is positively charged. This positive charge is unfavorable, and neutrality is achieved by loss of a proton which yields the intermediate hemiacetal. Remember that the reaction mixture is acidic so that a lone pair of electrons on the hemiacetal –OH can be protonated, which converts a poor leaving group into a good leaving group. Once again, this increases the electrophilicity of the carbon and makes it more susceptible to a second nucleophilic attack by an alcohol molecule. All that remains is for the positively charged oxygen from the attacking alcohol to lose a proton which yields the acetal product.

The Overall Reaction

The Mechanism

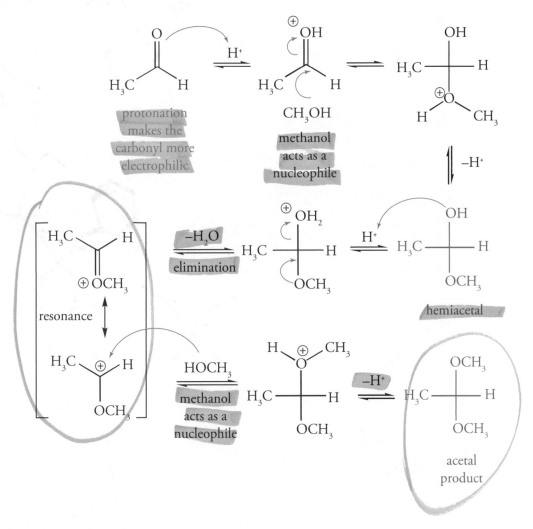

Example 6-3: Predict the acetal product from the following reactions:

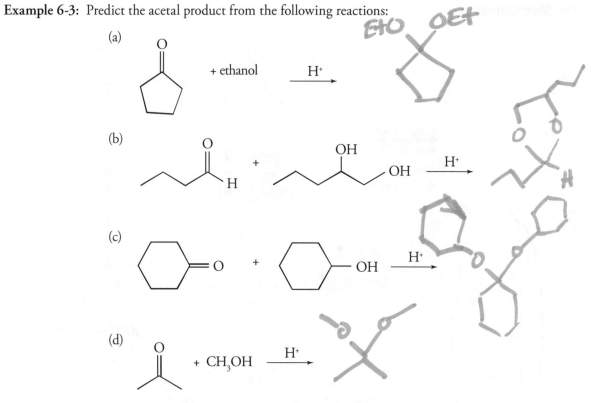

(a)

+ ethanol →(H⁺)

(b)

+ (pentanediol) →(H⁺)

(c)

+ (cyclohexanol) →(H⁺)

(d)

+ CH₃OH →(H⁺)

Solution:

(a) C₂H₅O   OC₂H₅

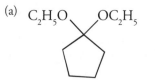

(b)

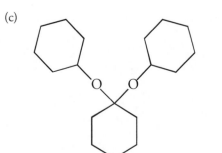

(c)

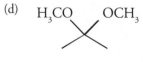

(d) H₃CO   OCH₃

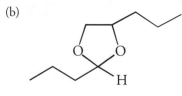

Imine Formation

A reaction that closely resembles acetal formation is the reaction of aldehydes or ketones with primary amines (R–NH$_2$). In this reaction, which is catalyzed by a weakly acidic buffer system (like an acetic acid/acetate buffer, pH about 4-5), an aldehyde or ketone reacts with a primary amine (R–NH$_2$) to form an imine. As in the acetal formation reaction, whatever is originally attached to the carbonyl carbon (other than the oxygen) stays attached in the product (an alkyl group or a hydrogen) and a molecule of water is produced. A brief examination of the reaction mechanism will help illustrate these common features.

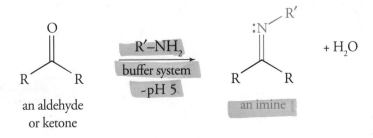

The Mechanism

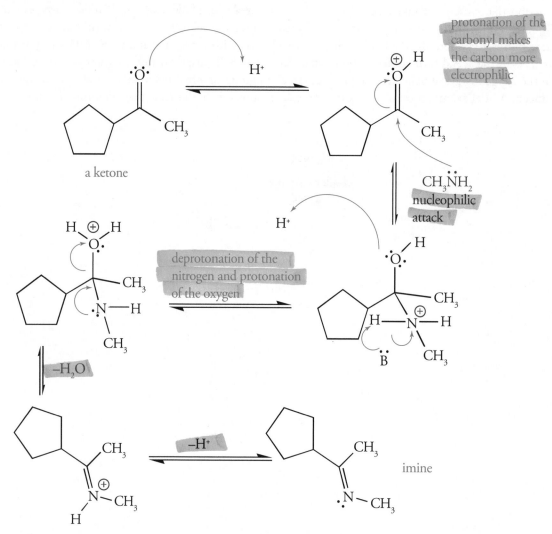

In the first step of this reaction, a lone pair of electrons on the carbonyl oxygen is protonated by the acidic medium. As in acetal formation, protonation of the carbonyl oxygen makes the carbonyl carbon more electrophilic and therefore more susceptible to nucleophilic attack. This time, the nucleophile is an amine (R–NH$_2$) so the nucleophilic nitrogen attacks the electrophilic carbon, resulting in a tetrahedral inter-mediate. The tetrahedral intermediate is then deprotonated at the nitrogen and protonated at the oxygen, thus converting a poor leaving group (–OH) into a good leaving group (–OH$_2^+$). Next, the oxygen de-parts with its electrons as a neutral water molecule and leaves behind a carbocation that is stabilized by resonance by the lone pair of electrons from the nitrogen. (*Note*: Only the more stable resonance form is shown in the mechanism above.) The imine product is then formed by deprotonation.

Example 6-4: Predict the major organic product of each of the following reactions:

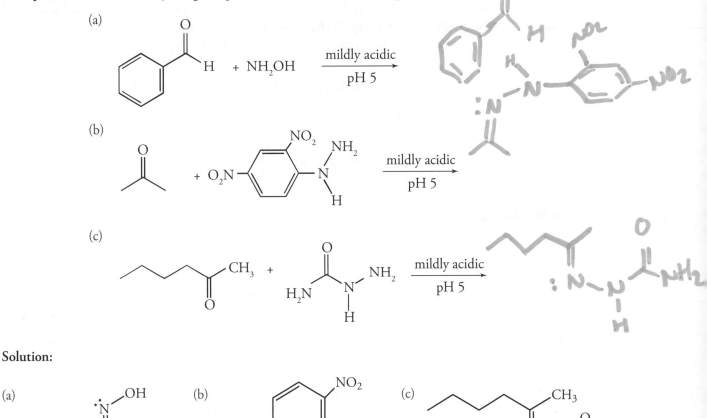

(a)

(b)

(c)

Solution:

(a)

(b)

(c)

Aldol Condensation

A classic reaction in which the enolate anion of one carbonyl compound reacts with the carbonyl group of another carbonyl compound is called the aldol condensation. This reaction combines the two types of aldehyde/ketone reactivities: the acidity of the α-proton, and the electrophilicity of the carbonyl carbon.

In the first step of this reaction, a strong base removes an α-proton from the aldehyde, resulting in the formation of a resonance-stabilized enolate anion. This corresponds to the first type of reactivity of aldehydes and ketones, deprotonation of the α-carbon atom. (Remember, the enolate anion is nucleophilic and usually reacts at the carbon atom which was deprotonated.) Next, the α-carbon of the enolate anion attacks the carbonyl carbon of another aldehyde molecule, thereby generating an alkoxide ion that is subsequently protonated by a molecule of water. This results in the formation of a general class of molecules referred to as β-hydroxy carbonyl compounds. There are three important points to note about this reaction. First, it requires a strong base (typically hydroxide, OH⁻ or an alkoxide ion RO⁻) to remove an α-proton adjacent to the carbonyl group. Second, one of the aldehydes or ketones must act as a source for the enolate ions while the other aldehyde or ketone will come under nucleophilic attack by the enolate carbanion. Third, the aldol condensation does not require the two carbonyl groups that participate in the reaction to be the same. When they are different, it is called a **crossed aldol condensation** reaction. In order to avoid obtaining a complex mixture of products in a crossed aldol condensation, it is often the case that one of the carbonyl compounds is chosen such that it does not have any acidic α-protons, and therefore *cannot* act as the nucleophile (enolate ion), it *must* be the electrophile.

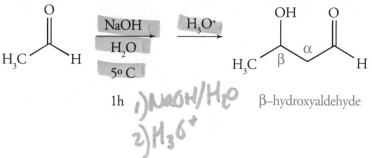

β–hydroxyaldehyde

The Mechanism

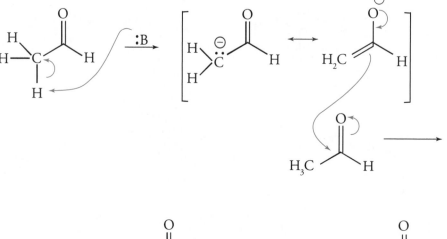

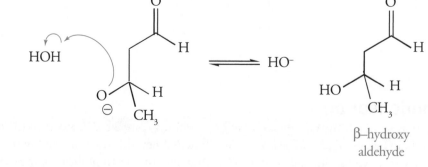

β–hydroxy
aldehyde

If the β-hydroxyaldehyde or ketone products are heated, they will undergo an elimination reaction (dehydration) to form an **α,β-unsaturated carbonyl compound**. Notice that the newly formed carbon-carbon π bond is in conjugation with the carbonyl group; this stabilizes the molecule.

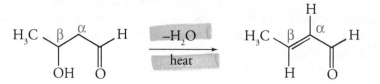

β-hydroxy carbonyl   α,β-unsaturated carbonyl compound
(some *Z* compound will also form)

Example 6-5: Predict the condensation products of each of the following reactions. Show both the β-hydroxy carbonyl product and the elimination product.

(a)

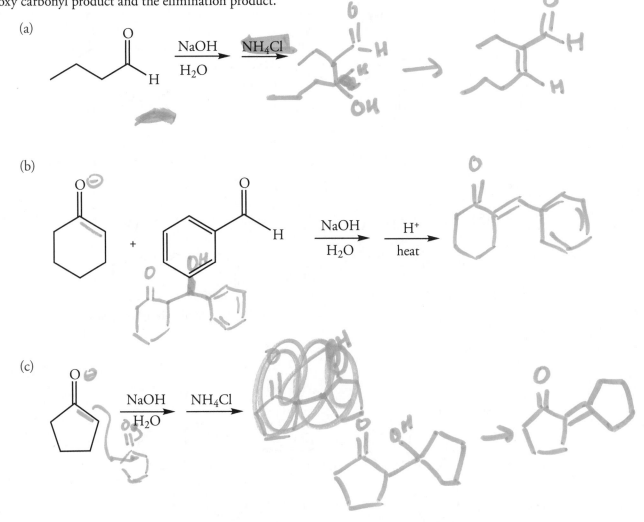

(b)

(c)

(d)

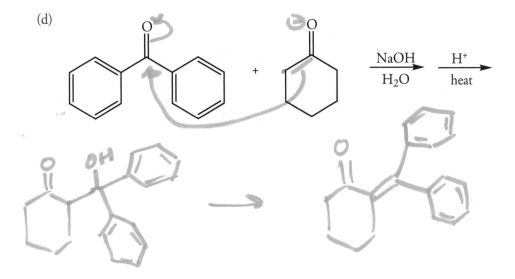

Solution:

(a)

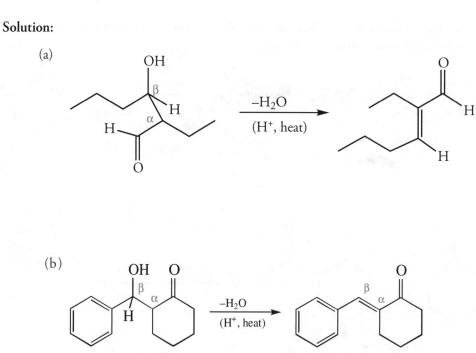

(b)

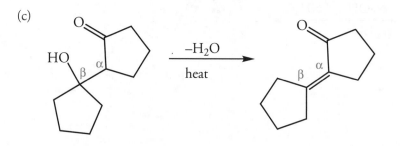

α,β-unsaturated carbonyl compound

(c)

(d)

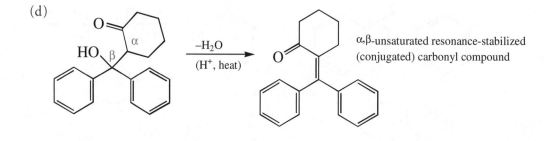

α,β-unsaturated resonance-stabilized (conjugated) carbonyl compound

Conjugate Addition to α,β-Unsaturated Carbonyl Compounds

The products of aldol condensations are not ordinary aldehydes (or ketones), they have a unit of unsaturation (the C=C double bond) between the α- and β-carbon atoms. These molecules display reactivity different from that of both the aldehydes (ketones) and alkenes we have encountered so far. This is best described by drawing resonance structures for the α,β-unsaturated carbonyl compound.

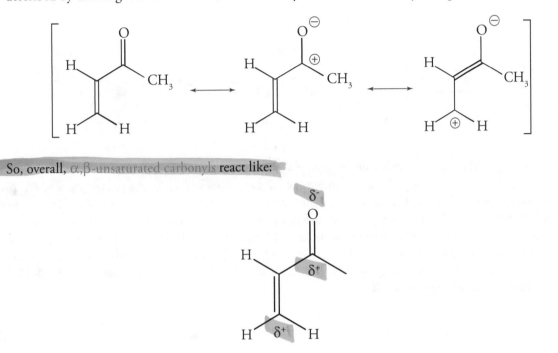

So, overall, α,β-unsaturated carbonyls react like:

The resonance forms shown above clearly predict that α,β-unsaturated carbonyl compounds could have two sites of electrophilicity (δ⁺), and therefore should have two sites available for nucleophilic attack. Although *some* nucleophilic reagents will attack the carbon of the carbonyl, *most nucleophiles attack the β-carbon atom.* This should seem strange based on all we've seen on the reactivity of alkenes. Recall that alkenes *usually* react as *nucleophiles.* However, in α,β-unsaturated carbonyl compounds, the alkene is in conjugation with the carbonyl group, thereby rendering it a good *electrophile.* Remember, α,β-unsaturated carbonyl compounds act neither as normal alkenes nor as normal carbonyl compounds.

As an example of the reactivity of α,β-unsaturated carbonyl compounds, we'll look at the acid catalyzed addition of dimethylamine to methyl vinyl ketone.

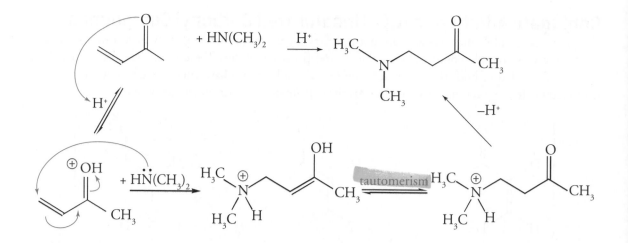

In the first step of the reaction, the carbonyl oxygen atom is protonated, thus making the β-carbon more electrophilic. In the second step, the nitrogen atom of dimethylamine attacks the β-carbon atom of the protonated methyl vinyl ketone, generating an enol intermediate. Since enols are not stable, the enol intermediate tautomerizes to the ketone. The ammonium ion is then deprotonated to form the product of the reaction. The overall reaction involves the addition of –N(CH$_3$)$_2$ and –H from HN(CH$_3$)$_2$ across the C=C double bond of the α,β-unsaturated unit of methyl vinyl ketone. Reactions where the nucleophile becomes attached to the β-carbon atom of an α,β-unsaturated carbonyl compound are termed 1,4-addition (or conjugate addition) reactions.

Example 6-6: Predict the product of each of the following conjugate addition reactions:

(a)

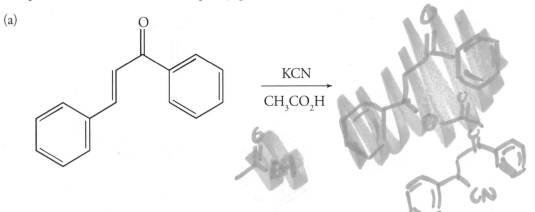

$$\frac{KCN}{CH_3CO_2H}$$

(b)

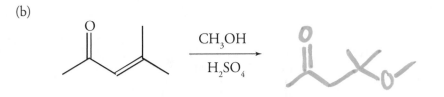

$$\frac{CH_3OH}{H_2SO_4}$$

(c)

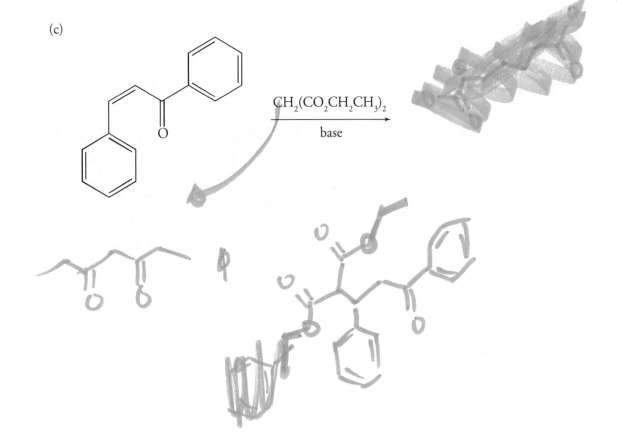

$$\frac{CH_2(CO_2CH_2CH_3)_2}{base}$$

Solution:

(a)

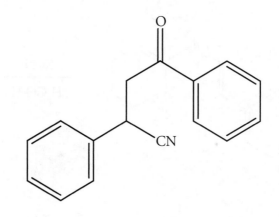

(b)

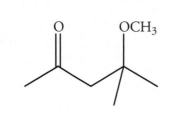

(c)

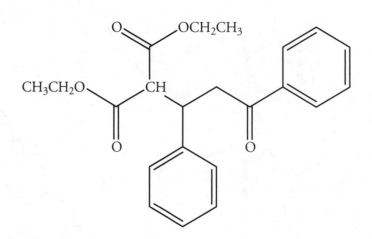

6.2 CARBOXYLIC ACIDS

Carboxylic acids are of fundamental importance in many biological systems. Fatty acids, for example, are long chain carboxylic acids that play important roles in both cellular structure and metabolism (as we'll see in Section 8.4). In the following sections, we'll explore the basic physical properties and common chemical reactions of carboxylic acids and their derivatives.

Acidity and Hydrogen Bonding

As we've already learned, the acidity of carboxylic acids results from the resonance stability of the carboxylate anion. When the carboxylic acid donates its acidic proton, the oxygen becomes negatively charged and this resulting negative charge can be delocalized into the adjacent π system. Two resonance structures of equivalent energy can be drawn. Remember that resonance structures of equivalent energy result in stability.

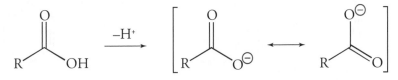

Inductive Stabilization of Carboxylate Ions by Electron-Withdrawing Groups

Electron-withdrawing groups increase the acidity of carboxylic acids by increasing the stability of the negative charge of the carboxylate anion. This is known as an **inductive effect** (as opposed to a *resonance effect*) and it exerts its effect by withdrawing electrons through σ bonds (single bonds). Inductive effects decrease with increasing distance; the closer the electron withdrawing group is to the acid, the greater the effect. The following order of acidity for the isomers of fluorobutanoic acid should help clarify this point.

Inductive Effect of Substituents:

> Electron-withdrawing groups
> *stabilize*
> the negative charge of the carboxylate anion.

Order of Acidity

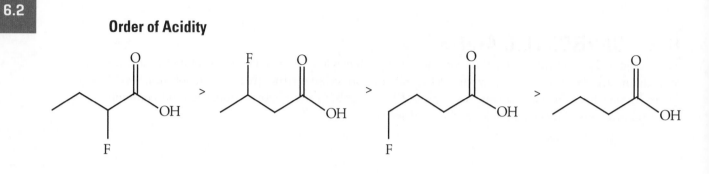

most acidic   least acidic

Example 6-7: Rank the following nine compounds in order of decreasing acidity.

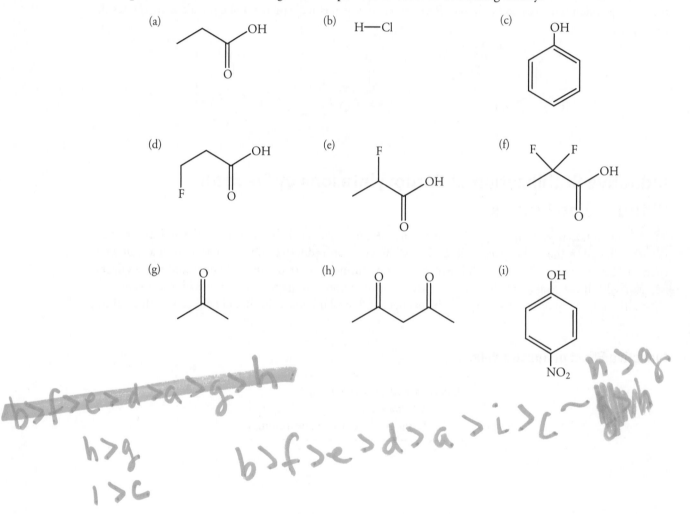

Solution:

(b) > (f) > (e) > (d) > (a) ────┐

strong   diflourinated   monoflourinated   monoflourinated   carboxylic
acid   carboxylic   carboxylic acid   carboxylic acid   acid
            acid   in α position   in β position

┌──> > (i) > (c) ~ (h) > (g)

phenol with   phenol   diketone with   ketone
electron   2 α protons
withdrawing   adjacent to
nitro group   2 carbonyls

Hydrogen Bonding in Carboxylic Acids

Carboxylic acids form strong hydrogen bonds because the carboxylate group contains both a hydrogen bond donor and a hydrogen bond acceptor. This can be seen in the inter-molecular hydrogen bonding of acetic acid. Notice that the acidic proton is the hydrogen bond donor and a lone pair of electrons on the carbonyl oxygen is the hydrogen bond acceptor. For this reason, they can form stable hydrogen bonded dimers.

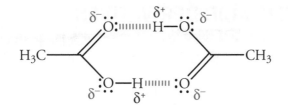

Decarboxylation Reactions of β-Keto Acids

Carboxylic acids that have carbonyl groups β to the carboxylate are unstable because they are subject to decarboxylation. The reaction proceeds through a cyclic transition state and results in the loss of carbon dioxide from the β-keto acid.

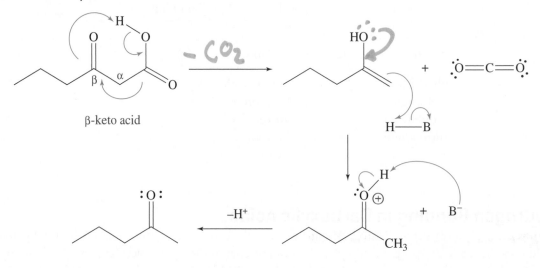

β-keto acid

6.3   CARBOXYLIC ACID DERIVATIVES

Carboxylic acid derivatives include acid chlorides, acid anhydrides, esters, and amides. The general chemical structures for these acid derivatives are:

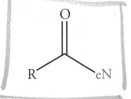

(eN = electronegative group)

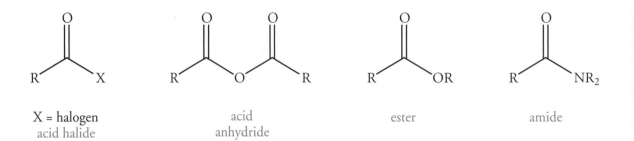

X = halogen
acid halide

acid
anhydride

ester

amide

Like aldehydes and ketones, acid derivatives often undergo nucleophilic addition reactions (see next page). This is because they are very electrophilic at the carbonyl carbon atom. However, unlike reactions with aldehydes and ketones, nucleophilic addition reactions to carboxylic acid derivatives are usually followed by elimination. This is because the tetrahedral intermediate formed upon attack of the nucleophile on the carbonyl carbon has both a negatively charged oxygen atom (the former carbonyl oxygen), and a good leaving group (the eN-group of the carboxylic acid derivative). This elimination by the electrons on the oxygen atom regenerates the carbonyl, thereby displacing the leaving group (eN⁻). This is called a **nucleophilic addition-elimination reaction.**

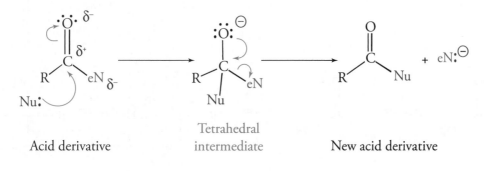

| Acid derivative | Tetrahedral intermediate | New acid derivative |

Esterification Reactions

An **esterification reaction** occurs when a carboxylic acid reacts with an alcohol in the presence of a catalytic amount of acid. The protonation of the carbonyl oxygen makes the carbonyl carbon more electrophilic, and nucleophilic attack by the oxygen of the alcohol results in a tetrahedral intermediate that is neutralized by deprotonation. An oxygen of the tetrahedral intermediate is then protonated and converts a poor leaving group (–OH) into a good one –OH_2^+). As a result, the water molecule departs with its electrons, and leaves behind a resonance-stabilized carbocation. Deprotonation of the carbonyl oxygen yields the ester product.

Esterification

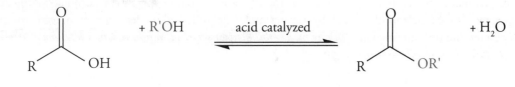

| a carboxylic acid | an alcohol | | an ester |

6.3

The Acid-Catalyzed Mechanism

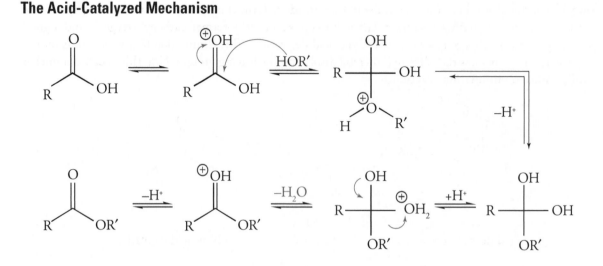

Acidic and Basic Hydrolysis of Esters

Let's now examine both the acidic and basic hydrolysis of the ester *methyl benzoate* to form the carboxylic acid and alcohol. First, we look at the acid-catalyzed reaction:

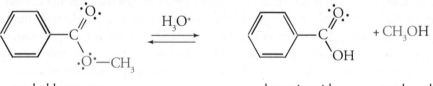

methyl benzoate   benzoic acid   methanol

In the first step of this reaction, the carbonyl oxygen is protonated. As before, the protonation of the carbonyl oxygen makes the carbon even more electrophilic and therefore susceptible to nucleophilic attack by a water molecule. Nucleophilic attack by a water molecule, followed by deprotonation, leads to the formation of a tetrahedral intermediate. *In any nucleophilic addition-elimination reaction of an acid derivative, there will always be a tetrahedral intermediate.*

Acid-Catalyzed Ester Hydrolysis Mechanism

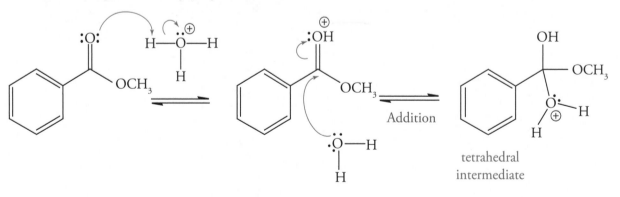

tetrahedral
intermediate

Next, the leaving group of the tetrahedral intermediate is protonated under the acidic reaction conditions. Notice that protonation of the hydroxyl oxygens can also occur. This leads to the reverse reaction. Protonation of the leaving group converts a poor leaving group (RO⁻, an alkoxide ion) into a good one (ROH, a neutral alcohol molecule). The alcohol leaves and yields a protonated acid that only has to undergo a deprotonation to give the carboxylic acid product.

Acid-Catalyzed Mechanism, Continued

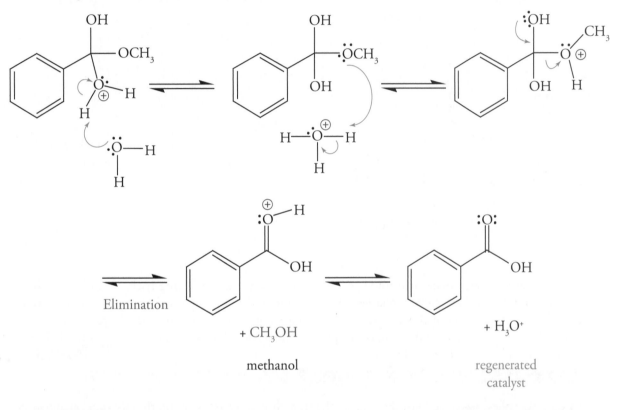

We now consider the corresponding *base*-mediated hydrolysis of methyl benzoate. In the first step of the reaction, the strongly nucleophilic hydroxide ion directly attacks the electrophilic carbonyl carbon. The nucleophilic attack results in the formation of a tetrahedral intermediate.

Base-Mediated Ester Hydrolysis Mechanism

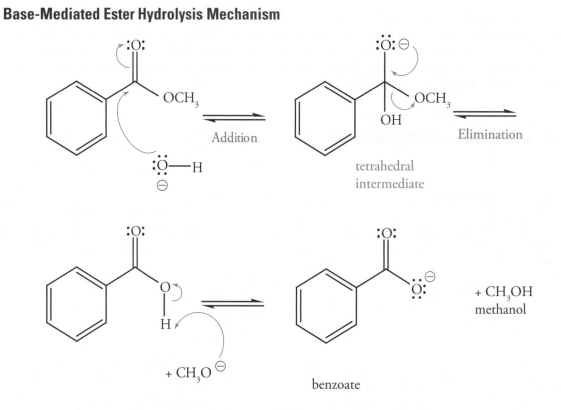

The tetrahedral intermediate then undergoes an elimination reaction, giving back the carbonyl when a pair of electrons on the negatively charged oxygen of the tetrahedral intermediate regenerates the carbon-oxygen π bond. This eliminates the alkoxide ion as a leaving group. However, since the reaction is carried out under basic conditions and the alkoxide ion is a strong enough base to deprotonate the newly formed carboxylic acid, the final step of the mechanism is the acid-base reaction shown above. In order to recover the carboxylic acid from this process, the reaction must have a final aqueous acidic workup.

In summary, these two reactions, the acid-catalyzed hydrolysis of an ester and the base-mediated hydrolysis of an ester, display the most common reactivities of all of the carboxylic acid derivatives. Both of these reactions give the same products, but by different mechanisms; and both of the mechanisms proceed by nucleophilic addition and elimination steps. A good understanding of these two reaction mechanisms leads to a solid understanding of all of the reactions of carboxylic acids and their derivatives.

Saponification: An Example of a Base-Mediated Ester Hydrolysis Reaction

The hydrolysis of fats and glycerides is a chemical reaction that has been practiced for many centuries in the process of making soap. Typically, large vats of animal fat are treated with lye (NaOH or KOH) and stirred over a roaring fire. This bubbling cauldron liberates free fatty acids from the animal fat, which then can be utilized as soap.

Upon inspection, it is clear that this ancient method is simply the basic hydrolysis of a triacylglyceride to yield a molecule of glycerol and three fatty acids. This is the reaction mechanism we just reviewed.

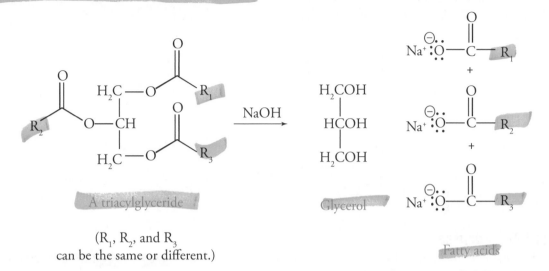

A triacylglyceride

(R₁, R₂, and R₃ can be the same or different.)

Glycerol

Fatty acids

The three electrophilic carbonyl carbons of the triacylglyceride sequentially undergo nucleophilic attack by hydroxide ions to produce an oxy-anion tetrahedral intermediate. Then the tetrahedral intermediate eliminates the –OR portion of the ester as an alkoxide ion which is then protonated to form the alcohol. This happens three times to ultimately yield glycerol and three molecules of fatty acid.

Recall that fatty acids are **amphipathic** molecules, because they contain a negatively charged carboxylate group that is hydrophilic and a long saturated or unsaturated hydrocarbon tail that's hydrophobic. As a result, these amphipathic fatty acid molecules form micelles in water that have hydrophobic tails associating with one another to exclude water, while the charged carboxylate groups are localized on the exterior of the micelles. Greases and fats are adsorbed by the fatty portion of these micelles and the whole micelle is later "washed" away by water. This is the physical basis of soap. We will discuss this further in Chapter 8.

Synthesis of the Carboxylic Acid Derivatives

Now that we understand the how the electronic structure of the carboxylic acid derivatives relates to their reactivity, the synthesis of carboxylic acid derivatives should be straightforward. For the most part, we shall only be concerned with the interconversion of one derivative to another. By the end of this section, you should be able to convert any carboxylic acid derivative into any other!

Acid Halides

Carboxylic acid halides are made from the corresponding carboxylic acid and either $SOCl_2$ or PX_3 (X = Cl, Br). This is very similar to the way alkyl halides are prepared from alcohols (Section 4.5).

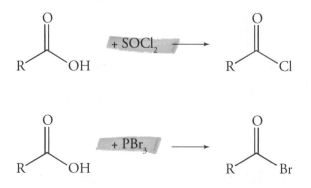

Acid Anhydrides

As their name implies, anhydrides (meaning "without water") can be prepared by the condensation of two carboxylic acids with the loss of water.

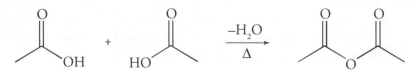

Acid anhydrides are also prepared from addition of the corresponding carboxylic acid (or carboxylate ion) to the corresponding acid halide.

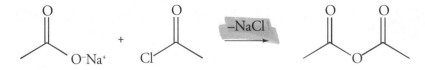

Esters

Esters are most easily synthesized from the corresponding carboxylic acid and an alcohol, as we saw earlier. This reaction is referred to as **esterification**. Esters can also be prepared from an acid halide or an anhydride and a corresponding alcohol.

Amides

Amides can be prepared from the corresponding acid halide, anhydride, or ester with the desired amine. They *cannot* be prepared from the carboxylic acid directly. This is because amines are very basic, and carboxylic acids are very acidic; an acid-base reaction occurs much faster than the desired addition-elimination reaction. For more on direct condensation of an amine and an acid, see the protein discussion in Chapter 6.

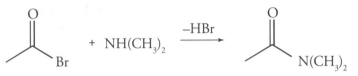

Carboxylic Acids

Carboxylic acids can be prepared from *any* of the derivatives merely by heating the derivative in acidic aqueous solutions.

Relative Reactivity of Carboxylic Acid Derivatives

Now that we are familiar with the general reactivity of carboxylic acid derivatives, nucleophilic addition-elimination reactions, we will examine how chemical *structure* affects the *relative* chemical reactivity of common acid derivatives. The order of reactivity in nucleophilic substitution reactions for acid derivatives is:

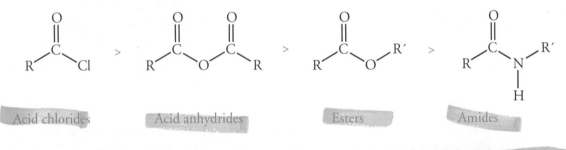

If we examine the leaving groups of these acid derivatives, it is clear that the reactivity of acid derivatives in nucleophilic substitution reactions decreases with increasing basicity of the leaving group.

Acid Derivative Reactivity

Acid Derivative	*Leaving Group*	
acid chloride	 Cl⁻	Chloride anion is a very good leaving group. It is a very weak base since it is the conjugate base of the strong acid HCl ($pK_a = -7$).
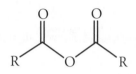 acid anhydride	(image)	This is a fairly good leaving group. It is the conjugate base of the weakly acidic carboxylic acid ($pK_a = 4\text{--}5$).
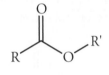 ester	(image)	An alkoxide ion is a rather poor leaving group. It is moderately basic since it is the conjugate base of alcohol, which is a fairly weak acid ($pK_a = 15\text{--}19$).
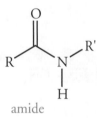 amide	(image)	This is a horrible leaving group. It is strongly basic since it is the conjugate base of an amine, which is a terrible acid ($pK_a = 35\text{--}40$).

Acid chlorides are *so* reactive in nucleophilic addition-elimination reactions that they are readily hydrolyzed in cold water.

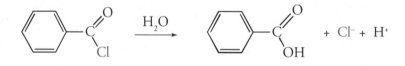

However, in order to hydrolyze amides and esters, heating with aqueous acid or base is required.

6.4 CYCLOADDITION REACTIONS

Concerted reactions are reactions that occur in one step without the formation of any intermediates. They usually occur with a high degree of stereoselectivity. Concerted reactions often occur via cyclic transition states by the reorganization of σ and π bonds. A typical concerted reaction will be illustrated with the **Diels-Alder reaction.**

In a Diels-Alder reaction, a cyclohexene ring is formed from the cycloaddition of a diene with a dienophile:

a diene   a dienophile

Since one molecule involved (the diene) contributes four π electrons, and the other molecule (the dienophile) contributes two π electrons, this reaction is denoted a [4+2] cycloaddition reaction. Although this reaction occurs both stereoselectively and regioselectively, these finer points are beyond the scope of the MCAT, so we will not discuss them further in this text.

Example 6-8: Predict the product of the following Diels-Alder cycloaddition reactions:

6.4

(a)

(b)

(c)

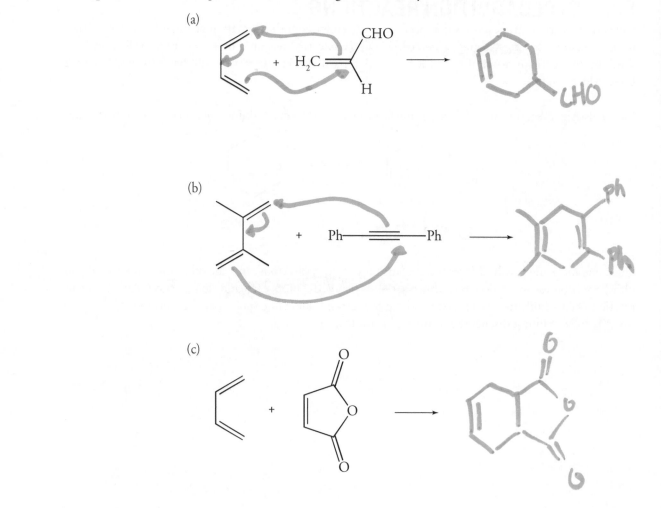

Solution:

(a)

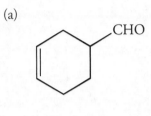

(b)

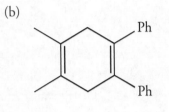

(c)

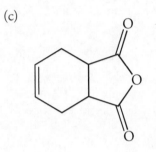

Chapter 6 Summary

- The C=O bond is very polarized due to the high electronegativity of oxygen, resulting in the carbon of the carbonyl group being electrophilic.

- Protons α to a carbonyl are acidic and can be removed by a strong base to yield a nucleophilic carbanion, or enolate.

- Keto-enol tautomerism is the rapid equilibration of the more stable keto form of a carbonyl and the less stable enol form where the α-proton shifts to the carbonyl oxygen.

- Nucleophilic additions involve the attack of a nucleophile on the carbon of an aldehyde or ketone; these reactions break one π bond to form two σ bonds.

- Hydride reduction, a type of nucleophilic addition, can convert ketones or aldehydes into alcohols; alcohols can be converted back to carbonyl compounds using oxidizing agents.

- An aldol condensation is a C—C bond forming reaction where the carbonyl carbon of one molecule is the electrophile, while the α-carbon of another carbonyl is the nucleophile.

- α,β-Unsaturated carbonyl compounds are electrophilic at the β-carbon and undergo Michael, or conjugate, addition reactions.

- Acidity of carboxylic acids results from the resonance stability of the carboxylate anion.

- Electron withdrawing groups increase the acidity of carboxylic acids by stabilizing the negative charge of the carboxylate anion via the inductive effect.

- The reactivity of carboxylic acid derivatives decreases as follows: acid halide > acid anhydride > ester > amide

- Nucleophilic addition to the carbonyl carbon in a carboxylic acid derivative is usually followed by elimination due to the presence of a good electronegative leaving group.

CHAPTER 6 FREESTANDING PRACTICE QUESTIONS

1. Rank the protons from least acidic to most acidic.

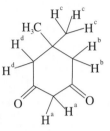

A) $H^a < H^b = H^d < H^c$
B) $H^c < H^d < H^b < H^a$
C) $H^c < H^b = H^d < H^a$
D) $H^c < H^b < H^d < H^a$

2. Predict a possible product of the following reaction:

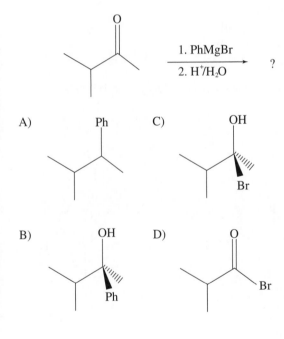

A)

Ph

C)

OH

Br

B)

OH

Ph

D)

O

Br

3. The enol and keto tautomers of 3-pentanone (shown below) are best described as:

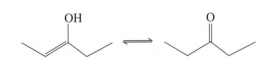

A) resonance structures.
B) geometric isomers.
C) constitutional isomers.
D) diastereomers.

4. Which of the following carbonyl compounds cannot undergo a symmetrical aldol condensation?

A) 2,2,4,4-tetramethylpentan-3-one
B) 1,2,2-triphenylethanone
C) *tert*-butyl acetate
D) pentan-2-one

5. Which of the following carbonyl compounds most favorably undergoes hydration?

A)

O

Cl
Cl Cl

C)

O

B)

O

F
F F

D)

O

H

CHAPTER 6 PRACTICE PASSAGE

Carboxylic acids play a large role in many biological pathways, including the synthesis of amino acids. Carboxylic acids and their derivatives are unlike aldehydes and ketones because they undergo addition-elimination reactions rather than simple additions. This is due to the fact that carboxylic acids and their derivatives contain a leaving group. The leaving group, in large part, determines the reactivity of the molecule. The better the leaving group is, the more reactive the molecule will be.

Carboxylic acids can be used to synthesize carboxylic acid derivatives. For example, one way to form an amide is shown in Figure 1.

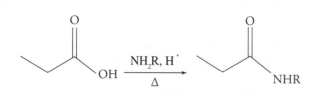

Amide Synthesis

Figure 1 Amide Synthesis

As their name implies, carboxylic acids have acidic properties. The first step in the reaction shown above is, in fact, an acid-base reaction that forms a salt. However, by using an excess of the amine, high temperatures, and long reaction times, the salt can be converted to the amide product. This method of amide formation is not regularly used since amides are more easily produced by reacting an amine with another carboxylic acid derivative.

1. Rank the following reagents in order of decreasing reactivity with methylamine to form a new amide product.

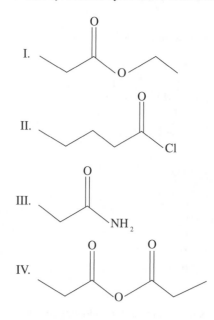

A) IV > II > I > III
B) II > IV > III > I
C) II > IV > I > III
D) IV > I > III > II

2. Which of the following carboxylic acids is most acidic?

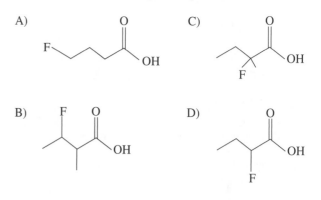

3. In Figure 1 the amine acts as the:

A) electrophile.
B) leaving group.
C) catalyst.
D) nucleophile.

4. Why do carboxylic acids have a higher boiling point than esters?

A) Carboxylic acids have electronegative oxygen atoms.
B) Carboxylic acids have intermolecular hydrogen bonding.
C) Carboxylic acids are larger in size.
D) Esters have significantly larger dipole moments than do carboxylic acids.

5. Predict the product of the following reaction:

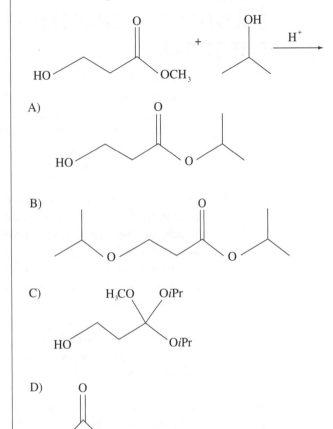

A)

B)

C)

D)

SOLUTIONS TO CHAPTER 6 FREESTANDING PRACTICE QUESTIONS

1. **C** Because H^a is bound to a carbon that is adjacent to two carbonyl groups, it is the easiest proton for a base to abstract since the conjugate base has the most resonance structures. Therefore, you can eliminate choice A. Because this molecule has a mirror plane, H^b and H^d are equivalent, so you can eliminate choices B and D, which leaves choice C as the correct choice. H^c is on a carbon that is not adjacent to any electron withdrawing groups or pi electrons, so it is the least acidic.

2. **B** This is an addition reaction involving a ketone and a Grignard reagent (RMgX). The R-group in the Grignard reagent, in this case the phenyl, adds on to the carbonyl carbon, and the acid workup step is used to protonate the carbonyl oxygen into an alcohol. This gives the product shown in choice B. Choice A can be eliminated as ketones cannot undergo substitution reactions with Grignard reagents due to lack of an appropriate leaving group. Choices C and D can be eliminated since the halogen is not the nucleophilic atom in a Grignard reagent.

3. **C** Tautomers do not have the same connectivity of atoms; they are constitutional isomers which are in equilibrium with one another. Choices A, B, and D all have the same connectivity of atoms.

4. **A** A symmetrical aldol condensation is the same thing as a self-condensation reaction; it is an aldol condensation between two of the same molecule. In order for an aldol condensation to occur, at least one of the carbonyl compounds must be able to form an enolate through deprotonation of an α-carbon. Since 2,2,4,4-tetramethylpentan-3-one contains no α-hydrogens, it cannot form an enolate, and therefore cannot undergo a self-condensation reaction. All of the other molecules listed to have at least one α-hydrogen, and therefore can undergo self-condensation reactions.

5. **B** Hydration is a reaction that involves the nucleophilic attack of water on a carbonyl carbon to form a diol. The most favorable reaction will be the one in which there is the largest net gain in stability upon hydration of the carbonyl compound. The more unstable the carbonyl starting material, the more favorable hydration will be, as it will result in a greater net stability change. Due to the partial positive charge on the carbonyl carbon, electron-withdrawing substituents destabilize carbonyl compounds. Therefore, choices C and D can be eliminated, since they do not contain electron-withdrawing groups, while choices A and B do. Since F is more electronegative than Cl, it is more electron withdrawing, making choice B the best answer. It should also be considered that the inductive ability of the substituents plays a more significant role in the relative stabilities of the carbonyl reactants than the diol products. This is why the favorability of this reaction can be considered based on the stability of the carbonyl starting materials, rather than on the stability of the diol products.

SOLUTIONS TO CHAPTER 6 PRACTICE PASSAGE

1. **C** The passage mentions that acid derivatives can be combined with amines to form amides, and that the reactivity of carboxylic acid derivatives is largely determined by the leaving group. The halides are the best leaving groups due to their low basicity, and anionic stability. Therefore, Item II is the most reactive (choices A and D can be eliminated). Item I has a leaving group that contains an oxide, while Item III has a leaving group that contains a nitride. Oxide is less basic than a nitride, which makes it a better leaving group. Therefore Item III would be the least reactive, so choice B can be eliminated.

2. **D** The carboxylic acids in question differ in the placement of the fluorine atom on the molecule. As we know, inductive effects can dramatically affect the acidity of a compound. In this case, fluorine is highly electronegative, so it will pull electron density toward itself and weaken the O—H bond. The strongest effect will occur when the fluorine is on the carbon next to the carbonyl carbon so choices A and B can be eliminated. The difference between choices C and D is the presence of the methyl group on compound C. Since methyl groups are electron donating, they will mitigate the effect of the fluorine atom and make the acid weaker, so choice C can be eliminated.

3. **D** Glancing at Figure 1, we see that the amine ends up in the product. Therefore, choice C can be eliminated because catalysts are never consumed in a reaction. Choice B can be eliminated because the leaving group cannot contain nitrogen since the starting material is a carboxylic acid. Finally, choice A can be eliminated because an electrophile is an electron pair acceptor. The amine has a lone pair, which it donates.

4. **B** Recall that boiling point increases with overall size and increasing strength of intermolecular interactions. Choice A can be eliminated since both carboxylic acids and esters have electronegative oxygen atoms. Choice C can be eliminated because no size is specified. If choice D were true, esters would have the higher boiling points. Carboxylic acids can hydrogen bond with one another; esters cannot. Therefore, choice B is the best answer.

5. **A** This question tests your knowledge of the addition-elimination reaction referred to in the passage. The conditions shown will make an ester instead of an amide. The nucleophile attacks the carbonyl group and replaces the methoxy leaving group, giving us choice A. Choice B can be eliminated because in addition to the transesterification, it shows the formation of an ether via a substitution reaction, which is unlikely under these conditions. Choice C can be eliminated as it is suggestive of acetal formation, a functional group formed from acid catalyzed reaction of alcohols with aldehydes or ketones. Choice D can be eliminated because it shows in intramolecular esterification, which is highly unlikely because of the strain associated with a four-membered ring.

Chapter 7
Lab Techniques and Spectroscopy

7.1 SEPARATIONS

Extractions

One of the more useful techniques in experimental organic chemistry is solvent extraction. Isolation of natural products from marine organisms, plants, and other natural sources is facilitated by exploiting the particular solubilities of organic compounds in various solvents. Complex mixtures of organic compounds can be separated using careful choice of solvents based on the differential solubilities of the various components of the mixture. We'll see that the acid/base properties of organic molecules play an important role in the extraction process.

Extraction allows the chemist to separate one substance from a mixture of substances by adding a solvent in which the compound of interest is highly soluble. If the solution containing the compound of interest is shaken with a second solvent (completely immiscible with the first) and allowed to separate into two distinct phases, the compound of interest will distribute itself between the two phases based upon its solubility in each of the individual solvents. This is called a **liquid-liquid extraction**. The ratio of the substance's solubilities in the two solvents is called the **distribution** (or **partition**) **coefficient**.

The simplest liquid-liquid extraction is accomplished when an organic compound is extracted with water. A simple water extraction can remove substances that are highly polar or charged, including inorganic salts, strong acids and bases, and polar, low molecular weight compounds (less than five carbons) such as alcohols, amines, and carboxylic acids.

A second class of organic extraction involves the use of acidic or basic water solutions. Organic compounds that are basic (e.g., amines) can be extracted from mixtures of organic compounds upon treatment with dilute acid (usually 5–10% HCl). This treatment will protonate the basic functional group, forming a positively charged ion. The resulting cationic salts of these basic compounds are usually freely soluble in aqueous solution and can be removed from the organic compounds that remain dissolved in the organic phase.

Extraction of Organic Amines

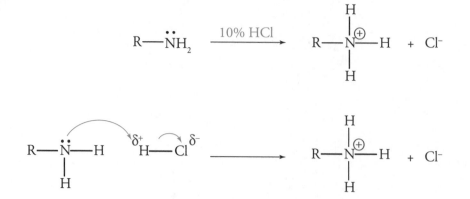

On the other hand, extraction with a dilute weak base—typically 5 percent sodium bicarbonate ($NaHCO_3$)—results in converting organic acids into their corresponding anionic salts.

Extraction of Carboxylic Acids

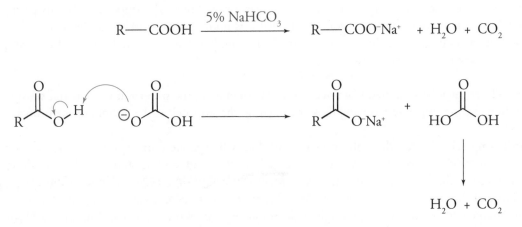

These anionic salts are generally soluble in aqueous solution and can be removed from the organic compounds that remain dissolved in the organic phase. Dilute sodium hydroxide could also be used for this kind of extraction, but it is basic enough to also convert phenols into their corresponding anionic salts. When phenols are present in a mixture of organic compounds and need to be removed, a dilute sodium hydroxide solution (usually about 10%) will succeed in converting phenols into their corresponding anionic salts. The anionic salts of the phenols are generally soluble in the aqueous phase and can therefore be removed from the organic phase.

Extraction of Phenols

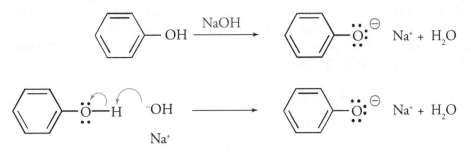

(*Note:* NaOH will also extract carboxylic acids.)

The apparatus in which these extractions are typically carried out is called a **separatory funnel**. To perform a solvent-solvent extraction, the solution containing the mixture of organic compounds and the extraction solvent of choice are poured into the separatory funnel, and the apparatus is fitted with a stopper. The partial vapor pressures of the two solvents add upon mixing because the vapors of both solvents are now in equilibrium with the solution. This causes a pressure increase which may be alleviated by "venting" the separatory funnel (inverting it and letting the gas escape out of the stopcock). At this point, vigorous shaking and venting should be continued until it is no longer possible to audibly detect the escape of gases upon venting. Once this has occurred, the mixing has come to equilibrium and the two phases should be allowed to fully separate.

The two layers may be separated from one another by removing the stopper at the top and slowly collecting each phase into separate receiving flasks by opening the stopcock at the bottom of the funnel.

As an example, let us step through an extraction that will separate four organic compounds from one another. The original mixture consists of *para*-cresol, benzoic acid, aniline, and naphthalene, all of which are dissolved in diethyl ether. This mixture is first extracted with an equal volume of aqueous sodium bicarbonate. The weakly basic bicarbonate is sufficiently basic to deprotonate benzoic acid and convert it to an anionic salt, but not strong enough to deprotonate *para*-cresol (a phenol). Likewise, a bicarbonate extraction will not affect aniline (a base itself) or naphthalene (a hydrocarbon). Thus, *para*-cresol, aniline, and naphthalene will remain dissolved in the ether phase, while the benzoic acid, now in its anionic salt form, will be extracted into the aqueous layer.

The ether layer, which now contains three components, is extracted with a sodium hydroxide solution. The strongly basic hydroxide ion is strong enough to deprotonate *para*-cresol and convert it to its anionic salt form. The basic conditions will not affect aniline or naphthalene so *para*-cresol is the only compound that is extracted into the aqueous phase, and the aniline and naphthalene will remain dissolved in the ether layer.

Finally, the remaining two components can be separated from one another by an acidic extraction with a 10% HCl solution. The solution is acidic enough to protonate the lone pair of electrons of aniline and to convert aniline to its cationic salt. Naphthalene will not be affected and will remain dissolved in the ether layer. The final extraction of aniline into the aqueous phase completes the separation. Naphthalene can be isolated by evaporating off the diethyl ether.

These steps are summarized on the following page.

All four components dissolved in diethyl ether

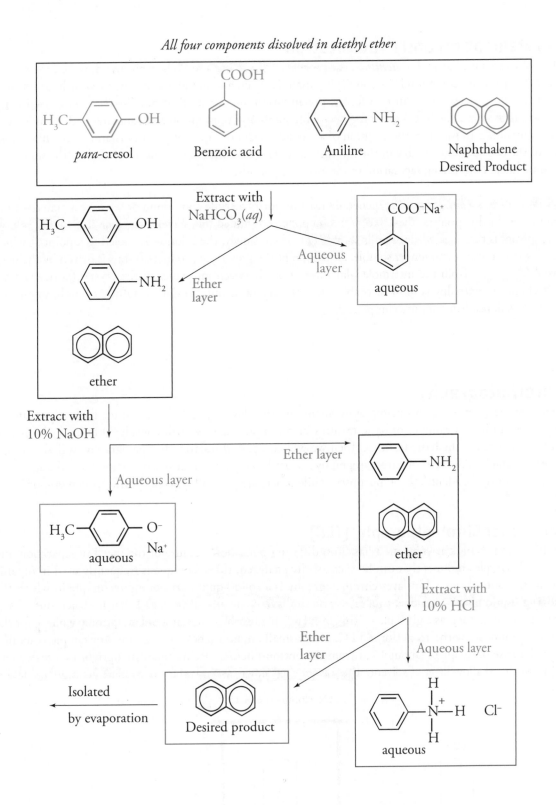

Crystallization and Precipitation

Most of us are familiar with *dissolution*, the process of dissolving a solid in a solvent. However, the reverse process, separating compounds by solidifying material from a liquid phase, is much less utilized in everyday life. This process comes in two forms, **precipitation** and **crystallization**. *Precipitation* is used when one wants to separate two compounds of variable solubility in given solvents. Starting with a mixture of two compounds in solution, the addition of a second solvent of different polarity than the first may make one of the two solutes insoluble in the mixture, forcing it to crash out of solution as a solid. The solids can then be filtered off, giving separation of the two compounds.

Crystallization is a similar process, generally used to purify a crude compound or separate a material from impurities. In this process, the mixture of components is added to a solvent in which it is mildly soluble. This solvent is then heated until all is solubilized. Then, slowly, the solution is cooled to a point at which the desired product is no longer soluble. At this point the growth of product crystals is driven by the negative $\Delta H_{crystallization}$, from the intermolecular interactions between molecules in the crystal (lattice energy). This change in enthalpy is most favorable when the crystal is pure. If done carefully enough, impurities are excluded, resulting in pure compound.

Chromatography

There are many types of chromatography, including thin layer, gas, and column (or flash) chromatography. They all have a number of basic features in common. First, we will consider thin-layer chromatography to enunciate the basic features. Then we will compare thin-layer chromatography to flash and gas chromatography. All types of chromatography are used to separate mixtures of compounds, though some are used mostly for identification purposes, while others are generally used as purification methods.

Thin-Layer Chromatography (TLC)

In TLC, compounds are separated based on differing polarities. Because of the speed of separation and the small sample amounts that can be successfully analyzed, this technique is frequently used in organic chemistry laboratories. Thin-layer chromatography is a solid-liquid partitioning technique in which the **moving liquid phase** ascends a thin layer of absorbant (generally silica, SiO_2) that is coated onto a supporting material such as a glass plate. This thin layer of absorbant acts as a **polar stationary phase** for the sample to interact with. To perform TLC, a very small amount (about 1 microliter) of sample is spotted near the base of the plate (about 1 cm from the bottom) before placing the plate upright in a sealed container with a shallow layer of solvent. The solvent then slowly ascends the coated plate via capillary action.

Developing the plate

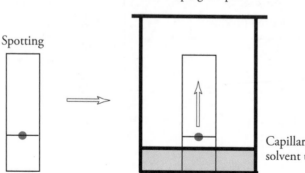

Spotting

Capillary action draws the solvent up the plate.

As the solvent slowly ascends the plate via capillary action, the components of the spotted sample are partitioned between the moving liquid phase and the stationary solid phase. This process is referred to as **developing**, or **running**, a thin layer plate. Each component of the sample experiences many equilibrations between the moving and the stationary phases as the development proceeds.

Separation of the compounds occurs because different components travel along the plate at different rates. The more polar components of the mixture interact more with the polar stationary phase and travel at a slower rate. The less polar components have a greater affinity for the solvent than the stationary phase and travel with the mobile solvent at a faster rate than the more polar components. The thin layer plate is then removed and allowed to dry when the solvent front approaches a few centimeters from the top of the plate. If the compounds in the mixture that was spotted are colored, we would see a vertical series of spots on the plate; however, it is more likely that the components are not colored and need to be detected by some other means. Visualization methods include shining ultraviolet light on the plate, placing the thin layer plate in the presence of iodine vapor, and a host of other chemical staining techniques.

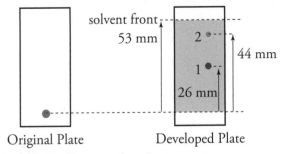

Once the separated components have been visualized, R_f values can be computed. This "ratio to front" value (R_f) is simply the distance traveled by an individual component divided by the distance traveled by the solvent front. For example, from the illustration above, we would find

$$R_f \text{ (Compound 1)} = \frac{26 \text{ mm}}{53 \text{ mm}} = 0.49 \qquad R_f \text{ (Compound 2)} = \frac{44 \text{ mm}}{53 \text{ mm}} = 0.83$$

(Note that R_f is always positive and never greater than 1.)

Column (Flash) Chromatography

While TLC is a good technique for separating very small amounts of material in order to assess how many compounds make up a mixture, it's not a good technique for isolating bulk compounds. A common technique known as column or flash chromatography employs the idea behind TLC toward just such a goal. Shown below is a chromatography column. This column is filled with silica gel (predominantly SiO_2, as in the TLC plate). The silica gel is saturated with a chosen organic solvent, and the mixture of compounds is then added to the top and allowed to travel down through the silica-packed column. Excess solvent is periodically added to the top of the column, and the flow of solvent (along with the separated compounds) is collected from the bottom. Just as is the case in TLC, polar compounds will spend more time adsorbed on the polar solid phase, and as such travel more slowly down the column than nonpolar compounds. Therefore, compounds can be expected to leave the column, and be collected, in order of polarity (least polar to most polar).

Column Chromatography

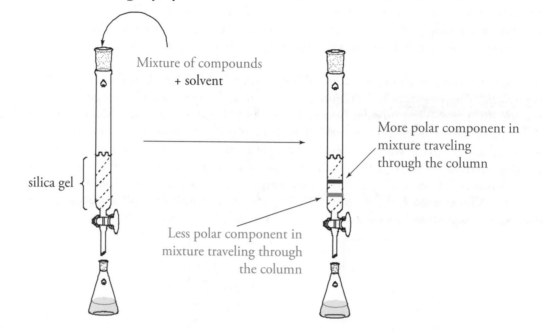

Mixture of compounds + solvent

silica gel

More polar component in mixture traveling through the column

Less polar component in mixture traveling through the column

Gas Chromatography

Gas chromatography (GC) is a form of column chromatography in which the partitioning of the components to be separated takes place between a **moving gas phase** and a **stationary liquid phase**. This partitioning, or separation, between mixtures of compounds occurs based on their *different volatilities*. In a typical gas chromatograph, a sample is loaded into a syringe and injected into the device through a rubber septum. The sample is then vaporized by a heater in the injection port and carried along by a stream of inert gas (typically helium). The vaporized sample is quickly moved by the inert stream into a column composed of particles that are coated with a liquid absorbant. As the components of the sample pass through the column, they interact differently with the absorbant based on their relative volatilities. Each component of the sample is subjected to many gas-liquid partitioning processes which separates the individual components.

As each component exits the column, it is burned, and the resulting ions are detected by an electrical detector that generates a signal that is recorded by a chart recorder. The chart recorder printout enables us to determine the number of components and their relative amounts.

Let's now take a closer look at the separation process by examining a typical GC column. In order to examine the separation process we will consider a mixture of two individual components. As the mixture enters the column, it begins to interact with the stationary phase, which is composed of support material coated with a liquid absorbant. The liquid absorbants can range from hydrocarbon mixtures that are very nonpolar to polyesters that are polar. As the mixture passes through the column, the components equilibrate between the carrier gas and the liquid phase. The less volatile components will spend more time dissolved in the liquid stationary phase than the more volatile components that will be carried along by the carrier gas at a faster rate. It is this equilibrium between the components (the absorbed liquid phase and the carrier gas mobile phase) that results in the separation of the mixture. If the interactions of the substrates with the column are similar (this is usually the case with most GC columns), the more volatile components emerge from the column first, while the less volatile components emerge from the column later.

Distillations

Distillation is the process of raising the temperature of a liquid until it can overcome the intermolecular forces that hold it together in the liquid phase. The vapor is then condensed back to the liquid phase and subsequently collected in another container.

Simple Distillation

A simple distillation is performed when trace impurities need to be removed from a relatively pure compound, or when a mixture of compounds with significantly different boiling points needs to be separated.

Fractional Distillation

Fractional distillation is a different type of distillation process that is used when the difference in boiling points of the components in the liquid mixture is not large. A fractional distillation column is packed with an appropriate material, such as glass beads or a stainless steel sponge. The packing of the column results in the liquid mixture being subjected to many vaporization-condensation cycles as it moves up the column toward the condenser. As the cycles progress, the composition of the vapor gradually becomes enriched in the lower boiling component. Near the top of the column, nearly pure vapor reaches the condenser and condenses back to the liquid phase where it is subsequently collected in a receiving flask.

Example 7-1: A chemist wishes to separate a mixture of Compounds A and B. He decides to distill the mixture; however, he is unsure of their respective boiling points. After several minutes of heating, he collects the distillate, takes a small sample, and injects it into a gas chromatograph. The output is:

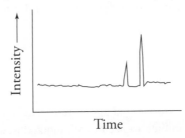

What can this chemist conclude about the separation, and how could it be improved?

Solution: Based on the data from the GC, his separation was only partial (because two different peaks are recorded). Because the second peak is larger than the first, the distillate consists primarily of one of the two compounds, but their boiling points may have been similar enough such that a complete separation was not possible. Perhaps the chemist should try fractional distillation.

7.2 SPECTROSCOPY

A basic understanding of the general principles of spectroscopy will enable you to answer important questions regarding the structure of organic molecules. In this chapter, we'll examine the general principles of both infrared (IR) spectroscopy and nuclear magnetic resonance (NMR) spectroscopy with the goal of interpreting the spectra of simple organic molecules.

Most types of spectroscopy that we will discuss are examples of absorption spectroscopy. A short explanation of the molecular events involved in absorption spectroscopy will help you remember the details of IR and NMR spectroscopy. Molecules normally exist in their lowest energy form, called their **ground state**. When a molecule is exposed to light it *may* absorb a photon, provided that the energy of this photon matches the energy between two of the fixed electronic energy levels of the molecule. When this happens, the molecule is said to be in an **excited state**. Molecules tend to prefer their ground state to an excited state, but in order for them to return to their ground state, they must lose the energy they have gained. This loss of energy can occur by the emission of heat, or less commonly, light. In absorption spectroscopy, scientists induce the absorption of energy by a sample of molecules by exposing the sample to various forms of light, thereby exciting molecules to a higher energy state. They then measure the energy released as the molecules relax back to their ground state. This measured energy can reveal structural features of the molecules in the sample.

There are many different forms of light, as displayed in the electromagnetic spectrum. In principle, any of these forms of light could be used to do absorption spectroscopy on molecules, and, in fact, many are! The different forms of light induce different transitions in ground state molecules to different excited states of the molecules and allow for the acquisition of different structural information about the molecules.

Mass Spectrometry

Mass spectrometry is a very useful technique that allows researchers to determine the mass of compounds in a sample. Within the mass spectrometer, molecules are ionized in a high vacuum, usually by bombarding them with high energy electrons. Once ionized, compounds enter a region of the spectrometer where they are acted on by a magnetic field. This field causes the flight path of the charged species to alter, and the degree to which the path is changed is determined by the mass of the ion. This difference is detected and translated into a mass readout in the detector.

On the following page is a schematic of a portion of the mass spectrum for *n*-nonane (MW = 128 g/mol).

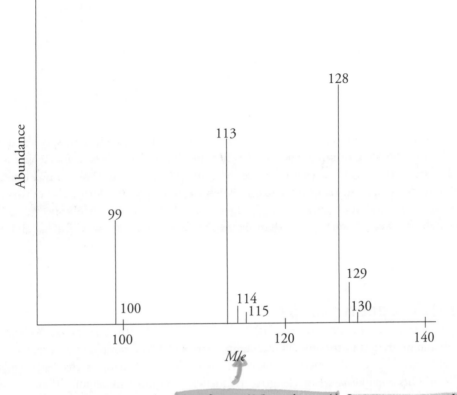

The *M/e* label on the *x*-axis represents the ratio of mass (*M*) to charge (*e*). In most cases *e* = +1, so peaks can simply be viewed as molecular mass. The *y*-axis represents the relative abundance of each species of a particular mass detected in the sample. Masses, though generally not labeled as such, are measured in amu.

Two aspects of the above spectrum may be puzzling: 1) If the molecular weight of nonane is 128 g/mol, why are there peaks greater than this value, and 2) why are there significant peaks in the sample with masses lower than 128?

Remember, atoms can come in a number of different isotopes. For example, the most prevalent mass of hydrogen in nature is 1, but deuterium has an extra neutron and weighs 2 (natural abundance = .015%). Likewise, the most abundant isotope of carbon is ^{12}C, but ^{13}C exists as 1.1% of all carbon atoms. So, the small peaks with masses larger than the main peak represent molecules that have one or more of these less abundant isotopes.

The masses lower than 128 in the above scan represent the masses of molecular fragments. The high energy beam of electrons used to ionize molecules in the mass spectrometer can cause the molecule to break into smaller parts. The figure below shows where *n*-nonane might have been broken to produce peaks with the masses found above. The outer, curved brackets represent a fragment which has lost the terminal CH_3 group and hence is 15 less than the peak at 128. The inner, square brackets show a fragment weighing 99, having lost CH_2CH_3.

Particular atoms present in a molecule may give characteristic peaks in their mass spectra thanks to isotopic ratios. The two most important are Br and Cl. Bromine naturally occurs in two isotopes (79 and 81) of nearly identical natural abundance. This means that any mass spectrum involving a brominated compound will have two major peaks, nearly equal in height, 2 amu apart. Chlorine also occurs as two main isotopes; 35 (75% natural abundance) and 37 (25% natural abundance). Mass spectra for chlorinated molecules will have a peak 2 amu heavier than the main peak, and about one-third its height.

Infrared (IR) Spectroscopy

Electromagnetic radiation in the infrared (IR) range λ = 2.5 to 20 μm has the proper energy to cause bonds in organic molecules to become vibrationally excited. When a sample of an organic compound is irradiated with infrared radiation in the region between 2.5 and 20 μm, its covalent bonds will begin to *vibrate at distinct energy levels* (wavelengths, frequencies) within this region. These wavelengths correspond to frequencies in the range of 1.5×10^{13} Hz to 1.2×10^{14} Hz. In IR spectroscopy, vibrational frequencies are more commonly given in terms of the **wavenumber**. Wavenumber ($\overline{\nu}$) is simply the reciprocal of wavelength:

$$\overline{\nu} = \frac{1}{\lambda} = \frac{1}{c}\nu$$

and is therefore directly proportional to both the frequency (since $\lambda\nu = c = 3 \times 10^{10}$ cm/sec) and the energy of the radiation (since $E = h\nu$). That is, the higher the wavenumber, the higher the frequency and the greater the energy. Wavenumbers are usually expressed in *reciprocal centimeters*, cm⁻¹, and MCAT IR spectra will typically cover the range from 4000 to 1000 cm⁻¹.

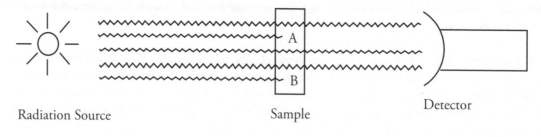

Radiation Source   Sample   Detector

When a bond absorbs IR radiation of a specific frequency, that frequency is not recorded by the detector and is thus seen as a peak in the IR spectrum (since low transmittance corresponds, naturally, to absorbance):

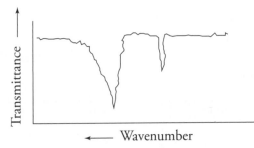

Important Stretching Frequencies

In order to do well on the MCAT, it is important that you know the stretching frequencies of the common functional groups. The most important ones are listed below.

The Double Bond Stretch

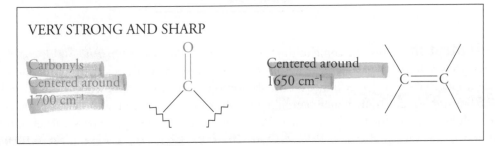

We'll begin by examining the carbonyl, or C=O, stretch. The carbonyl stretch is centered around 1700 cm⁻¹ and is very **strong** and very **intense**. *Strength* is reflected in the percent absorbance (or transmittance). *Intensity* is reflected in the sharpness or distinctiveness ("V" shape) of the spike appearing on the spectrum. The carbonyl stretch is one of the most important absorptions, and you should commit its location to memory. In any spectrum, always look for this stretch first. If it is *not* present, you can eliminate a wide range of compounds that contain a carbonyl group, including aldehydes, ketones, carboxylic acids, acid chlorides, esters, amides, and anhydrides. On the other hand, if the carbonyl stretch *is* present, you know that one of the carbonyl-containing functional groups is indeed present.

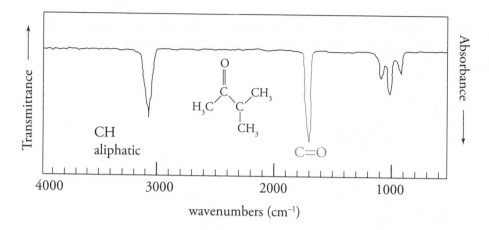

The Triple Bond Stretch

The next stretch to consider is the triple bond. This is an easy one because few molecules possess these functional groups. If they are present, however, the following characteristic stretches will be seen:

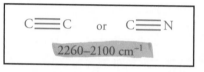

The O—H Stretch

Next we come to the hydroxyl stretch. *The O—H stretch is strong and very broad.* **Strength** is reflected as the degree of absorption a peak displays in the spectrum. **Broadness** is reflected as a wide "U"-shaped appearance on the absorption spectrum, as opposed to a "V," or spiked shape. The broadness is due to hydrogen bonding. Like the carbonyl stretch that occurs at 1700 cm⁻¹, one should always look for the O—H stretch at 3600–3200 cm⁻¹. Amines also have stretches in this region although they vary in intensity. The C—O stretch of the alcohol appears in the 1260–1000 cm⁻¹ range of the spectrum, but is a much less important stretch for the MCAT.

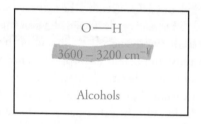

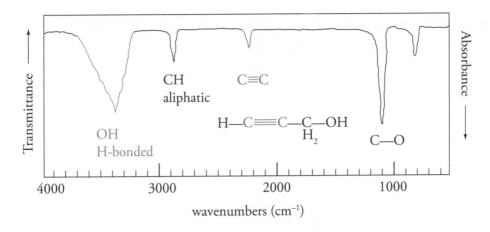

The C—H Stretches

Finally we come to the C—H stretching region (3300–2850 cm^{-1}). Since the vast majority of organic compounds contain C—H bonds, you will almost always see absorbances in this region. Even with the great number of these stretches, there are a few helpful characteristic absorptions in this region. Note that aliphatic C—H bonds stretch at wavenumbers a little less than 3000 cm^{-1}, and aromatic C—H bonds stretch at wavenumbers slightly greater than 3000 cm^{-1}.

C——H	for sp^3 carbon: 3000 – 2850 cm^{-1}
C——H	for sp^2 carbon: 3150 – 3000 cm^{-1}
C——H	for sp carbon: 3300 cm^{-1}

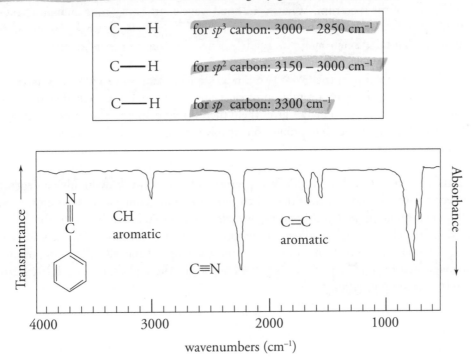

Summary of Relevant Infrared (IR) Stretching Frequencies

Bond	Frequency (Wavenumber) Range (cm^{-1})	Intensity
C$=$O	1735–1680	strong
C$=$C	1680–1620	variable
C$\equiv$C	2260–2100	variable
C$\equiv$N	2260–2220	variable
C—H	3300–2700	variable
N—H	3150–2500	moderate
O—H	3650–3200	broad

Ultraviolet/Visible (UV/Vis) Spectroscopy

UV/Vis spectroscopy is another type of absorption spectroscopy used in organic chemistry. It is very similar to IR, but instead focuses on the slightly shorter, more energetic wavelengths of radiation in the ultraviolet and visible area of the spectrum. Whereas infrared wavelengths are strong enough to induce bending and stretching of covalent bonds, the wavelengths in the UV and visible ranges are strong enough to induce electronic excitation, promoting ground state valence electrons into excited states.

In general, UV/Vis spectroscopy is used with two kinds of molecules. It is very useful in monitoring complexes of transition metals. The easy promotion of electrons from ground to excited states in the closely spaced *d*-orbitals of many transition metals gives them their bright color (by absorbing wavelengths in the visible region), and since many of these promotions involve energies in the UV range, these promotions allow study of these species.

More importantly in organic chemistry, UV/Vis spectroscopy is used to study highly conjugated organic systems. Molecular orbital theory tells us that when molecules have conjugated π-systems, orbitals form many bonding, non-bonding, and anti-bonding orbitals. These orbitals can be reasonably close together in energy, and in fact, close enough to allow promotion of electrons between electronic states through absorption of an ultraviolet photon. Though this is beyond the scope of the MCAT, it's important to know that highly conjugated organic systems can and will absorb in the UV range, and UV spectroscopy is often used to study their properties.

Proton (^{1}H) Nuclear Magnetic Resonance (NMR) Spectroscopy

Proton (^{1}H) NMR spectroscopy is the third type of absorption spectroscopy that we will consider. In all types of NMR spectroscopy, light from the radio frequency range of the electromagnetic spectrum is used to induce energy absorptions. The interpretation of ^{1}H NMR spectral data is important for the MCAT, but the theory underlying NMR spectroscopy is beyond the scope of the exam. Here, we'll only cover the interpretation of ^{1}H NMR spectra.

Four essential features of a molecule can be deduced from its ^1H NMR spectrum. First, the number of sets of peaks in the spectrum tells one the number of chemically nonequivalent sets of protons in the molecule. Second, the chemical shift values of those sets of peaks gives information about the environment of the protons in that set. Third, the mathematical integration of the sets of peaks indicates the relative numbers of protons in each set. Fourth, the splitting pattern of each set of peaks tells how many protons are interacting with the protons in that set. These four key features of ^1H NMR spectroscopy are explained in the next four sections.

Chemically Equivalent Protons

Determining which protons are **equivalent** in an organic molecule is the first important skill to master with respect to NMR spectroscopy. Equivalent protons in a molecule are those that have *identical electronic environments*. Such protons have identical locations in the ^1H NMR spectrum. Nonequivalent protons will have different locations in the ^1H NMR spectrum. One must be able to determine which protons (or, usually, groups of protons) are equivalent to which other groups, so that you can predict how many distinct NMR signals there will be in a molecule's ^1H NMR spectrum. Protons are considered equivalent if they can be interchanged by a free rotation or a symmetry operation (mirror plane or rotational axis). Check yourself on the following examples:

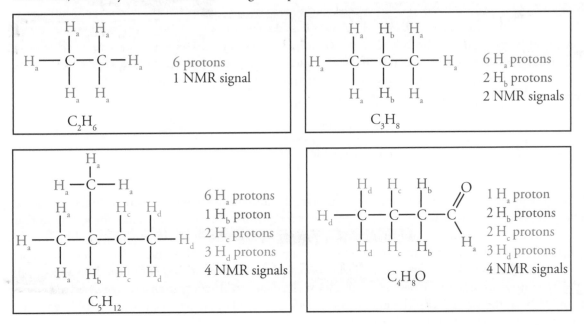

Example 7-2: A hydrocarbon C_5H_{12} shows only one peak on its NMR spectrum. Identify its structure.

Solution: Compute the degrees of unsaturation: $n = [2(\#C) + 2 - (\#H)]/2$. In this case, $n = 0$, so there are no double bonds or rings. Because there is only one peak in the NMR, all protons are equivalent, and thus our molecule must be:

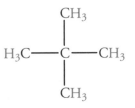

Example 7-3: C_5H_{10} also has an NMR spectrum showing only one peak. Identify.

Solution: Here, $n = [2(\#C) + 2 - (\#H)]/2 = 1$, so the molecule has a double bond or ring. All C_5H_{10} variations with a double bond have more than one type of proton. But in cyclopentane, all hydrogens are equivalent due to the presence of a five-fold axis of symmetry:

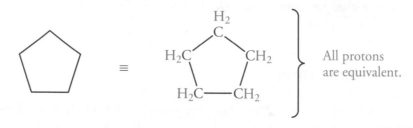

All protons are equivalent.

The Chemical Shift

The location of the resonance (set of peaks) in the ^1H NMR spectrum is referred to as its **chemical shift value**. Differences in the chemical shift values for different sets of protons in a molecule are the result of the differing electronic environments that different sets of protons experience. The magnetic field created by electrons near a proton will **shield** the nucleus from the applied magnetic field created by the instrument, shifting the resonance **upfield**. The more a proton is **deshielded** (i.e., the fewer electrons there are around it), the further **downfield** (to the left) in an NMR spectrum it will appear. For example, a set of protons *near* an electronegative group is said to be deshielded and will appear downfield (to the left) in the ^1H NMR spectrum, relative to a set of protons that are farther away from the electronegative group, which is more shielded and appears more upfield (to the right) in the ^1H NMR spectrum.

downfield   upfield

more deshielded | less deshielded

When obtaining the ^1H NMR spectrum of an organic molecule, a scientist usually includes a standard reference with the sample. It is with respect to this standard that chemical shift values for sets of protons in a molecule are determined. This standard is normally *tetramethylsilane*, $(CH_3)_4Si$ (TMS). TMS has 12 chemically equivalent protons that are arbitrarily assigned a chemical shift value of $\delta = 0$ ppm (parts per million). It turns out that the protons of TMS are very shielded compared to most other protons in common organic molecules, so the resonances of almost all protons will appear to the left (downfield, or more deshielded) of the TMS peak. The inclusion of TMS as a standard allows chemists to reliably compare their results with one another.

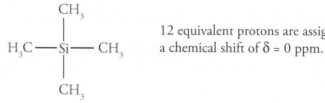

12 equivalent protons are assigned a chemical shift of $\delta = 0$ ppm.

Tetramethylsilane (TMS)

We now briefly examine the factors involved in proton deshielding. These include:

1. the electronegativity of the neighboring atoms,
2. hybridization, and
3. acidity and hydrogen bonding.

Electronegativity Effects on Chemical Shift Values

If an electronegative atom is in close proximity to a proton, it will decrease the electron density near the proton and thereby deshield it. This will result in a *down*field shift in the chemical shift value. Examples:

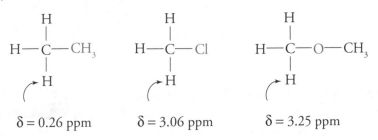

The spectrum of methyl acetate below shows how the two electronegative groups in the molecule (the O of the ester and the carbonyl) contribute to shifting both methyl signals downfield.

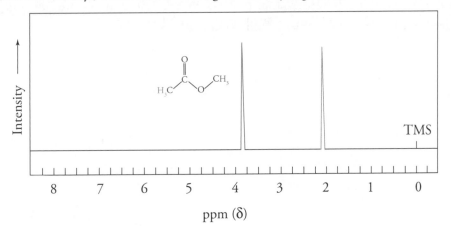

Hybridization Effects on Chemical Shift Values

The **hybridization effect** occurs as a result of the varying bond characteristics of carbon atoms *connected* to the hydrogens. The greater the *s*-orbital character of a C—H bond, the less electron density on the hydrogen. Thus, when considering the hybridization effect alone, the greater the *s*-orbital character, the more deshielded the set of protons is, which will result in a downfield shift for the peak corresponding to that set of protons. Here are two examples:

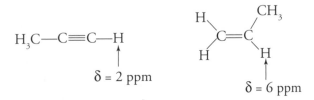

Hybridization effects alone would indicate the alkyne proton to be more deshielded than the alkene proton. However, due to a more complicated physical phenomenon (anisotropy), this turns out not to be the case. Another very characteristic chemical shift you should remember is that of the aromatic protons (δ = 6–8 ppm). A peak in an NMR spectrum in this region is highly indicative of an aromatic compound (usually a substituted benzene).

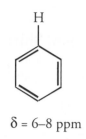

δ = 6–8 ppm

Acidity and Hydrogen Bonding Effects on Chemical Shift Values

Protons that are attached to **heteroatoms** (oxygen and nitrogen, for example) are quite deshielded. Acidic protons on a carboxylic acid are an extreme example of a very large downfield shift. In addition, hydrogen bonding can cause a wide variation of chemical shift. For example, the resonance of the alcohol proton in methanol varies with both solvent and temperature (different degrees of H bonding).

You should also be aware that the chemical shifts of alcohol and amine protons are quite variable depending upon the particular compound, but are in the range of δ = 1–5 ppm.

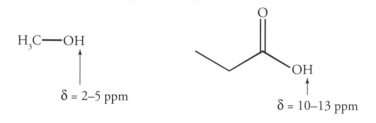

δ = 2–5 ppm

δ = 10–13 ppm

As with IR stretching frequencies, memorizing some commonly encountered ^1H NMR chemical shift values will be helpful. Below is a correlation chart for some common chemical shifts, the most important of which are in red:

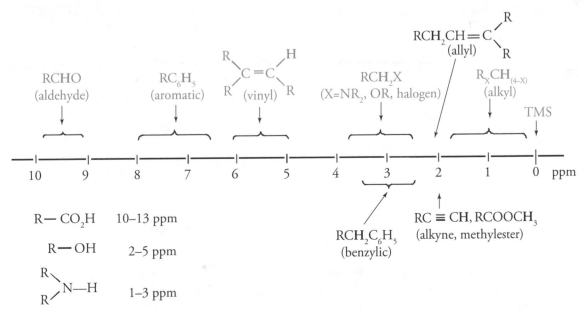

$R-CO_2H$ 10–13 ppm

$R-OH$ 2–5 ppm

R_2N-H 1–3 ppm

Integration

The third important piece of information obtained from the ^1H NMR spectrum of a molecule is the mathematical integration. As the NMR instrument obtains a spectrum of the sample, it performs a mathematical calculation, called an **integration**, thereby measuring the area under each absorption peak (resonance). The calculated area under each peak is proportional to the relative number of protons giving rise to each peak. Thus, the integration indicates the relative number of protons in each set in the molecule.

Splitting

The fourth and final aspect of NMR spectroscopy that you should be familiar with is the spin-spin splitting phenomenon. This occurs when protons interact with other protons that are not equivalent to it. Protons that are not equivalent can interact because the magnetic field felt by a proton is influenced by surrounding protons. This effect tends to fall off with distance, but it can often extend over two adjacent carbons. Nearby protons that are nonequivalent to the proton in question will cause a splitting in the observed ^1H NMR signal. The degree of splitting depends on the number of adjacent hydrogens, and a signal will be split $n + 1$ times, where n is the number of neighboring (interacting) protons. The important information one must determine is how a proton or a group of chemically equivalent protons will be split by their hydrogen neighbors.

This is best demonstrated by an example:

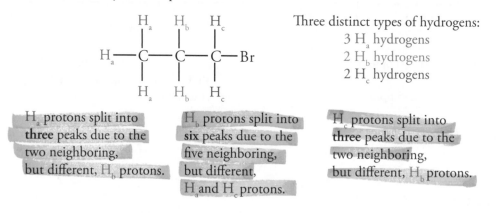

Three distinct types of hydrogens:

3 H_a hydrogens
2 H_b hydrogens
2 H_c hydrogens

H_a protons split into **three** peaks due to the two neighboring, but different, H_b protons.

H_b protons split into **six** peaks due to the five neighboring, but different, H_a and H_c protons.

H_c protons split into **three** peaks due to the two neighboring, but different, H_b protons.

Note that, for MCAT purposes, the H_a and H_c protons neighboring H_b do not have to be equivalent in order to add them together to get $n = 5$.

$n + 1$ RULE

n = Number of neighboring nonequivalent hydrogens	Splitting ($n + 1$)
0	1—Singlet
1	2—Doublet
2	3—Triplet
3	4—Quartet
4	5—Quintet (or multiplet)
5	6—Sextet (or multiplet)

Consider the NMR spectrum of CH_3CH_2I:

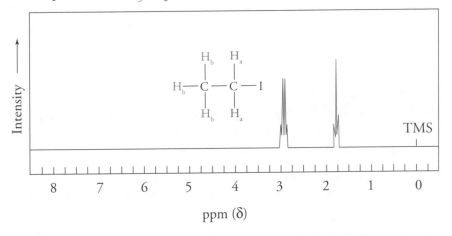

The α-hydrogens are farther downfield because they are closer to the electron-withdrawing iodine atom. They have three neighboring hydrogens and are therefore split into a quartet, according to the $n + 1$ rule. The β-hydrogens are split into a triplet because they have two neighboring hydrogens.

Example 7-4: How many ^1H NMR signals would you expect to find for the following molecules? What is the splitting pattern of each signal? Also indicate which protons would be shifted the farthest downfield.

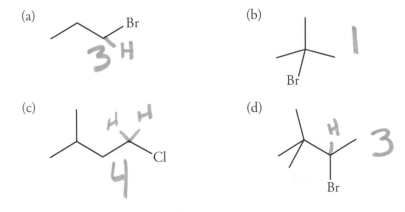

Solution:

(a) Three signals. C1's equivalent protons (which will be the farthest downfield) are split by two Hs on C2 to make a triplet. C2's protons (which are a bit more shielded than C1's) are split by a total of five Hs on C1 and C3 to make a sextet, or multiplet. C3's protons are split by two Hs on C2 to make a triplet.

(b) One signal; all are equivalent, therefore no splitting.

(c) Four signals. C1's equivalent protons are split by two Hs on C2 to make a triplet and appear the farthest downfield. C2's protons are split by a total of three Hs on C1 and C3 to make a quartet, which is more shielded. C3's proton is split by eight neighboring protons to make a multiplet. C4 and C5 have equivalent protons, split by C3's proton and forming the most shielded signal, a doublet.

(d) Three signals. The most downfield proton signal is from the one on C3 (the one bearing the Br). It is split by three Hs on C4 to make a quartet. Slightly more shielded are the Hs on C4, split by the one H on C3 to yield a doublet. The remaining Hs on the *tert*-butyl group are equivalent (nine total), are the most shielded and have no neighbors, making them appear as a singlet.

Carbon (^{13}C) Nuclear Magnetic Resonance (NMR) Spectroscopy

Carbon (^{13}C) spectroscopy is the third type of absorption spectroscopy that is important for the MCAT. Many of the same principles discussed for ^{1}H NMR also apply to ^{13}C NMR; there are, however, a few important differences.

Carbon (^{13}C) Chemical Shifts

The range of chemical shifts for ^{13}C nuclei is much larger than the range for ^{1}H nuclei. Typically, the ^{13}C can span a range of about 200 ppm. The same effects that shield and deshield ^{1}H nuclei affect ^{13}C nuclei as well. The following chart should give you a general idea of ^{13}C shifts:

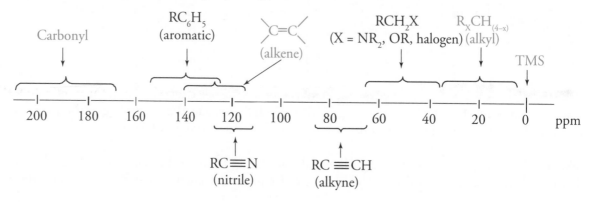

For example, the ^{13}C NMR spectrum of an ester is shown below.

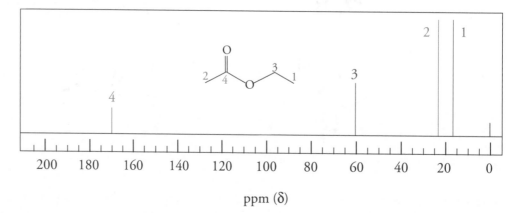

ppm (δ)

Integration

Unlike ^{1}H NMR, ^{13}C NMR spectra cannot be integrated meaningfully. The area under each peak is *not* exactly proportional to the number of carbons giving rise to that peak; however, the height of each peak does roughly correspond to the number of hydrogens that are attached to a particular carbon. The more hydrogens attached to a particular carbon, the taller the peak. So, a CH_3 peak would be taller than a CH_2 peak, which would be taller than a CH peak, and so on.

Splitting

Carbon NMR data are usually collected such that no splitting of the peaks occurs. As such each ^{13}C peak will appear as a singlet.

Example 7-5: How many ^{13}C signals would you expect to find for each of the following molecules?

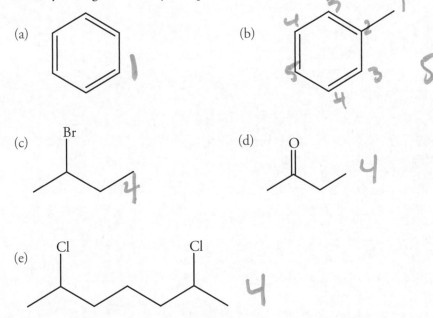

(a)

(b)

(c)

(d)

(e)

Solution:

(a)   One. All the carbon atoms in benzene are chemically equivalent.

(b)   Five. Toluene has a plane of symmetry, so there are two pairs of equivalent carbon atoms on either side of the ring.

(c)   Four. Each of the carbon atoms in 2-bromobutane are different.

(d)   Four. Each of the carbon atoms in 2-butanone are different.

(e)   Four. There's a plane of symmetry in 2,6-dichloroheptane, so the terminal methyl groups are equivalent, as are the carbon atoms bonded to chlorine and the outer methylene (CH_2) groups.

Chapter 7 Summary

- Organic compounds are separated via extraction based on their differing solubility in polar (aqueous) or nonpolar (organic) solvents.

- Organic acids (COOHs and PhOHs) and bases (amines) can undergo acid-base reactions to generate ions, which preferentially dissolve in the aqueous layer during an extraction.

- Thin layer chromatography (TLC) separates molecules based on polarity; the more polar compound travels the least distance up the plate and has the lowest R_f value.

- Distillation and gas chromatography separate compounds based on boiling point.

- IR spectroscopy identifies the functional groups present in molecules.

- The most common IR resonances tested on the MCAT are the C=O bond (~1700 cm^{-1}), the C=C bond (~1650 cm^{-1}) and the O—H bond (~3600 cm^{-1}).

- The number of resonances in a ^1H NMR spectrum indicates the number of non-equivalent hydrogens present in a molecule.

- The number of Hs each signal represents is determined by the integration of the peak.

- Protons that are more deshielded (near electronegative groups) will be further downfield (at higher ppm), and protons that are more shielded (near electron donating groups) will be more upfield (at lower ppm).

- Splitting in a ^1H NMR spectrum occurs when one H has non-equivalent protons located on an adjacent atom (signal will be split into $n + 1$ lines; n = # of nonequivalent adjacent hydrogens).

- The number of resonances in a ^{13}C NMR spectrum indicates the number of non-equivalent carbons present in a molecule.

CHAPTER 7 FREESTANDING PRACTICE QUESTIONS

1. The ^{13}C NMR spectrum for Compound X shows one peak at 128 ppm. If elemental analysis shows that the compound has an empirical formula of CH, how many possible stereoisomers could Compound X have?

A) 0
B) 1
C) 2
D) 4

2. How many resonances would appear in a ^1H NMR spectrum of the following compound?

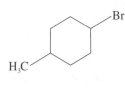

A) 3
B) 5
C) 7
D) 13

3. Consider the following reaction:

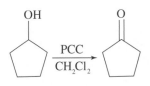

Which of the following observations about the infrared spectrum of the reaction mixture would indicate that the reaction above went to completion yielding the expected product?

A) The appearance of a stretch at 1700 cm^{-1}.
B) The disappearance of a stretch at 3300 cm^{-1}.
C) The disappearance of a stretch at 3300 cm^{-1} and the appearance of a stretch at 1700 cm^{-1}.
D) The disappearance of a stretch at 1700 cm^{-1} and the appearance of a stretch at 3300 cm^{-1}.

4. For the following reaction, how would the R_f value of the product compare to that of the starting material if monitored by TLC on a normal silica gel plate?

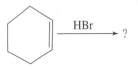

A) The R_f value of the product would be greater than that of the reactant because the product is more polar.
B) The R_f value of the product would be greater than that of the reactant because the product is less polar.
C) The R_f value of the product would be smaller than that of the reactant because the product is more polar.
D) The R_f value of the product would be smaller than that of the reactant because the product is less polar.

5. What will the ^1H NMR spectrum of isobutane show?

A) One 6 H triplet and one 4 H quartet
B) Two 3 H triplets and two 2 H quartets
C) One 9 H doublet and one 1 H multiplet
D) One 6 H triplet, one 2 H multiplet, and one 2 H triplet

CHAPTER 7 PRACTICE PASSAGE

The insecticide dichlorodiphenyltrichloroethane, more commonly known as DDT, was a great aid in slowing the spread of malaria during the 1940s and 1950s. However, it proved to be an environmental threat because it contaminated soils and had toxic effects on wildlife that fed on the crops and insects treated with the pesticide.

The toxin has been shown to be lethal to many animals and has been linked to diabetes and asthma in humans. To assess contamination in wildlife, levels of DDT are determined by taking samples of blood from the animals, treating them with 60% sulfuric acid, then extracting them with hexane, a non polar solvent with a boiling point of 69°C.

Dicofol is a synthetic analog of DDT and is commonly used as an insecticide targeting red spider mites. Like DDT, it has been shown to be mildly toxic to humans and other animals. However, dicofol is still a widely used pesticide in California and Florida.

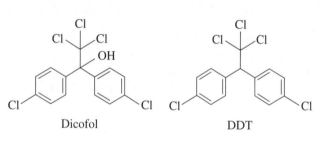

Figure 1   Dicofol and DDT

1. A scientist took a sample of blood from a bird to determine the level of toxins in the ecosystem. In which layers did she find DDT and dicofol after extraction of the blood with hexane?

A) The aqueous layer would contain dicofol, and the organic layer would contain DDT.
B) The aqueous layer would contain DDT, and the organic layer would contain dicofol.
C) Both compounds would be found in the aqueous layer.
D) Both compounds would be found in the organic layer.

2. How would the R_f values of DDT and dicofol differ when tested via TLC?

A) The R_f value of DDT would be larger than that of dicofol.
B) The R_f value of dicofol would be larger than that of DDT.
C) The R_f value would be negative for DDT and positive for dicofol.
D) The R_f values would be equal.

3. How many signals would you expect to see in the ^{13}C NMR spectra of DDT and dicofol?

A) 6 and 8 signals, respectively
B) 3 signals in each spectrum
C) 6 signals in each spectrum
D) 14 signals in each spectrum

4. Which of the following methods of identification would most conclusively determine the presence of DDT in a blood sample after extraction with hexane?

A) Mass spectroscopy
B) IR spectroscopy
C) Flash chromatography
D) Simple distillation

5. DDT and dicofol have melting points of 109°C and 79°C, respectively, and both compounds decompose before reaching their boiling points. Which of the following methods should be avoided when purifying the compounds?

    I.   Recrystallization
   II.   Gas chromatography
  III.   Fractional distillation

A) I only
B) I and II only
C) II and III only
D) I, II, and III

SOLUTIONS TO CHAPTER 7 FREESTANDING QUESTIONS

1. **A** One signal on the ^{13}C NMR spectrum implies that either the molecule has only one carbon, or that all carbons in the molecule are equivalent. Since the empirical formula of Compound X is CH and the molecule contains no electronegative elements to shift the signal downfield, the single peak, located in the region common for alkenes and aromatic carbons (128 ppm), must represent some sort of sp^2 hybridized carbon(s). Any compound with only sp^2 hybridized carbons will have no stereoisomers, and in this case, the compound is benzene (C_6H_6).

2. **B** By showing the hydrogens, one would expect the molecule to have five resonances in a ^1H NMR spectrum. Note the plane of symmetry through the molecule (as shown with the dotted line). Both sets of CH_2 hydrogens on the carbons adjacent to the bromo and methyl substituents are chemically equivalent to each other.

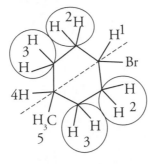

3. **C** The reaction is a transformation from an alcohol to a ketone. In an infrared spectrum, this can be noticed by the disappearance of the broad O—H stretch around 3300 cm^{-1}, and the appearance of the C=O stretch at 1700 cm^{-1}. Choices A and B are incorrect because the appearance of the C=O stretch does not automatically translate that the oxidation reaction went to completion and the disappearance of the O—H stretch doesn't mean that the desired product is formed. In order for the reaction to be complete, one must disappear as the other appears. Choice D is incorrect as the stretches that would appear and disappear are incorrect for the corresponding functional group transformation.

4. **C** TLC separates compounds based on their polarities. The more polar a compound is, the more it adheres to the silica gel plate, giving it a smaller R_f value. Choices A and D are inconsistent with this type of interaction. The product for this reaction is bromocyclohexane, which is more polar than the reactant due to the presence of the halogen.

5. **C** The structure of isobutane is shown below. All three terminal CH_3 groups are chemically identical, and will show up as one resonance. More specifically, they will correspond to a doublet as they are split by the sole proton on the central carbon. The proton on the central carbon will show up as a multiplet, as it is split by 9 equivalent H atoms. Thus, one 9H doublet and one 1H multiplet is the correct answer. Choice A, corresponds to *n*-butane.

SOLUTIONS TO CHAPTER 7 PRACTICE PASSAGE

1. **D** While the carbon-chlorine bonds do have dipole moments, they are not sufficiently large enough to overcome the effects of the nonpolar phenyl rings in DDT, so this compound is highly insoluble in water, eliminating choices B and C. Although the alcohol group present in dicofol makes it more polar than DDT, the effect does not override the nonpolar characteristics of the aromatic rings, so choice A can be eliminated.

2. **A** R_f values are never negative as they are a ratio of the distance the compound travels compared to the distance the solvent travels, so choice C can be eliminated. The R_f values of polar molecules are lower than the R_f values of nonpolar molecules because they travel a shorter distance up the plate. Dicofol has a hydroxyl group that allows it to interact more strongly with the stationary phase and results in a lower R_f value compared to DDT. Therefore, choices B and D can be eliminated.

3. **C** Both DDT and dicofol have a mirror plane that runs along C1 and C2 (see below).

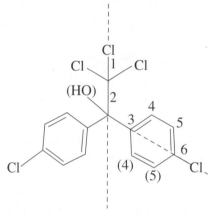

This makes the carbons on both phenyl rings equivalent to each other, so you can eliminate choice D. You might expect to see six signals in the aromatic region. However, because there is also symmetry within each aromatic ring, the two *ortho* carbons (C4, C(4)) and the two *meta* carbons (C5, C(5)) on each ring are equivalent to each other. Instead of seeing six unique signals in the aromatic region of the spectrum, you would only see four. This would give each compound six unique carbons, which eliminates choice A. Choice B is a trap answer that represents the number of ^{1}H NMR signals you would see in each molecule, so be sure to read the question carefully.

4. **A** Choices C and D are techniques used only for separating molecules, so they can be eliminated. IR spectroscopy is not the best option to conclusively identify a compound since it simply indicates the presence of functional groups. However, mass spectroscopy would indicate the exact mass of DDT, and is therefore the best choice.

5.   C   Since the compounds will decompose before reaching their boiling points, purification methods that require converting these compounds into the gas phase should be avoided. Distillation is a common purification technique that separates compounds based on their boiling points, so if Item III is a correct answer, you can eliminate choices A and B. It should then be clear that gas chromatography, which also converts compounds into the gas phase before separating them, must also be avoided as it appears in both remaining answers. The recrystallization of both DDT and dicofol is possible at temperatures below the melting points of the compounds, and there is no need to heat them close to their boiling points, so choice D can be eliminated.

Chapter 8
Biologically Important Organic Chemistry

INTRODUCTION

As you begin reading and working through this chapter of the text, you will notice that it is a little different than the other chapters. Up to now, this book has presented you with lots of information, then offered you practice questions and passages to help you test yourself. But this book's real purpose is not to just stuff you with detail—it is to make you think. Thus, this chapter is written in a style intended to do just that.

This chapter offers you *grillage*; that is, it puts you "on the grill" by asking you questions on the material you're reading and studying. In other words, the approach is Socratic. The grillage takes the form of questions between paragraphs, but also rears its head as queries that interrupt the flow of text. Some of the questions test factual knowledge that has already been presented. Others ask you to speculate, based on new information. Others force you to integrate factual knowledge and speculation. The idea is to wake you up and remind you that you're not supposed to be memorizing, but rather thinking about the information flowing past your eyes, speculating about it, integrating it with what you know, what you'd like to know, and what you'd like to do with all that knowledge (help sick people).

It is crucial that you take advantage of the grillage. How? When the book asks you a question, you'll usually find the answer in a footnote on the same page. DON'T READ THE FOOTNOTE UNTIL YOU'VE ANSWERED THE QUESTION! Some of the answers are as simple as "C" or "No," and others are complex conceptual explanations. In any case, take the time to formulate a thorough answer before you go to the footnote. If you think you're too rushed to "waste" time doing this, we've got news for you: You are studying the wrong way. The real waste of time is doing nothing but memorizing details. The profitable time is spent pondering concepts, as you'll do on the day of the MCAT. Though you shouldn't read the footnotes too soon, do be sure to read them, as sometimes they contain important information or vocabulary not given in the main body of the text.

8.1 AMINO ACIDS

Proteins are biological macromolecules that act as enzymes, hormones, receptors, antibodies, and support structures inside and outside cells. Proteins are composed of twenty different amino acids linked together in polymers. The composition and sequence of amino acids in the polypeptide chain is what makes each protein unique and enables it to fulfill its special role in the cell. In this section of Chapter 8, we will start with amino acids, the building blocks of proteins, and work our way up to three-dimensional protein structure and function.

Amino Acid Structure and Nomenclature

Understanding the structure of amino acids is key to understanding both their chemistry and the chemistry of proteins. The generic formula for all twenty amino acids is shown below.

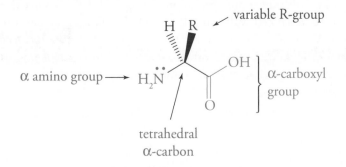

Generic Amino Acid Structure

All twenty amino acids share the same nitrogen-carbon-carbon backbone. The unique feature of each amino acid is its **side chain** (variable R-group), which gives it the physical and chemical properties that distinguish it from the other nineteen. Note that the α-carbon of each of the twenty amino acids is a stereocenter (has four different groups), except in the case of glycine, whose α-carbon is bonded to two hydrogen atoms. This means that all of the amino acids are chiral except for glycine.

L- and D-Amino Acids

Chemists often draw chiral molecules in their **Fischer projection** to illustrate stereochemistry. Let's review how Fischer projections denote the absolute stereochemistry of molecules. The conformation of a molecule that is shown in a Fischer projection happens to be the least stable, fully eclipsed form of the molecule. In Fischer projections the most oxidized carbon is at the top, and the structure is extended vertically until the final carbon atom is reached. This leaves the substituents on each carbon atom to occupy the horizontal positions of each carbon atom in the chain. This is illustrated below.

L-amino acid

D-amino acid

In the Fischer projection, it's understood that all horizontal lines are projecting from the plane of the page toward the viewer, and all vertical lines are projecting into the plane of the page, away from the viewer.

All animal amino acids are of the L-configuration, with the amino group drawn on the Left in Fischer nota-tion. Some **D**-amino acids, with the amino group on the right (*Dextro* in Greek), occur in a few special-ized structures, such as bacterial cell walls. The L and D classification system can be a source of great confusion. For the MCAT, it is most important to remember that *all animal amino acids have the L configuration and that all naturally occurring carbohydrates have the D configuration*. (Carbohydrates are discussed in a later section of this chapter.) For completeness, though, we'll take the time to discuss the meaning of D and L now.

Assigning the Configuration to a Chiral Center

L- and D-amino acids and L- and D-carbohydrates are **enantiomeric stereoisomers**. The simplest (small-est) carbohydrate has only three carbons and only one chiral center. It is called **glyceraldehyde**. Since it has one chiral center, this molecule can exist in one of two enantiomeric forms, (+)-glyceraldehyde and (–)-glyceraldehyde. In reactions occurring in living organisms, CHOH groups are added to carbon #1 of glyceraldehyde to form larger carbohydrate molecules with more than one chiral center. In this synthetic process the configuration at the original glyceraldehyde chiral carbon (#2) is not changed. So, if you start with (–)-glyceraldehyde and build a longer carbohydrate chain, that carbohydrate chain will have a pen-ultimate (second-to-last) carbon atom with the same configuration as (–)-glyceraldehyde. So why not just call the new, larger carbohydrate "(–)"? You cannot refer to the new carbohydrate as (–) because you have added several new chiral centers, and now if you put the new molecule in solution and measure its optical rotation with a polarimeter, the optical activity may in fact be (+). What is needed is a way to name a car-bohydrate that would specify that it had been built up from (–)- or (+)-glyceraldehyde without worrying about its actual optical activity.

L-(–)-Glyceraldehyde   D-(+)-Glyceraldehyde

The solution is to nickname (–)-glyceraldehyde as "L-glyceraldehyde," and to likewise refer to (+)-glyceraldehyde as "D-glyceraldehyde." Recall from the section on optical rotation that the letter L stands for "levorotatory," which means "left-rotating" (counter-clockwise-rotating), and the letter D stands for "dextrorotatory," which means "right-rotating." Now we can refer to all carbohydrates built up from (–)-glyceraldehyde as "L" carbohydrates, without specifying whether they rotate plane-polarized light to the left (–) or to the right (+). All we have to do is look at the last chiral carbon in the chain and decide whether it looks like C2 from L- or D-glyceraldehyde.

Once again, the important thing to remember is that *all animal amino acids are derived from L-glyceraldehyde* (because they share the same basic structure at the penultimate carbon). Hence, they all have the L configuration. *Animal carbohydrates are chemically derived from D-glyceraldehyde*, and are thus all D.

As we discussed in Chapter 3, there is another classification system, in which chiral centers are denoted either *R* or *S*. This system describes the *absolute configuration* of the chiral center; it refers to the actual three-dimensional arrangement of groups, as in a model or drawing; it says nothing about what the molecule will do to plane-polarized light.

In summary, you can see that three classification systems are used to organize amino acids and carbohydrates:

1. (+) and (–) describe optical activity;
2. *R* and *S* describe actual structure or absolute configuration; and
3. D and L tell us the basic precursor of a molecule (D- or L-glyceraldehyde).

You can also see that the three different classification systems don't describe each other in any way. A molecule that has the *R* configuration of its only stereocenter might rotate plane-polarized light *either* clockwise *or* counterclockwise, and hence be *either* (+) *or* (–). And a molecule that is experimentally determined to be (+) might be either D or L. However, two of the three classification systems go together for certain molecules. All D-sugars have the *R* configuration at the penultimate carbon atom because they are all derived from D-glyceraldehyde. Similarly, all L-sugars have the *S* configuration at the penultimate carbon atom. This is true only because carbohydrates are named according to the configuration of the last chiral center in the chain (which, remember, is synthetically derived from glyceraldehyde). By the same rationale, all L-amino acids are *S*, and all D-amino acids are *R*.

1) You crash-land on Mars without any food but notice that Mars is loaded with edible-looking plants. Martian life has evolved with all L-carbohydrates. Can you metabolize carbohydrates from Mars?[1]

Amino Acid Reactivity

Since amino acids are composed of an acidic group (the carboxylic acid) and a basic group (the amine), we must be sure to understand the acid/base chemistry of amino acids. Later, we will review amide bond formation by examining formation of the peptide bond in protein synthesis.

---

[1] No. Enzyme activity depends on three-dimensional shape, and all animal digestive enzymes have active sites specific for substrate carbohydrates with the D configuration.

Reviewing the Fundamentals of Acid/Base Chemistry

Before we can discuss amino acids, we must be sure to understand the fundamentals of acid/base chemistry because each amino acid is **amphoteric**, which means it has both acidic and basic activity. This should make sense since an amino acid contains the acidic carboxylic acid group and the basic amino group.

Remember from general chemistry that acids can be defined as proton (H^+) donors, and bases can be defined as proton acceptors. Thus, in the case of the equation below, H_2A^+ is a proton donor (acid), and A^- is a proton acceptor (base); HA may act as either acid or base. The equations below also show how to calculate the equilibrium constant (K) for an acid dissociation reaction. The equilibrium constant for an acid dissociation reaction is given a special name: **acid dissociation constant**, abbreviated "K_a." The equilibrium reactions for the first and second proton dissociation reactions are described by the equations for the acid dissociation constants K_{a1} and K_{a2}.

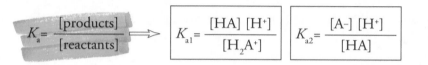

$$H_2A^+ \underset{(K_{a1})}{\rightleftharpoons} HA + H^+ \underset{(K_{a2})}{\rightleftharpoons} A^- + 2H^+$$

$$K_a = \frac{[\text{products}]}{[\text{reactants}]} \implies K_{a1} = \frac{[HA][H^+]}{[H_2A^+]} \quad K_{a2} = \frac{[A^-][H^+]}{[HA]}$$

The Acid Dissociation Reaction

2) In the equilibrium between H_2A^+, HA, and A^- above, which statement is true?[2]
   A. HA will act as a base by donating a proton.
   B. HA will act as an acid by accepting a proton.
   C. HA can act as either an acid or a base, depending on whether it accepts or donates a proton.
   D. HA is in chemical equilibrium with H_2A^+ and A^- and in that capacity cannot act as either an acid or a base.

Whether a molecule (or a functional group) is protonated depends on its affinity for protons, and the concentration of protons in solution that are available to it. Let's discuss both and do a few practice problems.

The concentration of available protons is simply $[H^+]$ (moles/liter), but it is usually expressed as **pH**, defined as $-log\ [H^+]$. If you're wondering why pH is used instead of $[H^+]$, it has to do with the fact that $[H^+]$ values tend to be clumsy numbers, so a logarithmic scale reduces the amount of writing we have to do; we use the *negative* logarithm simply to avoid writing an extra minus sign. For example, instead of writing "$[H^+] = 10^{-3.46}$," we can write "pH = 3.46." The pH inside cells is 7.4. This is often referred to as **physiological pH**, and is carefully regulated by buffers in the blood because extremes of pH disrupt protein structure.

---

[2] Choice C is correct: In the equilibrium shown, HA can either act as an acid by donating a proton (choice B is wrong) or as a base by accepting a proton (choice + is wrong). Remember also that equilibrium is not a fixed state; in other words, HA is not doomed to stay HA forever, it can move forward and back between the states shown (choice D is wrong).

The affinity of a functional group (such as an amino or carboxyl group) for protons is given by the acid dissociation constant K_a for that functional group, which is simply the equilibrium constant for the dissociation of the acid form (HA) into a proton (H⁺) plus the conjugate base (A⁻). The equilibrium constant describes a reaction's tendency to move right or left as it moves toward equilibrium from some starting point. This affinity can also be expressed as pK_a, defined as $-\log K_a$. Carboxyl groups of amino acids generally have a pK_a of about 2 (acidic), while the amino groups generally have a pK_a of 9 or 10 (basic).

The mathematical formula that describes the relationship between pH, pK_a, and the position of equilibrium in an acid-base reaction is known as the **Henderson–Hasselbalch** equation:

$$pH = pK_a + \log \frac{[A^-]}{[HA]} = pK_a + \log \frac{[\text{base form}]}{[\text{acid form}]}$$

Given the pH and the pK_a, we can calculate the ratio of the base and acid forms of a compound at equilibrium. Just remember these rules:

- Low pH means high [H⁺].
- Lower pK_a (same as higher K_a) describes a stronger acid that can donate a proton even when there are already excess protons (high [H⁺], low pH).

3) The text above states that physiological pH is 7.4. Is this more or less acidic—and are there more or fewer extra protons—than in pure water?[3]

4) Pure water at 25°C has a balance of 10^{-7} M H⁺ and 10^{-7} M OH⁻ resulting from the spontaneous breakdown of water itself. What pH does pure water have?[4]

5) What is the pH of a solution of 0.1 M HCl (assuming the HCl dissociates fully)?[5]

6) Acetic acid (CH_3COOH) has pK_a = 4.7. Calculate the equilibrium ratio of [CH_3COO^-] to [CH_3COOH] at pH 4.7.[6]

7) Which functional group on amino acids has a stronger tendency to accept protons: carboxyl groups (pK_a = 2.0) or amino groups (pK_a = 9)? Which group will donate protons at the lowest pH?[7]

---

[3] Remember that a larger pH implies *fewer* extra protons, since pH $= -\log[H^+]$. A pH of 7.4 describes a solution with slightly fewer extra free protons, i.e., a slightly less acidic (more basic) solution, relative to a pH 7.0 solution.

[4] Simply use the formula for pH. Pure water has a pH of $-\log (10^{-7}) = 7$.

[5] The solution will have a proton concentration equal to 0.1 or 10^{-1} M. The pH of a solution with [H⁺] $= 10^{-1}$ M is determined by the formula for pH: pH $= -\log(10^{-1}$ $M) = 1$.

[6] First, substitute into the equation: $4.7 = 4.7 + \log [CH_3COO^-]/[CH_3COOH]$. Then, solve:
$0 = \log [CH_3COO^-]/[CH_3COOH]$.
What has a log of 0? In other words, ten to the power of 0 is equal to what?
$10^0 = [CH_3COO^-]/[CH_3COOH] = 1.0$
So when the pH = pK_a, the ratio of base to acid is 1 to 1. That's a fact worth memorizing.

[7] A higher pK_a means that a higher proportion of the protonated form is present relative to the unprotonated form, according to the H-H equation. High pK_a indicates basicity. At normal pH ranges, bases do not donate protons, but rather accept them. Acids have low pK_as, and thus tend to deprotonate. Therefore, amino groups have a stronger tendency to accept protons and carboxyl groups will donate protons at the lowest pH (highest [H⁺]).

Application of Fundamental Acid/Base Chemistry to Amino Acids

With that review of acids and bases, we are now prepared to discuss amino acid reactivity. The review is important because all amino acids contain an amino group ($pK_a \approx 9$) that acts as a base and a carboxyl group ($pK_a \approx 2$) that acts as an acid. For example:

$$-NH_3^+ \rightleftharpoons -NH_2 + H^+ \qquad pK_a \approx 9$$

$$-COOH \rightleftharpoons -COO^- + H^+ \qquad pK_a \approx 2$$

8) Assuming a pK_a of 2, will a carboxylate group be protonated or deprotonated at pH 1.0?[8]
9) Will the amino group be protonated or deprotonated at pH 1.0?[9]
10) Glycine is the simplest amino acid, with only hydrogen as its R-group. Its only functional groups are the backbone groups discussed above (amino and carboxyl). What will be the net charge on a glycine molecule at pH 12?[10]
11) At pH 5.5, between the pK_as of the amino and carboxyl groups, what will be the net charge on a molecule of glycine?[11]

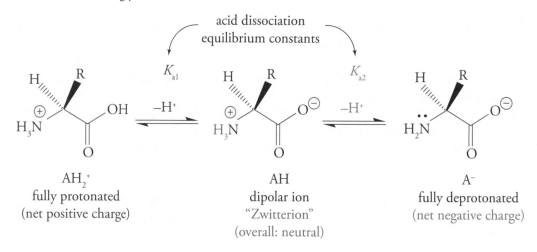

Important Amino Acid Conjugate Acid/Base Pairs

The Isoelectric Point of Amino Acids

There is a pH for every amino acid at which it has no overall net charge (the positive and negative charges cancel). A molecule with positive and negative charges that balance is referred to as a dipolar ion or zwitterion. The pH at which a molecule is uncharged (zwitterionic) is referred to as its isoelectric point (pI). "Zwitter" is German for "both," implying that an amino acid at its pI has both (+) and (–) charges.

---

[8] The pH is less than the pK_a here, so protonation wins over dissociation, and the group will be protonated. The correct answer is –COOH.

[9] The pH is much lower than the pK_a for the amino group, so the amino group is protonated: NH_3^+.

[10] Since pH 12 represents a very low [H^+], both groups will become deprotonated (COO^- and NH_2), creating a net charge of –1 per glycine molecule.

[11] The carboxyl group will be deprotonated (COO^-) with a charge of –1 and the amino group will be protonated (NH_3^+) with a charge of +1, creating a net charge of 0 per glycine molecule.

It is possible to calculate the pI of an amino acid—in other words, to figure out the pH value at which (+) and (–) charges balance (that's the definition of pI). For a molecule with two functional groups, such as glycine, the calculation is simple: just *average the pK$_a$s of the two functional groups*. The pI of more complex molecules can also be calculated, but the math is complex. For the MCAT, you should know how to calculate the pI of a molecule with two functional groups (with no acidic or basic functional groups in the side chain). Another important thing to know for the MCAT is how to compare the pH of a solution to the pK$_a$ of a functional group of an amino acid and determine if a site is mostly protonated or deprotonated. If the pH is higher than the pK$_a$, the site is mostly deprotonated; if the pH is lower than the pK$_a$, the site is mostly protonated. This can be illustrated in the titration curve for glycine:

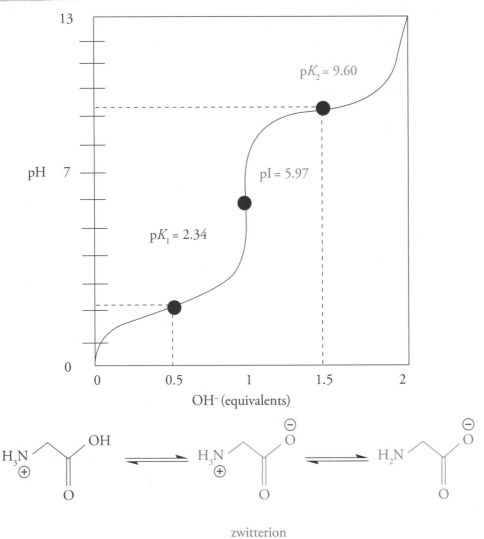

zwitterion

12) What is the pI of glycine?[12]

---

[12] To calculate the pI, just average the pK$_a$s of the two functional groups: $(9 + 2)/2 = 5.5$.

Classification of Amino Acids

Each of the twenty amino acids is unique because of its side chain. Each amino acid has a three-letter abbreviation and a one-letter abbreviation, which you do *not* need to memorize. Though they are all unique, many of them are similar in their chemical properties. It is *not* necessary to memorize all 20 side chains, but it is important to understand the chemical properties that characterize them. The important properties of the side chains include their varying *shape, charge, ability to hydrogen bond, and ability to act as acids or bases*. These side group properties are important in the structure of proteins.

We now consider the 20 amino acids, organizing them into broad categories.

Nonpolar, Hydrophobic | Polar, Neutral

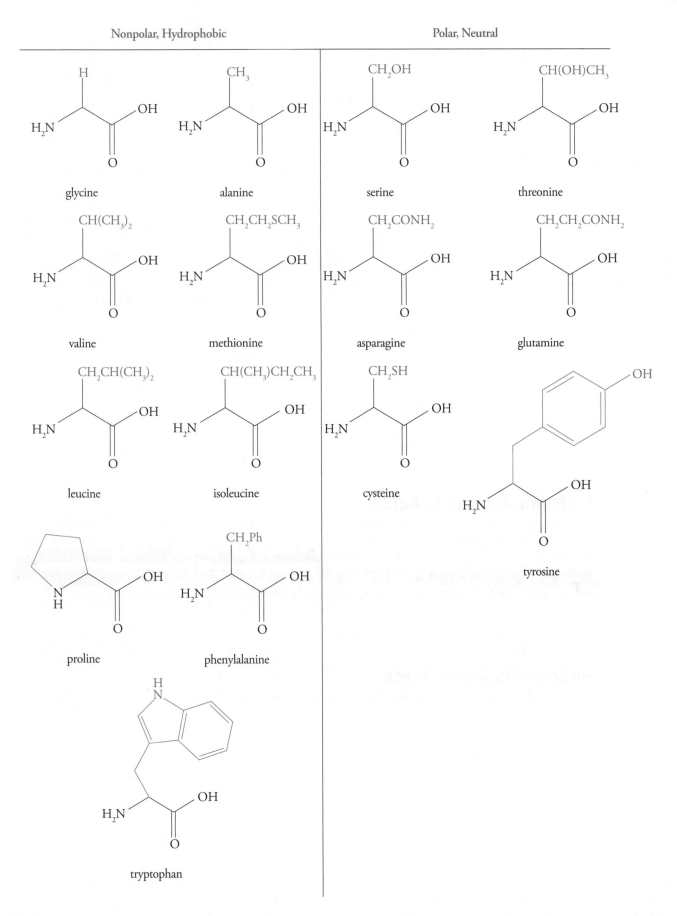

glycine

alanine

serine

threonine

valine

methionine

asparagine

glutamine

leucine

isoleucine

cysteine

tyrosine

proline

phenylalanine

tryptophan

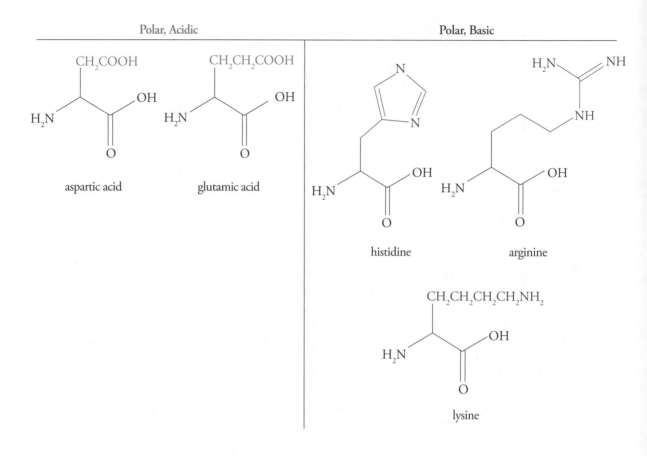

Polar, Acidic

aspartic acid

glutamic acid

Polar, Basic

histidine

arginine

lysine

Hydrophobic Amino Acids

Hydrophobic amino acids have either aliphatic (alkyl) or aromatic side chains. Amino acids with aliphatic side chains include glycine, alanine, valine, leucine, and isoleucine. Amino acids with aromatic side chains include phenylalanine, tyrosine, and tryptophan. Hydrophobic residues tend to associate with each other rather than with water, and therefore are found on the interior of folded globular proteins, away from water. The larger the hydrophobic group, the greater the hydrophobic force repelling it from water.

Hydrophilic Amino Acids

The hydrophilic, or water-loving side chains are categorized into three distinct categories: acidic, basic, and neutral polar residues.

Acidic Amino Acids

Glutamic acid and aspartic acid are the only amino acids with carboxylic acid functional groups ($pK_a \approx 4$) in their side chains, thereby making the side chains acidic. Thus, there are three functional groups in these amino acids that may act as acids or bases—the two backbone groups and the R-group. You may hear the terms glutam*ate* and aspart*ate*—these simply refer to the anionic (unprotonated) form of the molecule.

Basic Amino Acids

Lysine, arginine, and histidine have basic R-group side chains. The pK_as for the side chains in these amino acids are 10 for Lys, 12 for Arg, and 6.5 for His. Histidine is unique in having a side chain with a pK_a so close to physiological pH. At pH 7.4 histidine may be either protonated or deprotonated—we put it in the basic category, but it often acts as an acid, too. This makes it a readily available proton acceptor *or* donor, explaining its prevalence at **protein active sites** (discussed below). A mnemonic is "His goes both ways." This contrasts with amino acids containing –COOH or –NH$_2$ side chains, which are *always* anionic (RCOO$^-$) or cationic (RNH$_3^+$) at physiological pH. (By the way, *histamine* is a small molecule that has to do with allergic responses, itching, inflammation, and other processes. (You've heard of antihistamine drugs.) It is not an amino acid; don't confuse it with *histidine*.)

Polar Amino Acids

These amino acids are characterized by an R-group that is polar enough to form hydrogen bonds with water but not polar enough to act as an acid or base. This means they are hydrophilic and will interact with water whenever possible.

The hydroxyl groups of serine, threonine, and tyrosine residues are often modified by the attachment of a phosphate group by a regulatory enzyme called a **kinase**. The result is a change in structure due to the very hydrophilic phosphate group. This modification is an important means of regulating protein activity.

Sulfur-Containing Amino Acids

Amino acids with sulfur-containing side chains include cysteine and methionine. Cysteine, which contains a thiol (also called a sulfhydryl—like an alcohol that has an S atom instead of an O atom), is actually fairly polar, and methionine, which contains a thioether (like an ether that has an S atom instead of an O atom) is fairly nonpolar. This should make sense, based on the polarities of alcohols and ethers we discussed in Chapter 4.

Proline

Proline is unique among the amino acids in that its amino group is bound covalently to a part of the side chain, creating a secondary α-amino group and a distinctive ring structure. This unique feature of proline has important consequences for protein folding (see Section 8.2).

Hydrophobic	Hydrophilic		
Nonpolar	Polar	Acidic	Basic
Glycine	Serine	Aspartic acid	Lysine*
Alanine	Cysteine	Glutamic acid	Arginine
Valine*	Tyrosine		Histidine
Leucine*	Threonine*		
Isoleucine*	Asparagine		
Phenylalanine*	Glutamine		
Tryptophan*			
Methionine*			
Proline			

*Denotes one of the eight **essential** amino acids, those that cannot be synthesized by adult humans and must be obtained from the diet.

Summary Table of Amino Acids

Amino Acid Separation—Gel Electrophoresis

Gel electrophoresis is a technique that separates amino acids based on their charge. In general, when employing this technique, amino acids are loaded onto a gel that is held at a constant pH, then exposed to an electric field. When exposed to a pH different from their pI, each amino acid will bear an overall charge because pI is specific to the unique structure of the side chain of each amino acid. The amino acids will therefore migrate through the gel based on their charge and the external electric field. The MCAT tends to ask about how specific amino acids will migrate relative to each other in these separation conditions. In order to answer these questions, an understanding of the relationship between pH, pK_a, and pI (as discussed previously) is required. See the table below, which summarizes how pH will determine the direction of amino acid migration during an electrophoresis separation:

pH	Charge on Amino Acid	Direction of Migration
greater than pI	negative	toward positive electrode
lower than pI	positive	toward negative electrode
equal to pI	neutral (zwitterion)	no migration

13) A sample of glycine is loaded on a gel in a pH = 5.5 solution with a (+) electrode at one end and a (−) electrode at the other end. Will the majority of the glycine migrate toward the negative terminal, migrate toward the positive terminal, or not migrate in either direction?[13]

---

[13] At this pH level, glycine has a net charge of zero. Hence, it will not move in an electric field.

14) The pK_as for the three functional groups in aspartic acid are 9.8 for the amino group, 2.1 for the α–carboxyl, and 3.9 for the side chain carboxyl. What pole (– or +) will aspartic acid migrate toward in an electric field at physiological pH (7.4)?[14]

15) What pole (– or +) would aspartic acid migrate toward in an electric field in a pH 1.0 solution?[15]

16) Which of these amino acids is most likely to be found on the interior of a protein at pH 7.0?[16]
   A. Alanine
   B. Glutamic acid
   C. Phenylalanine
   D. Glycine

17) Which of the following amino acids is most likely to be found on the exterior of a protein at pH 7.0?[17]
   A. Leucine
   B. Alanine
   C. Serine
   D. Isoleucine

8.2 PROTEINS

There are two common types of covalent bonds between amino acids in proteins: the **peptide bonds** that link amino acids together into polypeptide chains and **disulfide bridges** between cysteine R-groups.

The Peptide Bond

Polypeptides are formed by linking amino acids together in peptide bonds. A peptide bond is formed between the carboxyl group of one amino acid and the α-amino group of another amino acid with the loss of water. This occurs by the same nucleophilic addition-elimination mechanism shown in Section 4.3 for formation of any one of the carboxylic acid derivatives from any other carboxylic acid derivative. Remember that a peptide bond is just an amide bond between two amino acids. The figure below shows the formation of a dipeptide from the amino acids glycine and alanine.

---

[14] The amino group will be protonated ($-NH_3^+$), and both carboxyl groups deprotonated ($-COO^-$), producing an average charge per aspartic acid molecule of –1. Thus, aspartic acid will migrate toward the oppositely charged (+) pole at pH 7.0.

[15] Both carboxyl groups would be protonated and uncharged (–COOH), and the amino group would be protonated and charged ($-NH_3^+$). The net charge is +1, so aspartic acid would migrate toward the (–) pole.

[16] Glu is incorrect, since this amino acid is charged at a pH of 7. Of the three remaining, phenylalanine has the largest hydrophobic group, and is therefore the most likely to be found on the interior of a protein. The answer is C.

[17] Leucine, alanine, and isoleucine are all hydrophobic residues more likely to be found on the interior than the exterior of proteins. Serine (choice C), which has a hydroxyl group that can hydrogen bond with water, is the correct answer.

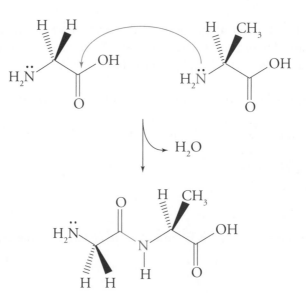

Peptide Bond (Amide Bond) Formation

Note: The above diagram showing formation of a peptide bond via a simple condensation reaction is not entirely accurate. As seen in the following graph, the formation of a peptide bond with two amino acids is not thermodynamically favorable and requires energy. This naturally oc-curring reaction, which takes place during translation in cells, involves enzyme catalysis, is RNA directed, and co-factor mediated.

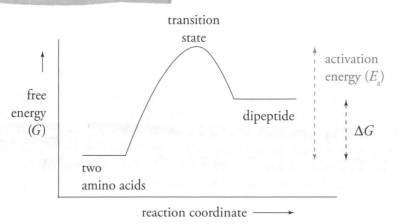

DCC Coupling

In order to synthesize peptides artificially in the laboratory, **DCC coupling** is used. In the first step of the coupling process, DCC, or dicyclohexyl carbodiimide, converts the OH of the caboxylate group in an amino acid into a good leaving group. In the next step, the amino group of a second amino acid attacks the carbonyl carbon of the "activated" amino acid. Finally, the DCC leaves with the oxygen to which it is bonded. To assure that amino acids are added in a unidirectional manner and in the proper order for the desired peptide, the reaction is run using protecting groups so that only one of the carboxyl groups and one of the amino groups are available to react. See the example reaction that follows.

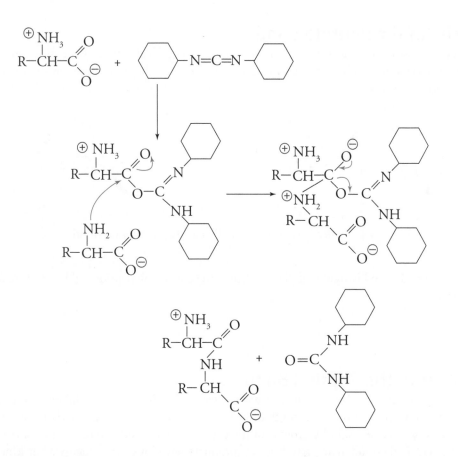

In a polypeptide chain, the N–C–C–N–C–C pattern formed from the amino acids is known as the **backbone** of the polypeptide. An individual amino acid is termed a **residue** when it is part of a polypeptide chain. The amino terminus is the first end made during polypeptide synthesis, and the carboxy terminus is made last. Hence, by convention, the amino-terminal residue is also always written first.

18) In the oligopeptide Phe-Glu-Gly-Ser-Ala, state the number of acid and base functional groups, which residue has a free α-amino group, and which residue has a free α-carboxyl group. (Refer to the beginning of the chapter for structures.)[18]

19) Thermodynamics states that free energy must decrease for a reaction to proceed spontaneously and that such a reaction will spontaneously move toward equilibrium. The diagram on page 266 shows the free energy changes during peptide bond formation. At equilibrium, which is thermodynamically favored: the dipeptide or the individual amino acids?[19]

20) In that case, how are peptide bonds formed and maintained inside cells?[20]

---

[18] As stated above, the amino end is always written first. Hence, the oligopeptide begins with an exposed Phe amino group and ends with an exposed Ala carboxyl; all the other backbone groups are hitched together in peptide bonds. Out of all the R-groups, there is only one acidic or basic functional group, the acidic glutamate R-group. This R-group plus the two terminal backbone groups gives a total of three acid/base functional groups.

[19] The dipeptide has a higher free energy, so its existence is less favorable. In other words, existence of the chain is less favorable than existence of the isolated amino acids.

[20] During protein synthesis, stored energy is used to force peptide bonds to form. Once the bond is formed, even though its destruction is thermodynamically favorable, it remains stable because the activation energy for the hydrolysis reaction is so high. In other words, hydrolysis is thermodynamically favorable but kinetically slow.

Planarity of the Peptide Bond

The peptide bond is planar and rigid because the resonance delocalization of the nitrogen's electrons to the carbonyl oxygen gives substantial double bond character to the bond between the carbonyl carbon and the nitrogen, as shown below. Hence there can be no rotation around the peptide bond.

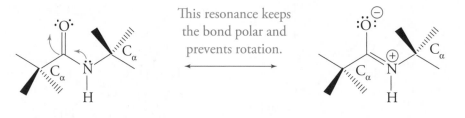

This resonance keeps the bond polar and prevents rotation.

Resonance Structure of the Planar, Rigid Peptide Bond

21) If the peptide bond is rigid and planar, then is the entire polypeptide rigid and incapable of rotation?[21]

Hydrolysis of the Peptide Bond

Hydrolysis refers to any reaction in which water is cleaved. We have already discussed the details of hydrolysis reactions in Chapter 6, which covered the hydrolysis of an ester under both acidic and basic reaction conditions (see Section 6.3). Hydrolysis of the peptide bond (amide bond) to form a free amine and a carboxylic acid is thermodynamically favored (products have lower free energy), but kinetically slow. There are two common means of accelerating the rate of peptide bond hydrolysis (i.e., two common ways to destroy proteins): strong acids and proteolytic enzymes.

Acid hydrolysis is the cleaving of a protein into its constituent amino acids with strong acid and heat. This is a non-specific means of cleaving peptide bonds. The amount of each amino acid present after hydrolysis can then be quantified to determine the overall amino acid content of the protein.

22) If a tripeptide of Gly-Phe-Ala is subjected to acid hydrolysis, can the order of the residues in the tripeptide be determined afterward?[22]

---

[21] No, only the peptide bond (between amino acids) is rigid due to resonance. The bonds to the α-carbon (within each amino acid) are free to rotate.

[22] No. After hydrolysis all amino acids are separate and have free amino and carboxyl groups.

Hydrolysis of a protein by another protein is called **proteolysis** or **proteolytic cleavage**, and the protein that does the cutting is known as a **proteolytic enzyme** or **protease**. Proteolytic cleavage is a specific means of cleaving peptide bonds. Many enzymes only cleave the peptide bond adjacent to a specific amino acid. For example, the protease trypsin cleaves on the carboxyl side of the positively charged (basic) residues arginine and lysine, while chymotrypsin cleaves adjacent to hydrophobic residues such as phenyl-alanine. (Do *not* memorize these examples.)

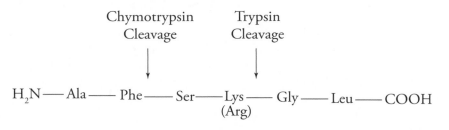

Specificity of Protease Cleavage

23) Based on the above, if the following peptide is cleaved by trypsin, what amino acid will be on the new N-terminus and how many fragments will result: Ala-Gly-Glu-Lys-Phe-Phe-Lys?[23]

The Disulfide Bond

Cysteine is an amino acid with a reactive thiol (sulfhydryl, SH) in its side chain. The thiol of one cysteine can react with the thiol of another cysteine to produce a covalent sulfur-sulfur bond known as a disulfide bond, as illustrated. The cysteines forming a disulfide bond may be located in the same or different poly-peptide chain(s). The disulfide bridge plays an important role in stabilizing tertiary protein structure; this will be discussed in the section on protein folding. Once a cysteine residue becomes disulfide-bonded to another cysteine residue, it is called *cystine* instead of cysteine.

---

[23] Trypsin will cleave on the carboxyl side of the Lys residue, with Phe on the N-terminus of the new Phe-Phe-Lys fragment. There will be two fragments after trypsin cleavage: Phe-Phe-Lys and Ala-Gly-Glu-Lys.

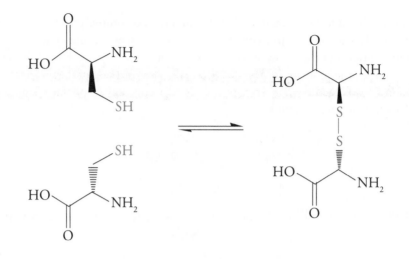

Formation of the Disulfide Bond

24) Which is more oxidized, the sulfur in *cysteine* or the sulfur in *cystine*?[24]
25) The inside of cells is known as a reducing environment because cells possess antioxidants (chemicals that prevent oxidation reactions). Where would disulfide bridges be more likely to be found, in extracellular proteins, under oxidizing conditions, or in the interior of cells, in a reducing environment?[25]

Protein Structure in Three Dimensions

Each protein folds into a unique three-dimensional structure that is required for that protein to function properly. Improperly folded, or **denatured**, proteins are non-functional. There are four levels of protein folding that contribute to their final three-dimensional structure. Each level of structure is dependent upon a particular type of bond, as discussed in the following sections.

Denaturation is an important concept. It refers to the **disruption of a protein's shape without breaking peptide bonds.** Proteins are denatured by *urea* (which disrupts hydrogen bonding interactions), by *extremes of pH*, by extremes of *temperature*, and by *changes in salt concentration (tonicity)*.

Primary (1°) Structure: The Amino Acid Sequence

The simplest level of protein structure is the order of amino acids bonded to each other in the polypeptide chain. This linear ordering of amino acid residues is known as primary structure. Primary structure is the same as sequence. The bond which determines 1° structure is the peptide bond, simply because this is the bond that links one amino acid to the next in a polypeptide.

---

[24] The sulfur in cysteine is bonded to a hydrogen and a carbon; the sulfur in cystine is bonded to a sulfur and a carbon. Hence, the sulfur in cystine is more oxidized. As a mnemonic, note that cysteine has an extra "e" because it's bonded to two hydrogens instead of an H and a sulfur.

[25] In a reducing environment, the S-S group is reduced to two SH groups. Disulfide bridges are found only in extracellular polypeptides, where they will not be reduced. Examples of protein complexes held together by disulfide bridges include antibodies and the hormone insulin.

Secondary (2°) Structure: Hydrogen Bonds Between Backbone Groups

Secondary structure refers to the initial folding of a polypeptide chain into shapes stabilized by hydrogen bonds between backbone NH and CO groups. Certain motifs of secondary structure are found in most proteins. The two most common are the α-helix and the β-pleated sheet.

All α-helices have the same well-defined dimensions that are depicted below with the R-groups omitted for clarity. The α-helices of proteins are always right handed, 5 angstroms in width, with each subsequent amino acid rising 1.5 angstroms. There are 3.6 amino acid residues per turn with the α-carboxyl oxygen of one amino acid residue hydrogen-bonded to the α-amino proton of an amino acid three residues away. (*Don't* memorize these numbers, but *do* try to visualize what they mean.)

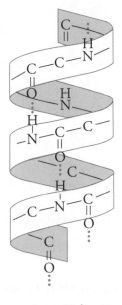

An α Helix

The unique structure of **proline** forces it to kink the polypeptide chain; hence proline residues never appear within the α-helix.

Proteins such as hormone receptors and ion channels are often found with α-helical transmembrane regions integrated into the hydrophobic membranes of cells. The α-helix is a favorable structure for a hydrophobic transmembrane region because all polar NH and CO groups in the backbone are hydrogen bonded to each other on the inside of the helix, and thus don't interact with the hydrophobic membrane interior. α-Helical regions that span membranes also have hydrophobic R-groups, which radiate out from the helix, interacting with the hydrophobic interior of the membrane.

β-Pleated sheets are also stabilized by hydrogen bonding between NH and CO groups in the polypeptide backbone. In β-sheets, however, hydrogen bonding occurs between residues distant from each other in the chain or even on separate polypeptide chains. Also, the backbone of a β-sheet is extended, rather than coiled, with side groups directed above and below the plane of the β-sheet. There are two types of β-sheets, one with adjacent polypeptide strands running in the *same* direction (**parallel** β-pleated sheet) and another in which the polypeptide strands run in *opposite* directions (**antiparallel** β-pleated sheet).

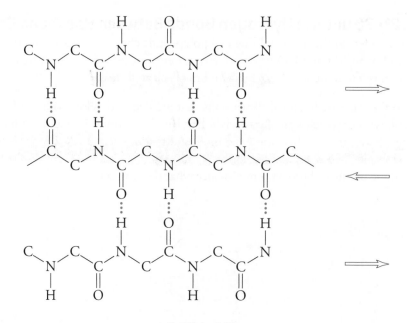

A β-Pleated Sheet

26) If a single polypeptide folds once and forms a β-pleated sheet with itself, would this be a parallel or antiparallel β-pleated sheet?[26]

27) What effect would a molecule that disrupts hydrogen bonding, e.g., urea, have on protein structure?[27]

Tertiary (3°) Structure: Hydrophobic/Hydrophilic Interactions

The next level of protein folding, tertiary structure, concerns interactions between amino acid residues located more distantly from each other in the polypeptide chain. The folding of secondary structures such as α-helices into higher order tertiary structures is driven by interactions of R-groups with each other and with the solvent (water). Hydrophobic R-groups tend to fold into the interior of the protein, away from the solvent, and hydrophilic R-groups tend to be exposed to water on the surface of the protein (shown for the generic globular protein).

---

[26] It would be antiparallel because one participant in the β-pleated sheet would have a C to N direction, while the other would be running N to C.

[27] Putting a protein in a urea solution will disrupt H-bonding, thus disrupting secondary structure by unfolding α-helices and β-sheets. It would not affect primary structure, which depends on the much more stable peptide bond. Disruption of 2°, 3°, or 4° structure without breaking peptide bonds is *denaturation*.

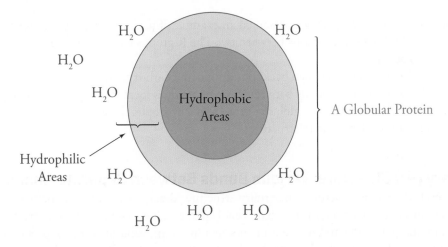

Folding of A Globular Protein in Aqueous Solution

Under the right conditions, the forces driving hydrophobic avoidance of water and hydrogen bonding will fold a polypeptide spontaneously into the correct conformation, the lowest energy conformation. In a classic experiment by Christian Anfinsen and coworkers, the effect of a denaturing agent (urea) and a reducing agent (β-mercaptoethanol) on the folding of a protein called ribonuclease were examined. In the following questions, you will reenact their thought processes. Figure out the answers before reading the footnotes.

28) Ribonuclease has eight cysteines that form four disulfides bonds. What effect would a reducing agent have on its tertiary structure?[28]

29) If the disulfides serve only to lock into place a tertiary protein structure that forms first on its own, then what effect would the reducing agent have on correct protein folding?[29]

30) Would a protein end up folded normally if you (1) first put it in a reducing environment, (2) then denatured it by adding urea, (3) next removed the reducing agent, allowing disulfide bridges to reform, and (4) finally removed the denaturing agent?[30]

31) What if you did the same experiment but in this order: 1, 2, 4, 3?[31]

The disulfide bridge is perhaps not a good example of 3° structure because it is a covalent bond, not a hydrophobic interaction. However, because the disulfide is formed after 2° structure and before 4° structure, it is usually considered part of 3° folding.

---

[28] The disulfide bridges would be broken. Tertiary structure would be less stable.

[29] The shape should not be disrupted if breaking disulfides is the only disturbance. It's just that the shape would be less sturdy—like a concrete wall without the rebar.

[30] No. If you allow disulfide bridges to form while the protein is still denatured, it will become locked into an abnormal shape.

[31] You should end up with the correct structure. In step one, you break the reinforcing disulfide bridges. In step two, you denature the protein completely by disrupting H-bonds. In step four, you allow the H-bonds to reform; as stated in the text, normally the correct tertiary structure will form spontaneously if you leave the polypeptide alone. In step three, you reform the disulfide bridges, thus locking the structure into its correct form.

32) Which of the following may be considered an example of tertiary protein structure?[32]
    I.   van der Waals interactions between two Phe R-groups located far apart on a polypeptide
    II.   Hydrogen bonds between backbone amino and carboxyl groups
    III.   Covalent disulfide bonds between cysteine residues located far apart on a polypeptide

33) What effect would dissolving a globular protein in a hydrophobic organic solvent such as hexane have on tertiary protein structure?[33]

Quaternary (4°) Structure: Various Bonds Between Separate Chains

The highest level of protein structure, quaternary structure, describes interactions between polypeptide subunits. A **subunit** is a single polypeptide chain that is part of a large complex containing many subunits (a **multisubunit complex**). The arrangement of subunits in a multisubunit complex is what we mean by quaternary structure. For example, mammalian RNA polymerase II contains twelve different subunits. The interactions between subunits are instrumental in protein function, as in the cooperative binding of oxygen by each of the four subunits of hemoglobin.

The forces stabilizing quaternary structure are generally the same as those involved in secondary and tertiary structure—non-covalent interactions (the hydrogen bond, the hydrophobic interaction, and the van der Waals interaction). However, covalent bonds may also be involved in quaternary structure. For example, antibodies (immune system molecules) are large protein complexes with disulfide bonds holding the subunits together. It is key to understand, however, that there is one covalent bond that may not be involved in quaternary structure—the peptide bond—because this bond defines sequence (1° structure).

34) What is the difference between a disulfide bridge involved in quaternary structure and one involved in tertiary structure?[34]

---

[32] This is a simple question provided to clarify the classification of the disulfide bridge. Item I is a good example of 3° structure. Item II is describes 2°, not 3°, structure. Item III describes the disulfide, which is considered to be tertiary because of when it is formed, despite the fact that it is a covalent bond.

[33] The protein would be turned inside out.

[34] Quaternary disulfides are bonds that form between chains that aren't linked by peptide bonds. Tertiary disulfides are bonds that form between residues in the same polypeptide.

8.3 CARBOHYDRATES

Carbohydrates are chains of hydrated carbon atoms with the molecular formula $C_nH_{2n}O_n$. The chain usually begins with an aldehyde or ketone and continues as a polyalcohol in which each carbon has a hydroxyl substituent. Carbohydrates are produced by photosynthesis in plants and by biochemical synthesis in animals. Carbohydrates can be broken down to CO_2 in a process called **oxidation**, which is also known as burning or combustion. Because this process releases large amounts of energy, carbohydrates serve as the principle energy source for cellular metabolism. Glucose in the form of the polymer cellulose is also the building block of wood and cotton. Understanding the nomenclature, structure, and chemistry of carbohydrates is essential to understanding cellular metabolism. This chapter will also help you understand key facts such as why we can eat potatoes and cotton candy but not wood and cotton T-shirts, and why milk makes some adults flatulent.

Structure and Nomenclature of Monosaccharides

A single carbohydrate molecule is a **monosaccharide** (meaning "single sweet unit"), also known as a **simple sugar**. Two monosaccharides bonded together form a **disaccharide**; several bonded together make an **oligosaccharide**, and many make a **polysaccharide**. If these polymers are subjected to strong acid, they are hydrolyzed to monosaccharides, which are not further hydrolyzed.

Classes of monosaccharides are given a two-part name. The first part is either "aldo" or "keto," depending on whether an aldehyde or a ketone is present. The second part reveals the number of carbon atoms in the chain: trioses are the smallest and have three carbons; tetroses have four, pentoses five, hexoses six, and heptoses seven. For example, the *polyhydroxy aldehyde glucose* is an *aldohexose* because it is a six-carbon chain beginning in an aldehyde. "Glucose" and "fructose" are examples of **common names**. IUPAC nomenclature is not usually used with individual carbohydrates because the systematic names are so long.

The carbons in monosaccharides are numbered beginning with carbon #1 at the *most oxidized end* of the carbon chain, which is the end with the aldehyde or ketone.

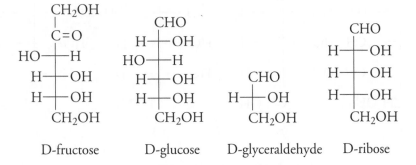

Some Metabolically Important Simple Sugars and Common Sugars on the MCAT

35) Which of the sugars in the figure above is a ketohexose?[35]
36) Which carbon (#?) is the most oxidized in fructose?[36]

---

[35] Fructose. It has six carbons, making it a hexose, and the carbonyl group is located on carbon #2, making it a ketose. Fructose is a polyhydroxy ketone, or a ketohexose.

[36] Carbon #2.

Absolute Configuration of Monosaccharides

Because carbohydrates contain chiral carbons, it is also necessary to classify them according to stereochemistry. Like amino acids, carbohydrates are assigned one of two configurations, either D or L, based on the configuration of the last chiral carbon in the chain (farthest from the aldehyde or ketone). By convention, this configuration is determined by comparison with glyceraldehyde. If a monosaccharide's last chiral carbon matches the chiral carbon of D-glyceraldehyde, it will be assigned the "D" label. The sugars in our bodies have the D configuration. When you are drawing a Fischer projection of a monosaccharide, put the aldehyde or ketone on top and the CH_2OH group (last carbon) on the bottom. The last chiral carbon will have its OH on the Left for L monosaccharides. However, we have only D-sugars in our bodies. Remember that we have only L-amino acids and only D-sugars.

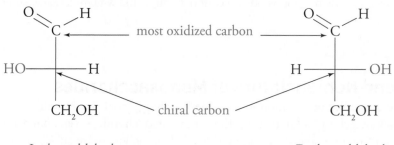

L-glyceraldehyde   D-glyceraldehyde

The Fischer Notation for Carbohydrates

For a given class of monosaccharide (like any other chiral molecule), there are 2^n different stereoisomers, where n is the number of chiral carbons.

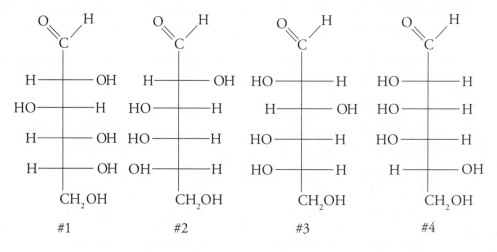

Four Monosaccharide Stereoisomers

37) Consider the four monosaccharides above. Which one of the following is correct?[37]
- A. Carbohydrate #2 is a D sugar and an enantiomer of #4.
- B. Carbohydrate #2 is an enantiomer of #3.
- C. Carbohydrates #1 and #3 are epimers and enantiomers.
- D. Carbohydrates #1 and #3 are enantiomers.

38) There are ___ aldohexoses and ___ D-aldohexoses (tough question but you *do* have all the information you need to figure it out).[38]

39) Is it possible to produce a diastereomer of D-glyceraldehyde? How about an epimer?[39]

Since we already discussed the relationships between the terms *isomer, stereoisomer, enantiomer,* and *diastereomer,* and *epimer* in Chapter 3, we will not discuss them again here. The following Venn diagram represents a concise way of categorizing these terms. It shows which groups are subsets of which. *Isomers* have the same atoms but different bonds, unless they are also stereoisomers. Stereoisomers have the same atoms and the same bonds, but different bond geometries. All stereoisomers are either enantiomers or diastereomers. Some diastereomers are epimers.

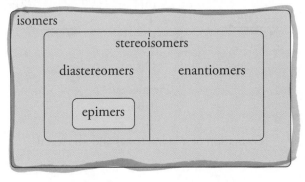

A Venn Diagram for Stereoisomers

Cyclic Structures of Monosaccharides

So far, we have represented the monosaccharides as straight chain structures. In solution, however, hexoses and pentoses spontaneously form five- and six-membered rings. In fact, the cyclic structures are thermodynamically favored, so that only a small percentage usually exist in the open chain form. The six-membered ring structures are termed **pyranoses** due to their resemblance to pyran, and five- membered sugar rings are termed **furanoses** due to their resemblance to furan.

---

[37] Sugar #2 is an L sugar, since the last chiral OH is on the left (choice A is false and can be eliminated). Sugars #2 and #3 are not mirror images, so they cannot be enantiomers (choice B is false and can be eliminated). Since sugars #1 and #3 are non-superimposable images, the are enantiomers (choice D is the correct statement), and remember that epimers are never enantiomers (choice C is false and can be eliminated).

[38] There are 2^4 aldohexoses, because there are 4 chiral carbons (#2, 3, 4, and 5). There are only 2^3 D-aldohexoses, because when you specify the "D" configuration, you leave only 3 variable chiral centers.

[39] No, it is not possible to make a glyceraldehyde diastereomer, because the molecule has only one chiral carbon. The only stereoisomer of D-glyceraldehyde is L-glyceraldehyde, an enantiomer. You can't make an epimer because the word "epimer" is reserved for sugars with more than one chiral center.

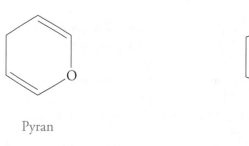

Pyran   Furan

Let's take glucose as an example. The ring forms when the OH on C5 nucleophilically attacks the carbonyl carbon (C1), forming a **hemiacetal**. The reactions involved, in which an alcohol reacts with an aldehyde to produce a hemiacetal (one –OR group and one –OH group) and subsequently an acetal (two –OR groups), are shown on the next page (see also Section 6.1). The difference between an acetal and a hemiacetal is that the hemiacetal is in constant equilibrium with the carbonyl form. The acetal form, in contrast, is quite stable, requiring an enzyme to react.

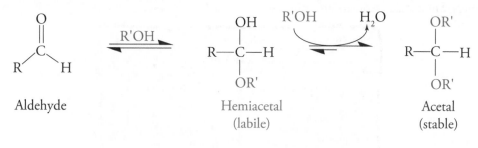

Aldehyde   Hemiacetal   Acetal
                            (labile)   (stable)

Formation of a Hemiacetal and an Acetal

The figure below shows the reaction for glucose. This manner of drawing ring structures is a modified form of Fischer notation, useful for indicating which carbons are involved in forming the cyclical structure, but unrealistic in terms of bond lengths and angles.

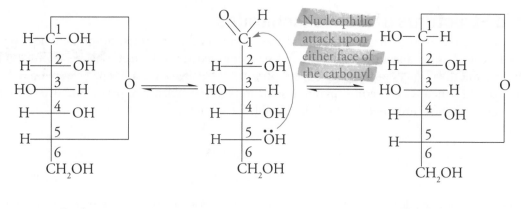

α-D-glucose   β-D-glucose

Glucopyranose Formation: A Nucleophilic Addition Reaction

The more realistic "chair" representations of these structures are shown on the next page. Note that two different ring structures are shown, α and β. The α or β ring is formed depending upon from which face of the carbonyl the C5-hydroxyl group attacks. If the attack comes from one face, the carbonyl oxygen will become an equatorial hydroxyl group; if the attack comes from the other face, the carbonyl oxygen will become an axial hydroxyl group. [To distinguish the forms, remember, "It's always better to βE up (happy)!" This will help you remember that in β-D-Glucose, the anomeric hydroxyl group is up.] The two forms are called **anomers**, and C1 (designated with an asterisk in the figures) is called the **anomeric carbon**. The anomeric carbon is always the carbonyl carbon, so in aldoses it is C1, but in ketoses it is C2. The interconversion between the two anomers is called **mutarotation**.

The groups on the *left* in Fischer notation are *above* the ring in chair notation. Also, remember that *axial* substituents on six-membered chair rings are those that point *straight up or down*. The *equatorial* substituents point *out* from the ring. Equatorial substituents have less steric hindrance with the ring and are thus thermodynamically more favorable.

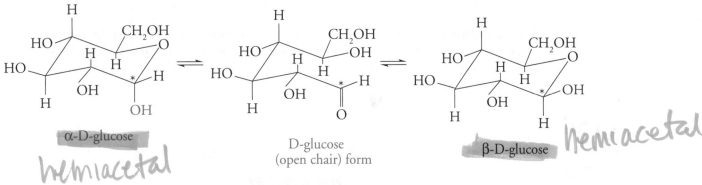

Chair Representation of Glucopyranose Formation

40) Why doesn't glucose cyclize into three- or four-membered rings?[40]
41) Are the OH's in β-D-glucopyranose axial or equatorial?[41]
42) A solution of glucose may contain both furanose and pyranose rings. How can the same sugar exist in both forms?[42]

Another way to represent cyclic sugars is called Haworth notation. The groups on the *left* in Fischer notation are *above* the ring in Haworth notation (as in the chair form). A summary of how to convert Fischer Projections of sugars to Haworth Projections is as follows:

1. Draw the basic structure of the sugar.
2. If the sugar is a D-sugar, place a –CH_2OH above the ring on the carbon to the left of the oxygen. For an L-sugar, place it below the ring.
3. For an α-sugar, place an –OH below the ring on the carbon to the right of the ring oxygen. For a β-sugar, place the –OH above the ring.
4. Finally, –OH groups on the right go below the ring and those on the left above, using the –CH_2OH group as the reference point for both projections.

---

[40] Smaller rings necessitate bond angles that are much narrower than the normal tetrahedral angle. Strained bonds are unfavorable because they are high energy.

[41] They are all equatorial. This makes it a very stable molecule, and may explain why it is the most prevalent sugar in nature. It stores a lot of energy, and yet is very stable. (Key fact.)

[42] The structure that forms depends on which OH attacks the carbonyl carbon (C#2). If OH4 attacks the carbonyl, the result will be a five-membered ring. If OH5 attacks, the result will be a six-membered ring. If you actually counted the structures in solution, you'd find more six-membered rings, since these are inherently more stable due to bond angles.

8.3

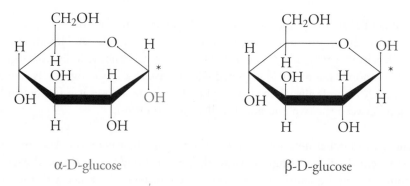

α-D-glucose   β-D-glucose

Haworth Representation of Glucopyranose

43) A monosaccharide is represented below in Haworth notation. What number is the carbon that the arrow is pointing toward? Is this a furanose or a pyranose? Is it the α- or β-anomer?[43]

44) Mentally unfold the Haworth projection and draw the Fischer notation. Is this a D- or L-sugar? How many chiral carbons does it have?[44]

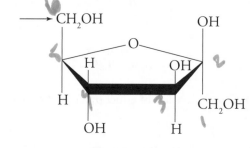

Structure and Nomenclature of Disaccharides

Recall that two monosaccharides bonded together form a disaccharide, a few form an oligosaccharide, and many form a polysaccharide. The bond between two sugar molecules is called a **glycosidic linkage**. This is a covalent bond, formed in a dehydration reaction that requires enzymatic catalysis.

Typically, the glycosidic bond joins C1 of one pyranose or furanose to C4 (sometimes C2 or C6) of another pyranose or furanose through an oxygen atom. Is the anomeric carbon in a hemiacetal form, or is it in an acetal form once it is part of a glycosidic bond? It has two –OR constituents, so it forms an acetal group. The significance of this is that the glycosidic linkage stays in the α or β configuration until an enzyme breaks the bond, because the acetal is a stable functional group. In other words, once a monosaccharide has attacked another sugar to form a glycosidic linkage, it is no longer free to mutarotate. This is an important concept, and we will discuss it further in the section on reducing sugars.

[43] It is the one farthest from the anomeric carbon, so it is #6. It is in a five-membered ring, so it is a furanose. The anomeric OH (former carbonyl O) is up, so it's β.

[44] It is D-fructose, with three chiral carbons (four when cyclic), and the Fischer structure is shown in Figure 18. The only way to determine that it's a D sugar is to identify the penultimate chiral carbon, mentally open the chain, and visualize it as a Fischer structure.

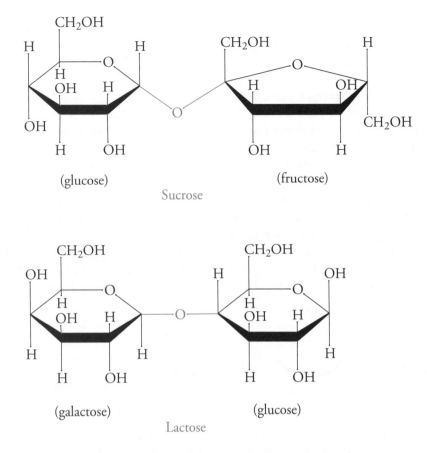

Disaccharides and the α- or β-Glycosidic Bond

Glycosidic linkages are named according to which carbon in each sugar comprises the linkage. The configuration (α or β) of the linkage is also specified. For example, lactose (milk sugar) is a disaccharide joined in a galactose-β-1,4-glucose linkage (above). Sucrose (table sugar) is also shown above, with a glucose unit and a fructose unit.

45)   Does sucrose contain an α- or β-glycosidic linkage?[45]

You should memorize the linkages of four disaccharides: sucrose (Glc-α-1,2-Fru), lactose (Gal-β-1,4-Glc), maltose (Glc-α-1,4-Glc), and cellobiose (Glc-β-1,4-Glc).

Polymers made from these disaccharides form important biological macromolecules. Glycogen serves as an energy storage carbohydrate in animals and is composed of thousands of glucose units joined in α-1,4 linkages; α-1,6 branches are also present. Starch is the same as glycogen (except that the branches are a little different), and serves the same purpose in plants. Cellulose is a polymer of cellobiose; the β-glycosidic bonds allow the polymer to assume a long, straight, fibrous shape. Wood and cotton are made of cellulose.

The hydrolysis of polysaccharides into monosaccharides is essential for monosaccharides to enter metabolic pathways (e.g., glycolysis) and be used for energy by the cell. Different enzymes catalyze the hydrolysis

---

[45] The anomeric carbon of glucose is pointing down, which means the linkage is α-1,2. So, sucrose is Glc-α-1,2-Fru.

of different linkages. The enzyme is named for the sugar it hydrolyzes. For example, the enzyme that catalyzes the hydrolysis of maltose into two glucose monosaccharides is called **maltase**. Each enzyme is highly specific for its linkage.

This specificity is a great example of the significance of stereochemistry. Consider cellulose. A cotton T-shirt is pure sugar. The only reason we can't digest it is that mammalian enzymes can't deal with the β-glycosidic linkages that make cellobiose from glucose. Cellulose is actually the energy source in grass and hay. Cows are mammals, and all mammals lack the enzymes necessary for cellobiose breakdown. To live on grass, cows depend on bacteria that live in an extra stomach called a rumen to digest cellulose for them. If you're really on the ball, you're next question is: Humans are mammals, so how can we digest lactose, which has a β linkage? The answer is that we have a specific enzyme, **lactase**, which can digest lactose. This is an exception to the rule that mammalian enzymes cannot hydrolyze β-glycosidic linkages. People without lactase are **lactose malabsorbers**, and any lactose they eat ends up in the colon. There it may cause gas and diarrhea, if certain bacteria are present; people with this problem are said to be **lactose intolerant**. People produce lactase as children so that they can digest mother's milk, but most adults naturally stop making this enzyme, and thus become lactose malabsorbers and sometimes intolerant.

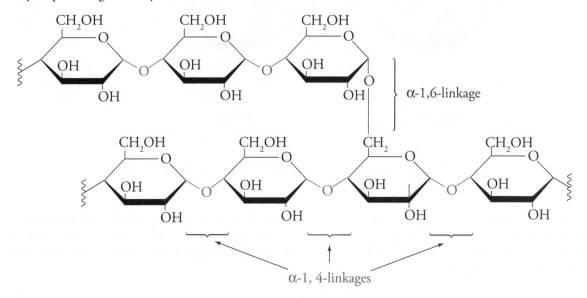

The Polysaccharide Glycogen

Hydrolysis of Glycosidic Linkages

Disaccharides and polysaccharides are broken down into their component monosaccharides by enzymatic hydrolysis. This just means water is the nucleophile, and one of the sugars is the leaving group (the one which was the attacker during bond formation). In other words, the cleavage reaction is precisely the reverse of the formation reaction.

Hydrolysis of polysaccharides into monosaccharides is favored thermodynamically. This means the hydrolysis of polysaccharides releases energy in the cell. However, it does not occur at a significant rate without enzymatic catalysis. As catalysts, enzymes increase reaction rates by lowering the activation energy but do not change final concentrations of reactants and products.

46) Which requires net energy input: polysaccharide synthesis or hydrolysis?[46]

47) If the activation energy of polysaccharide hydrolysis were so low that no enzyme was required for the reaction to occur, would this make polysaccharides better for energy storage?[47]

Reducing Sugars

This is a simple concept that often confuses students. **Benedict's test** is a chemical assay that detects the carbonyl units of sugars. It is useful because it distinguishes hemiacetals from acetals [only hemiacetals are in equilibrium with the carbonyl (open-chain) form]. For example, if you had a white powder that you knew to be composed of glucose, you would be able to say whether the glucose existed in the free monosaccharide form or was in the form of glycogen. How? Well, if it's in the monosaccharide form, there will be many hemiacetals, and Benedict's test will be strongly positive. However, if the powder consists of only relatively few glycogen molecules, Benedict's will be only weakly positive. This is because all the glucose units in a glycogen polymer are tied up in acetal linkages, except for the very first one in the chain (the one which was first attacked during polymerization).

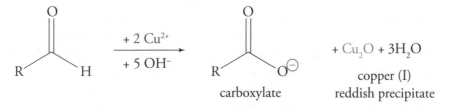

Benedict's Test for Reducing Sugars

Benedict's test is performed as follows: Benedict's reagent, an oxidized form of copper, is used to oxidize a sugar's aldehyde or ketone to the corresponding carboxylic acid, yielding a reddish precipitate. Any carbohydrate that can be oxidized by Benedict's reagent is referred to as a **reducing sugar** because it *reduces* the Cu^{2+} to Cu^{+} while itself being oxidized. All monosaccharides are reducing sugars. More generally, *all aldehydes, ketones, and hemiacetals give a positive result in Benedict's test for reducing sugars; acetals give a negative result because they do not react with Cu^{2+}, and they are not in equilibrium with the open-chain (carbonyl) form.*

48) Which carbon of glucose can be oxidized by Benedict's reagent? What about fructose?[48]

Recall that we've said once a monosaccharide has attacked another sugar to form a glycosidic linkage, it is no longer free to mutarotate. Now we can expand this statement as follows: Once a monosaccharide has attacked another sugar to form a glycosidic linkage, its anomeric carbon is in an acetal configuration and is thus no longer free to mutarotate *nor to reduce Benedict's reagent.*

---

[46] Because hydrolysis of polysaccharides is thermodynamically favored, energy input is required to drive the reaction toward polysaccharide synthesis.

[47] No, because then polysaccharides would hydrolyze spontaneously (they'd be unstable). The high activation energy of polysaccharide hydrolysis allows us to use enzymes as gatekeepers—when we need energy from glucose, we open the gate of glycogen hydrolysis.

[48] The anomeric carbon, which is #1 for aldoses like glucose and #2 for ketoses like fructose.

49) If 98% of a monosaccharide is present as the ring form at equilibrium in solution, then how much of the sugar can be oxidized in Benedict's reaction?[49]

50) Is lactose a reducing sugar? What about sucrose? (You may refer back to the text and figures above.)[50]

8.4 LIPIDS

Lipids are oily or fatty substances that play three physiological roles, summarized here and discussed below.

- In cellular membranes, phospholipids constitute a barrier between intracellular and extracellular environments.
- In adipose cells, triglycerides (fats) store energy.
- Finally, cholesterol is a special lipid that serves as the building block for the hydrophobic steroid hormones.

The cardinal characteristic of the lipid is its **hydrophobicity**. Hydrophobic means *water-fearing*. It is important to understand the significance of this. Since water is very polar, polar substances dissolve well in water; these are known as *water-loving*, or **hydrophilic** substances. Carbon-carbon bonds and carbon-hydrogen bonds are nonpolar. Hence, substances that contain only carbon and hydrogen will not dissolve well in water. Some examples: table sugar dissolves well in water, but cooking oil floats in a layer above water or forms many tiny oil droplets when mixed with water. Cotton T-shirts become wet when exposed to water because they are made of glucose polymerized into cellulose, but a nylon jacket does not become wet because it is composed of atoms covalently bound together in a nonpolar fashion. A synonym for hydrophobic is **lipophilic** (which means lipid-loving); a synonym for hydrophilic is **lipophobic**. We return to these concepts below.

Fatty Acid Structure

Fatty acids are composed of long unsubstituted alkanes that end in a carboxylic acid. The chain is typically 14 to 18 carbons long, and because they are synthesized two carbons at a time from acetate, only *even-numbered* fatty acids are made in human cells. A fatty acid with no carbon-carbon double bonds is said to be **saturated** with hydrogen because every carbon atom in the chain is covalently bound to the maximum number of hydrogens. **Unsaturated** fatty acids have one or more double bonds in the tail. These double bonds are almost always (Z) (or *cis*). The position of a double bond in the alkyl chain of a fatty acid is denoted by the symbol Δ and the number of the first carbon involved in the double bond. Carbons are numbered starting with the carboxylic acid carbon. For example, a (Z) double bond between carbons 3 and 4 in a fatty acid would be referred to as $(Z)\text{-}\Delta^3$ (or *cis*-Δ^3).

---

[49] 100% will be oxidized. In a monosaccharide, the ring form is in equilibrium with the open chain form. So when the open chain form is used up in the oxidation reaction, it will be replenished by other rings opening up (Le Châtelier's principle).

[50] Lactose (Gal-β-1-4-Glc) is a reducing sugar. Although the attacking anomeric carbon becomes locked in an acetal, the anomeric carbon of the *attacked* monosaccharide is still free to mutarotate or react with Benedict's reagent. Sucrose (Glc-α-1-2-Fru) is not a reducing sugar, because it is made of glucose and fructose, which are both joined at their anomeric carbons. Carbon #1 of glucose is the anomeric carbon, since glucose is an aldose; carbon #2 of fructose is the anomeric carbon, since fructose is a ketose.

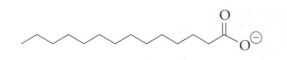

Saturated fatty acid

Unsaturated fatty acid

51) What is the correct nomenclature for the double bond in the unsaturated fatty acid above?[51]
52) How does the shape of an unsaturated fatty acid differ from that of a saturated fatty acid?[52]
53) If fatty acids are mixed into water, how are they likely to associate with each other?[53]

The drawing on the next page illustrates how free fatty acids interact in an aqueous solution; they form a structure called a **micelle**. The force that drives the tails into the center of the micelle is called the **hydrophobic interaction**. The hydrophobic interaction is a complex phenomenon. In general, it results from the fact that water molecules must form an orderly **solvation shell** around each hydrophobic substance. The reason is that H_2O has a dipole that "likes" to be able to share its charges with other polar molecules. A solvation shell allows for the most water-water interaction and the least water-lipid interaction. The problem is that forming a solvation shell is an increase in order and thus a decrease in entropy ($\Delta S < 0$), which is unfavorable according to the second law of thermodynamics, $\Delta G = \Delta H - T\Delta S$. In the case of the fatty acid micelle, water forms a shell around the spherical micelle with the result being that water interacts with polar carboxylic acid head groups while hydrophobic lipid tails hide inside the sphere.

Soaps are the sodium salts of fatty acids ($RCOO^-Na^+$). They are **amphipathic**, which means both hydrophilic and hydrophobic.

---

[51] This double bond extends between carbons 7 and 8, and is *cis*. The bond therefore is *cis*-Δ^7.

[52] An unsaturated fatty acid is bent, or "kinked," at the *cis* double bond.

[53] The long hydrophobic chains will interact with each other to minimize contact with water, exposing the charged carboxyl group to the aqueous environment.

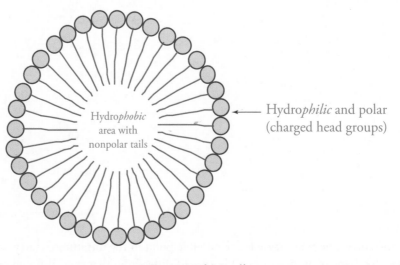

Hydro*philic* and polar
(charged head groups)

Hydro*phobic*
area with
nonpolar tails

A Fatty Acid Micelle

54) How does soap help to remove grease from your hands?[54]

Triacylglycerols (TG)

The storage form of the fatty acid is fat. The technical name for fat is **triacylglycerol** or **triglyceride** (shown below). The triglyceride is composed of three fatty acids esterified to a glycerol molecule. Glycerol is a three-carbon triol with the formula $HOCH_2–CHOH–CH_2OH$. As you can see, it has three hydroxyl groups that can be esterified to fatty acids. It is necessary to store fatty acids in the relatively inert form of fat because free fatty acids are reactive chemicals.

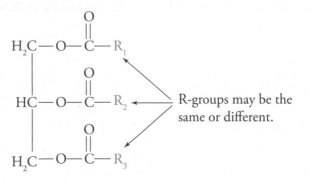

R-groups may be the
same or different.

A Triglyceride (Fat)

---

[54] Grease is hydrophobic. It does not wash off easily in water because it is not soluble in water. Scrubbing your hands with soap causes micelles to form around the grease particles.

The triacylglycerol undergoes reactions typical of esters, such as base-catalyzed hydrolysis. Soap is economically produced by base-catalyzed hydrolysis of triglycerides from animal fat into fatty acid salts (soaps). This reaction is called **saponification** and is illustrated below.

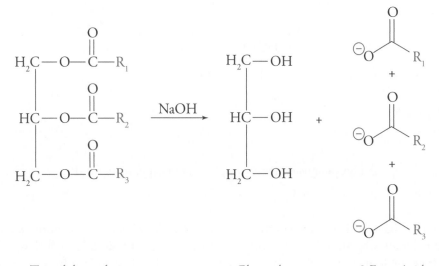

Triacylglycerol Glycerol 3 Fatty Acids

Saponification

Lipases are enzymes that hydrolyze fats. Triacylglycerols are stored in fat cells as an energy source. Fats are more efficient energy storage molecules than carbohydrates for two reasons: packing and energy content.

Packing: Their hydrophobicity allows fats to pack together much more closely than carbohydrates. Carbohydrates carry a great amount of water-of-solvation (water molecules hydrogen bonded to their hydroxyl groups). In other words, the amount of carbon per unit area or unit weight is much greater in a fat droplet than in dissolved sugar. If we could store sugars in a dry powdery form in our bodies, this problem would be obviated.

Energy content: All packing considerations aside, fat molecules store much more energy than carbohydrates. In other words, regardless of what you dissolve it in, a fat has more energy carbon-for-carbon than a carbohydrate. The reason is that fats are much more *reduced*. Remember that energy metabolism begins with the *oxidation* of foodstuffs to release energy. Since carbohydrates are more oxidized to start with, oxidizing them releases less energy. Animals use fat to store most of their energy, storing only a small amount as carbohydrates (glycogen). Plants such as potatoes commonly store a large percentage of their energy as carbohydrates (starch).

Introduction to Lipid Bilayer Membranes

Membrane lipids are **phospholipids** derived from diacylglycerol phosphate or DG-P. For example, phosphatidyl choline is a phospholipid formed by the esterification of a choline molecule [$HO(CH_2)_2N^+(CH_3)_3$] to the phosphate group of DG-P. Phospholipids are **detergents**, substances that efficiently solubilize oils while remaining highly water-soluble. Detergents are like soaps, but stronger.

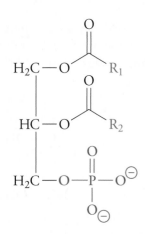

A Phosphoglyceride (Diacylglycerol Phosphate, or DGP)

We saw above how fatty acids spontaneously form micelles. Phospholipids also minimize their interactions with water by forming an orderly structure—in this case, it is a **lipid bilayer** (below). Hydrophobic interactions drive the formation of the bilayer, and once formed, it is stabilized by van der Waals forces between the long tails.

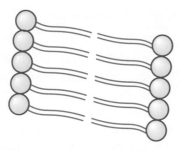

A Small Section of a Lipid Bilayer Membrane

55)   Would a saturated or an unsaturated fatty acid residue have more van der Waals interactions with neighboring alkyl chains in a bilayer membrane?[55]

A more precise way to give the answer to the question above is to say that double bonds (unsaturation) in phospholipid fatty acids *tend to increase membrane fluidity*. Unsaturation prevents the membrane from solidifying by disrupting the orderly packing of the hydrophobic lipid tails. This decreases the melting point. The right amount of fluidity is essential for function. Decreasing the *length* of fatty acid tails also increases fluidity. The steroid **cholesterol** (discussed in the next section) is a third important modulator of membrane fluidity. At low temperatures, it increases fluidity in the same way as kinks in fatty acid tails; hence, it is known as membrane antifreeze. At high temperatures, however, cholesterol attenuates (reduces) membrane fluidity. Don't ponder this paradox too long; just remember that cholesterol keeps fluidity at an *optimum level*. Remember, the structural determinants of membrane fluidity are: degree of saturation, tail length, and amount of cholesterol.

---

[55]   The bent shape of the unsaturated fatty acid means that it doesn't fit in as well and has less contact with neighboring groups to form van der Waals interactions. Unsaturation makes the membrane less stable, less solid.

The lipid bilayer acts like a plastic bag surrounding the cell in the sense that it seals the interior of the cell from the exterior. However, the cell membrane is much more complex than a plastic bag. Since the plasma bilayer membrane surrounding cells is impermeable to charged molecules such as Na^+, protein gateways such as ion channels are required for these molecules to enter or exit cells. Proteins that are integrated into membranes also transmit signals from the outside of the cell into the interior. For example, certain hormones (peptides) cannot pass through the cell membrane due to their charged nature; instead, protein **receptors** in the cell membrane bind these hormones and transmit a signal into the cell in a **second messenger cascade**.

8.5 STEROIDS

Steroids are included here because of their hydrophobicity, and, hence, similarity to fats. Their structure is otherwise unique. All steroids have the basic tetracyclic ring system (see below), based on the structure of **cholesterol**, a polycyclic amphipath. (Polycyclic means several rings, and amphipathic means displaying both hydrophilic and hydrophobic characteristics.)

As discussed above, the steroid cholesterol is an important component of the lipid bilayer. It is obtained from the diet and synthesized in the liver. It is carried in the blood packaged with fats and proteins into **lipoproteins**. One type of lipoprotein has been implicated as the cause of atherosclerotic vascular disease, which refers to the build-up of cholesterol "plaques" on the inside of blood vessels.

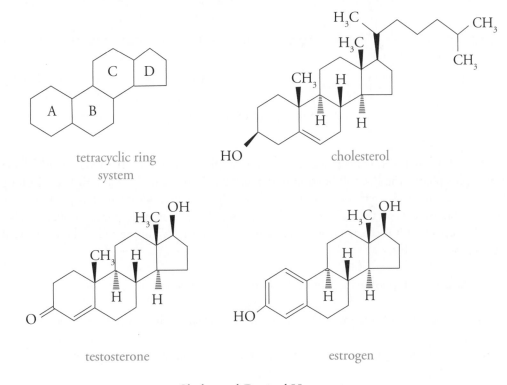

Cholesterol-Derived Hormones

Steroid hormones are made from cholesterol. Two examples are **testosterone** (an androgen or male sex hormone) and **estradiol** (an estrogen or female sex hormone). There are no receptors for steroid hormones on the surface of cells. If this is true, how can they exert an influence on the cell? Because steroids are highly hydrophobic, they can diffuse right through the lipid bilayer membrane into the cytoplasm. The receptors for steroid hormones are located within cells rather than on the cell surface. This is an important point! You must be aware of the contrast between *peptide* hormones, such as insulin, which exert their effects by binding to receptors at the cell-surface, and *steroid* hormones, such as estrogen, which diffuse into cells to find their receptors.

8.6 NUCLEIC ACIDS

Before we can talk about nucleic acids, we must first briefly review some background.

Phosphorus-Containing Compounds

Phosphoric acid is an *inorganic* acid (it does not contain carbon) with the potential to donate three protons. The K_as for the three acid dissociation equilibria are 2.1, 7.2, and 12.4. Therefore, at physiological pH, phosphoric acid is significantly dissociated, existing largely in anionic form.

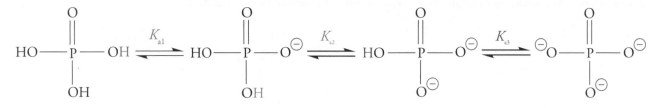

Phosphoric Acid Dissociation

Phosphate is also known as orthophosphate. Two orthophosphates bound together via an **anhydride linkage** form **pyrophosphate**. The P–O–P bond in pyrophosphate is an example of a **high-energy phosphate bond**. This name is derived from the fact that the hydrolysis of pyrophosphate is thermodynamically extremely favorable (shown on the next page). The $\Delta G°$ for the hydrolysis of pyrophosphate is about –7 kcal/mol. This means that it is a very favorable reaction. The actual $\Delta G°$ in the cell is about –12 kcal/mol, which is even more favorable.

There are three reasons that phosphate anhydride bonds store so much energy:

1. When phosphates are linked together, their negative charges repel each other strongly.
2. Orthophosphate has more resonance forms and thus a lower free energy than linked phosphates.
3. Orthophosphate has a more favorable interaction with the biological solvent (water) than linked phosphates.

The details are not crucial. What is essential is that you fix the image in your mind of linked phosphates acting like compressed springs, just waiting to fly open and provide energy for an enzyme to catalyze a reaction.

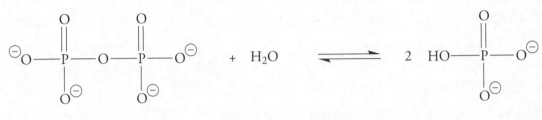

The Hydrolysis of Pyrophosphate

Nucleotides

Nucleotides are the building blocks of nucleic acids (RNA and DNA). Each nucleotide contains a **ribose** (or **deoxyribose**) **sugar** group; a **purine** or **pyrimidine base** joined to carbon number one of the ribose ring; and one, two, or three **phosphate units** joined to carbon five of the ribose ring. The nucleotide **a**denosine **tri**phosphate (ATP) plays a central role in cellular metabolism in addition to being an RNA precursor.

ATP is the universal short-term energy storage molecule. Energy extracted from the oxidation of foodstuffs is immediately stored in the phosphoanhydride bonds of ATP. This energy will later be used to power cellular processes; it may also be used to synthesize glucose or fats, which are longer-term energy storage molecules. This applies to *all* living organisms, from bacteria to humans. Even some viruses carry ATP with them outside the host cell, though viruses cannot make their own ATP.

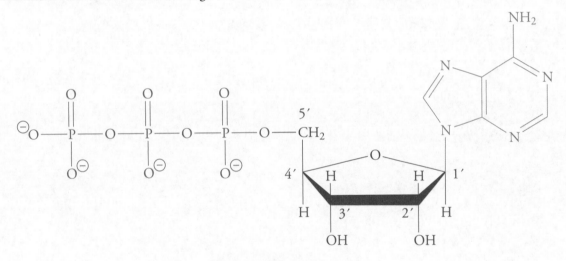

Adenosine Triphosphate (ATP)

Chapter 8 Summary

- Amino acids (AAs) consist of a tetrahedral α-carbon connected to an amino group, a carboxyl group, and a variable R group, which determines the AA's properties.

- The isoelectric point of an AA is the pH at which the net charge on the molecule is zero; this structure is referred to as the *zwitterion*.

- Electrophoresis separates mixtures of AAs and is conducted at buffered pH. Positively charged AAs move to the "–" end of the gel, and negative AAs move to the "+" end.

- Proteins consist of amino acids linked by peptide bonds, or amide bonds, which have partial double bond characteristics, lack rotation and are very stable.

- The secondary structure of proteins (α-helices and β-sheets) is formed through hydrogen bonding interactions between atoms in the backbone of the molecule.

- The most stable tertiary protein structure generally places polar AAs on the exterior and nonpolar AAs on the interior of the protein. This minimizes interactions between nonpolar AAs and water, while optimizing interactions between side chains inside the protein.

- All animal amino acids are L-configuration and all animal sugars are D-configuration.

- Carbohydrates are chains of hydrated carbon atoms with the molecular formula $C_nH_{2n}O_n$.

- Sugars in solution exist in equilibrium between the straight chain form and either the furanose (five-atom) or pyranose (six-atom) cyclic forms.

- The anomeric forms of a sugar differ by the position of the OH group on the anomeric carbon; OH down = α, OH up = β.

- All monosaccharides will give a positive result in a Benedict's test because they contain an aldehyde, ketone or hemiacetal, and are therefore reducing sugars.

- The glycosidic linkage in a disaccharide is named based on which anomer is present for the sugar containing the acetal and the numbers of the carbons linked to the bridging O.

- Saponification (base mediated hydrolysis) of a triglyceride produces three equivalents of fatty acid carboxylates. These amphipathic molecules form micelles in solution.

- The building blocks of nucleic acids (DNA and RNA) are nucleotides, which are comprised of a pentose sugar, a purine or pyrimidine base, and 2-3 phosphate units.

CHAPTER 8 FREESTANDING PRACTICE QUESTIONS

1. Which of the following best explains the strength of the peptide bond in a protein?

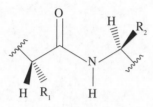

A) The steric bulk of the R groups prevents nucleophilic attack at the carbonyl carbon.
B) The electron pair on the nitrogen atom is delocalized by orbital overlap with the carbonyl group.
C) Peptide bonds are never exposed to the exterior of a protein.
D) The peptide bond is resistant to hydrolysis by many biological molecules.

2. Why is ATP known as a "high energy" structure at neutral pH?

A) It exhibits a large decrease in free energy when it undergoes hydrolytic reactions.
B) The phosphate ion released from ATP hydrolysis is very reactive.
C) It causes cellular processes to proceed at faster rates.
D) Adenine is the best energy storage molecule of all the nitrogenous bases.

3. Which of the following best describes the secondary structure of a protein?

A) Various folded polypeptide chains joining together to form a larger unit
B) The amino acid sequence of the chain
C) The polypeptide chain folding upon itself due to hydrophobic/hydrophilic interactions
D) Peptide bonds hydrogen-bonding to one another to create a sheet-like structure

4. Which of the following fatty acids has the highest melting point?

A) 4,5-dimethylhexanoic acid
B) octanoic acid
C) 2,3-dimethylbutanoic acid
D) hexanoic acid

5. Which of the following terms best describes the interconversion between α-D-glucose and β-D-glucose?

A) Tautomerism
B) Nucleophilic addition
C) Mutarotation
D) Elimination

CHAPTER 8 PRACTICE PASSAGE

In the body, proteins are constantly being synthesized and degraded in order to maintain and modulate protein concentration and enzyme activity levels. In eukaryotic cells, a 76-residue protein called *ubiquitin* is used as a tag to label proteins destined for degradation.

Ubiquitin forms an amide bond between its glycine residue at position 76 and the side chain of a lysine residue of the target protein. Three enzymes are required in the attachment of ubiquitin to the target protein. The steps of ubiquitination at pH 7 are shown in Figure 1. The first step is coupled to ATP hydrolysis.

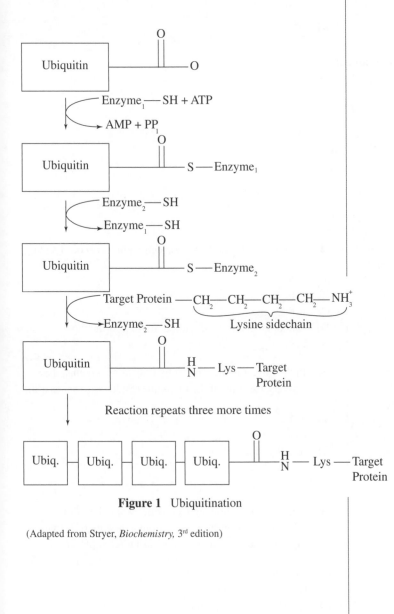

Figure 1 Ubiquitination

(Adapted from Stryer, *Biochemistry,* 3rd edition)

First, a single ubiquitin is attached to the target protein via the reaction shown in Figure 1. Subsequently, a second ubiquitin is attached to a lysine residue of the first ubiquitin, a third ubiquitin is attached to a lysine residue of the second ubiquitin, and so on, until a chain consisting of four ubiquitin monomers is attached to the target protein (Figure 1). The ubiquitinated protein is then sent to the proteosome where it is degraded into single amino acids. In the proteosome, threonine proteases cleave solvent-exposed peptide bonds using a threonine active site residue. A representative cleavage of a diglycine peptide at pH 7 is shown in Figure 2.

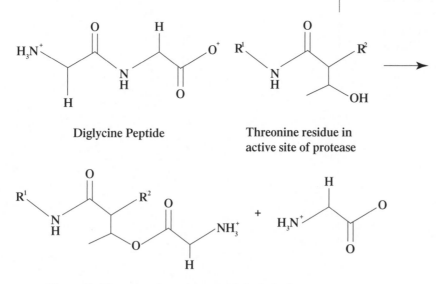

Diglycine Peptide

Threonine residue in active site of protease

Figure 2 Threonine-dependent peptide hydrolysis

1. The amide bond between ubiquitin and its target protein is formed between the side chain of a lysine residue and the:

   A) C-terminus of glycine 76.
   B) N-terminus of glycine 76.
   C) side chain of glycine 76.
   D) α–carbon of glycine 76.

2. In Step 2 of ubiquitination, the ubiquitin is transferred from Enzyme$_1$ to Enzyme$_2$. This reaction is most accurately described as:

   A) nucleophilic substitution.
   B) transesterification.
   C) trans(thio)esterification.
   D) nucleophilic addition.

3. In the absence of ATP, the ubiquitination reaction would:

   A) occur more slowly than in the presence of ATP.
   B) occur more quickly than in the presence of ATP.
   C) not be affected.
   D) not occur.

4. Compared to lysine, the isoelectric point (pI) of glycine

   A) is lower.
   B) is higher.
   C) is the same.
   D) cannot be determined without more information.

5. In the threonine-dependent hydrolysis of proteins, the primary function of the threonine residue is to act as a(n):

   A) acid.
   B) base.
   C) nucleophile.
   D) electrophile.

6. Which of the following techniques would be most effective in separating lysine from a mixture of lysine, glycine, and threonine in aqueous buffer at pH 7?

   A) Extraction
   B) Gel electrophoresis
   C) Column chromatography
   D) Distillation

SOLUTIONS TO CHAPTER 8 FREESTANDING PRACTICE QUESTIONS

1. **B** Because the peptide bond is delocalized, the C—N bond has double-bond character and is difficult to break. Choice A can be eliminated because steric hindrance describes the electron density surrounding an atom, not the density associated with bonds. Choice C can be eliminated because the folding of a peptide within a protein does not affect bond strength. Choice D can be eliminated because proteins are susceptible to hydrolysis from enzymes.

2. **A** Choice A is the best because it directly addresses the energetics of ATP hydrolysis. Choice B discusses the reactivity of the released phosphate ion and not the structure of ATP itself, so it can be eliminated. Choice C can be eliminated because it describes the rate of cellular processes not the energy of ATP. Choice D can be eliminated because the structure of adenine is not related to why ATP is a good energy storage molecule.

3. **D** The secondary structure of proteins is the initial folding of the polypeptide chain into α-helices or β-pleated sheets. Choice A describes the formation of a quaternary protein, choice B can be eliminated because it describes the primary protein structure, and choice C can be eliminated because it describes the tertiary protein structure.

4. **B** Two points to consider in the melting point of fatty acids are 1) molecular weight, and 2) branching. Choices A and B both consist of eight carbons, while choices C and D each have six. Thus, it is likely that choice A or B will be the better choice based on molecular weight. Since choice A is branched and choice B is not, choice A has the lower melting point. Although all four structures may be drawn to answer this question, it is not necessary. The carbons can be counted based on the names (2 *methyl* = 2 carbons + *hexan* = 6 carbons or *but* = 4 carbons), and the methyl substituents are indicative of branching in choices A and C.

5. **C** The interconversion between α and β anomers of the same sugar is known as mutarotation. Although the mechanism of mutarotation involves both elimination, then nucleophilic addition, individually each of these two answers is incomplete (eliminate choices B and D). Tautomerism describes the equilibration between structural isomers (eliminate choice A), not anomers, which are stereoisomers.

SOLUTIONS TO CHAPTER 8 PRACTICE PASSAGE

1. **A** Since proteins are written from N-terminus to C-terminus, glycine 76 is the C-terminal residue with the free carbonyl shown (eliminate choice B). Glycine does not have a side chain (its R group attached to the α-carbon is a single H) so choice C can be eliminated. The α-carbon of an amino acid is next to the carbonyl, not the carbonyl carbon itself, so choice D can be eliminated.

2. **C**   At the beginning of Step 2, the ubiquitin is linked to Enzyme₁ through a thioester bond, not a simple ester, due to the presence of sulfur in the molecule. At the end of the reaction it emerges linked to Enzyme₂ through a new thioester bond. Transesterification and trans(thio)esterification involve the exchange of one alcohol or thiol group, respectively, on one ester compound for another. Therefore, this reaction is best described as a trans(thio) esterification (eliminate choice B). Substitution is a tempting answer since one enzyme has been replaced by another, maintaining the same number of sigma bonds from reactant to product. However, since the interconversion of carboxylic acid derivatives occurs through an addition-elimination mechanism, choice C is a more specific answer, and choice A can be eliminated. Choice D can be eliminated since it only describes part of the mechanism.

3. **D**   ATP coupling is used to drive thermodynamically unfavorable reactions that would otherwise be nonspontaneous. Therefore, in the absence of ATP this reaction would not occur. Choices A and B imply that the kinetics of the reaction would change, not the thermodynamics, and can therefore be eliminated.

4. **A**   The isoelectric point (pI) of an amino acid is the pH at which it has an overall neutral charge. Differences in pI between the amino acids are due to differences in the side chains, since all amino acids have both an amino and carboxyl group that behave similarly in terms of their protonation states. In the passage, the side chain of lysine at pH 7 is shown in Figure 1; it is protonated and carries a positive charge. The side chain of glycine, a hydrogen, is shown in Figure 2, carries a neutral charge. Since the side chains are different and have different overall charges at pH 7, their pIs are not the same, and choice C can be eliminated. Since the side chain of lysine is still charged at pH 7, in order to deprotonate this side chain so that the overall amino acid carries a neutral charge, the pH must be raised. Therefore, the pH at which glycine carries an overall neutral charge is lower than the pH at which lysine carries an overall neutral charge, so the pI of glycine is lower than that of lysine.

5. **C**   The hydroxyl group on the threonine side chain carries two lone pairs and can act as a nucleophile. Reaction 2 shows that this hydroxyl group attacks the electrophilic carbonyl carbon of the peptide bond, further implicating threonine as a nucleophile. While there is some proton transfer in this reaction, the main function of threonine is not to act as an acid or base (eliminate choices A and B), but to cause the cleavage of the peptide bond via nucleophilic addition-elimination.

6. **B**   The major physical difference between lysine and the other two amino acids at pH 7 is that lysine carries an overall positive charge, as shown in Figures 1 (lysine side chain) and 2 (threonine and glycine). Gel electrophoresis separates molecules with different charges, and therefore would be the best choice for the separation. Extraction would not be effective since all of the species are charged and soluble in aqueous solution at pH 7 (eliminate choice A). Silica gel is a polar substance that would strongly attract all of the amino acids, therefore it would be very difficult to separate them using silica-based chromatography (eliminate choice C). The high molecular weight of the amino acids and ionic interactions between them will cause them to have a high vaporization point, making them nearly impossible to distill (eliminate choice D).

Organic Chemistry
Glossary

After each entry, the section number in *MCAT Organic Chemistry Review* where the term is discussed is given.

1,3-diaxial interaction
A destabilizing interaction between substituents that occupy axial positions on the same side of a cyclohexane ring. [**Section 3.4**]

achiral
A molecule that is superimposable on its mirror image. [**Section 3.4**]

aldehyde
A functional group where a carbonyl is attached to one carbon group and one hydrogen. [**Section 6.1**]

aldol condensation
A reaction in which the enolate anion of one carbonyl reacts with the carbonyl of another compound. [**Section 6.1**]

alkanes
Saturated hydrocarbons of the form C_nH_{2n+2}. [**Section 3.5**]

alkyl radicals
Neutral species that contain an unpaired electron on a carbon atom. [**Section 3.6**]

amphipathic
A molecule that is both hydrophilic and hydrophobic. [**Section 6.3**]

anomeric center
The orientation at the anomeric center distinguishes anomers from one another. [**Section 3.4**]

anomers
Epimers formed by ring closure. [**Section 3.4**]

anti **conformation**
A conformation in which the two largest groups are 180° apart. [**Section 3.4**]

axial
A substituent orientation on rings where the group is pointed up or down, perpendicular to the plane of the ring. [**Section 3.4**]

Benedict's test
A test to detect aldehydes, ketones, and hemiacetals in sugars. [**Section 8.3**]

boiling point
The temperature at which a compound changes from a liquid into a gas. [**Section 3.5**]

bond dissociation energy
The energy required to break a bond homolytically (producing two radicals). [**Section 3.3**]

bond length
The distance between two nuclei that are bonded to one another. [**Section 3.3**]

Cahn-Ingold-Prelog rules
A set of rules for assigning absolute configuration to a stereocenter. [**Section 3.4**]

carbanions
Negatively charged species with a full negative charge on carbon. [**Section 3.6**]

carbocations or carbonium ions
Positively charged species with a full positive charge on carbon. [**Section 3.6**]

carbohydrate
A chain of hydrated carbon atoms with the molecular formula $C_nH_{2n}O_n$. [**Section 8.3**]

chair conformation
The most stable conformation of cyclohexane. [**Section 3.4**]

chemical shift
The location of a resonance in a NMR spectrum. [**Section 7.2**]

chiral
A molecule that cannot be superimposed on its mirror image is chiral. Most frequently this refers to an sp^3 hybridized carbon with four different groups attached to it. [Section 3.4]

cis
Substituents on the same side of a double bond. [Section 3.4]

concerted reactions
Reactions that occur in one step without the formation of any intermediates. [Section 6.4]

conformational isomers
Any compounds that have the same molecular formula and the same connectivity but that differ from one another by rotation about a σ bond. [Section 3.4]

constitutional isomers
Any compounds with the same molecular formula but whose atoms have different connectivity. [Section 3.4]

crystallization
A purification method that relies on slow crystal formation to exclude impurities. [Section 7.1]

degree of unsaturation
A degree of unsaturation is either one ring or one π bond in a molecule. The degree of unsaturation can be calculated using the formula $[(2n + 2) - x]/2$, where n is the number of carbon atoms and x is the number of hydrogen atoms. [Section 3.2]

delocalized
Electrons that are allowed to interact with orbitals on adjacent atoms are said to be delocalized. [Section 3.6]

diasteromers
Stereoisomers that are not enantiomers. [Section 3.4]

Diels-Alder reaction
A concerted reaction between a diene and a dienophile that forms a cyclohexene ring. [Section 6.4]

disaccharide
Two monosaccharides bonded together. [Section 8.3]

distillation
A purification method based on a difference in boiling points. [Section 7.1]

disulfide bonds
A sulfur-sulfur bond between two cysteines that stabilizes protein structure. [Section 8.2]

E1 reaction
Unimolecular elimination. A two-step process that occurs by ionization of the leaving group to leave a planar carbocation; a base then removes a proton on a carbon adjacent to the positive charge, forming a double bond. [Section 4.3]

E2 reaction
Bimolecular elimination. A one-step process that involves simultaneous ionization of the leaving group and deprotonation of an adjacent carbon to form a double bond. [Section 4.3]

(E)-alkenes
Alkenes where the two higher priority groups are on the opposite side of the double bond. [Section 3.4]

electron-donating groups
Groups that push electrons away from themselves through σ bonds. [Section 3.6]

electron-withdrawing groups
Groups that pull electrons toward themselves through σ bonds. [Section 3.6]

electrophiles
Electrophiles ("electron loving") are electron-deficient and typically react with nucleophiles by accepting electrons. [Section 4.1]

electrophilic aromatic substitution
Substitution with a very electrophilic species on a normally unreactive π bond of an aromatic ring. [**Section 5.2**]

enantiomers
Molecules whose mirror images are non-superimposable. [**Section 3.4**]

enolate ion
A resonance-stabilized anion resulting from the deprotonation of a carbon atom adjacent to a carbonyl functional group. [**Section 6.1**]

epimeric center
The stereocenter at which the configuration differs in epimers. [**Section 3.4**]

epimers
Diastereomers that differ in configuration at only one of many chiral centers. [**Section 3.4**]

equatorial
A substituent orientation on rings where the group is pointed away from the center of the ring. [**Section 3.4**]

extraction
A separation technique that relies on relative solubilities of the two solvents used. [**Section 7.1**]

gas chromatography
A method that separates compounds based on their volatilities. [**Section 7.1**]

gauche **conformation**
A conformation in which the two largest groups are 60° apart. [**Section 3.4**]

geometric isomers
Diastereomers that differ in orientation of substituents around a ring or double bond. [**Section 3.4**]

glycosidic linkage
The bond between two saccharides. [**Section 8.3**]

half-chair conformation
The high-energy intermediate conformation of cyclohexane as it converts from one chair conformation into the other. [**Section 3.4**]

heterolytic bond cleavage (dissociation)
In heterolytic bond cleavage, a bond breaks such that both of the electrons that make up the bond end up on the same atom; this usually forms an anion and a cation. [**Section 3.3**]

homolytic bond cleavage
In homolytic bond cleavage, a bond breaks such that one electron of the two that make up the bond end up on each atom; this process forms two radicals. [**Section 3.3**]

Hückel numbers
In order for a delocalized π system to be aromatic, it must contain a Hückel number of π electrons: $4n + 2$, where $n = 0, 1, 2, 3, \ldots$. [**Section 5.2**]

hybrid orbitals
Hybrid orbitals are a mathematical combination of atomic orbitals centered on the same atom. The total number of orbitals is conserved in their formation (i.e., the number of atomic orbitals equals the number of hybrid orbitals). [**Section 3.1**]

hydrophilic
Literally "water loving." [**Section 8.4**]

hydrophobic
Literally "water fearing." [**Section 8.4**]

imine formation
A reaction between an aldehyde or ketone and a primary amine to form an imine. [**Section 6.1**]

inductive effect
The sharing of electrons through σ bonds. [**Section 3.6**]

infrared spectroscopy
A method that detects the vibrations of covalent bonds and can differentiate their frequencies, which is related to the type of bond. [**Section 7.2**]

isomers
Any compounds that have the same molecular formula. [Section 3.4]

ketone
A functional group in which a carbonyl is attached to two carbon groups. [Section 6.1]

Lindlar catalyst
A catalyst used in the hydrogenation of alkynes to (Z) or *cis* alkenes. [Section 5.1]

lipase
Enzymes that hydrolyze fats. [Section 8.4]

lipids
Oily or fatty substances that are part of cellular membranes (phospholipids), can store energy as triglycerides (in adipose cells), and can serve as the building block for steroid hormones (cholesterol). [Section 8.4]

lipid bilayer
A double layer of lipids where the polar groups line the outside and the non-polar tails compose the inside. [Section 8.4]

localized
Electrons that are confined to one orbital, either a bonding orbital or a lone-pair orbital. [Section 3.6]

Markovnikov's rule
The formation of the most stable carbocation intermediate. [Section 5.1]

melting point
The temperature at which a compound changes from a solid into a gas. [Section 3.5]

meso
A molecule that contains chiral centers and an internal plane of symmetry. [Section 3.4]

meta
Two substituents, on carbons separated by one carbon atom of an aromatic ring, are meta to one another. [Section 5.2]

meta-directing
Groups that favor electrophilic aromatic substitution at the meta position. [Section 5.2]

monosaccharide
Literally a "single sweet unit", also known as a simple sugar (e.g., fructose, glucose, etc.). [Section 8.3]

mutarotation
Interconversion between anomers. [Section 8.3]

nucleophile
Nucleophiles ("nucleus loving") have an unshared pair of electrons or a π bond and react with electrophiles by donating these electrons. [Section 4.1]

nucleotides
The building blocks of nucleic acids. [Section 8.6]

oligosaccharide
Several monosaccharides bonded together. [Section 8.3]

optically active
Compounds that rotate the plane of polarized light are optically active. A pair of enantiomers will rotate the plane of polarized light in equal, but opposite directions. [Section 3.4]

ortho
Two substituents, on adjacent carbons of a benzene ring, are ortho to one another. [Section 5.2]

ortho, para-directing
Groups that favor electrophilic aromatic substitution at the ortho and para positions. [Section 5.2]

para
Two substituents on opposite carbons of a benzene ring are para to one another. [Section 5.2]

peptide bond
The bond that links amino acids together formed between the carboxyl group of one amino acid and the amino group of another. [**Section 8.2**]

pi (π) bonds
A π bond consists of two electrons localized above and below a nodal plane; π bonds are formed from overlap of two unhybridized *p* orbitals on adjacent atoms. [**Section 3.1**]

polysaccharide
Many monosaccharides bonded together.
[**Section 8.3**]

protease
A protein enzyme that performs proteolysis.
[**Section 8.2**]

proteolysis
Hydrolysis of a protein by another protein.
[**Section 8.2**]

racemic mixture
An equal mixture of two enantiomers is said to be racemic; racemic mixtures do not rotate the plane of polarized light because one enantiomer cancels out the rotation of the other. [**Section 3.4**]

resonance
The sharing of electrons through π bonds.
[**Section 3.6**]

ring-activating
Substituents that make electrophilic aromatic substitution less difficult. [**Section 5.2**]

ring-deactivating
Substituents that make electrophilic aromatic substitution more difficult. [**Section 5.2**]

ring strain
Instability due to deviation of bond angles from optimal geometry. [**Section 3.6**]

S_N1 reaction
Unimolecular nucleophilic substitution reaction. A two-step reaction in which a planar carbocation is initially formed and then trapped with a nucleophile producing a racemic mixture.
[**Section 4.2**]

S_N2 reaction
Bimolecular nucleophilic substitution reaction. A one-step reaction that proceeds with inversion of configuration at the carbon. [**Section 4.2**]

saponification
The hydrolysis of esters by treatment with a basic solution. [**Section 6.3**]

saturated
A molecule is saturated if it contains no π bonds and no rings. [**Section 3.2**]

sigma (σ) bonds
A σ bond consists of two electrons localized between two nuclei; σ bonds are formed by overlap of two hybridized orbitals. [**Section 3.1**]

stereoisomers
Any compounds with the same molecular formula and connectivity that differ only in the spatial arrangement of atoms, are known as stereoisomers. Note that if the compounds only differ by rotation around a sigma bond they are not stereoisomers but *conformational* isomers.
[**Section 3.4**]

tautomers
Readily interconvertible constitutional isomers.
[**Section 6.1**]

thin-layer chromatography (TLC)
A rapid technique used to separate compounds based on their polarity. [**Section 7.1**]

trans
Substituents on opposite sides of a double bond.
[**Section 3.4**]

twist boat conformation
The local energy minimum for cyclohexane as it converts from one chair conformation to the other. [**Section 3.4**]

unsaturated
A molecule is unsaturated if it contains at least one π bond or ring. [**Section 3.2**]

van der Waals forces
A general term for intermolecular forces, often used to describe London dispersion forces: forces between temporary dipoles formed in nonpolar molecules formed because of a temporary asymmetric electron distribution. [**Section 3.5**]

wavenumber
The reciprocal of wavelength, expressed in reciprocal centimeters (cm^{-1}). [**Section 7.2**]

(Z)-alkenes
Alkenes where the two high priority groups are on the same side of the double bond. [**Section 3.4**]

zwitterion
A molecule with both positive and negative formal charges. [**Section 8.1**]

Summary of Reactions

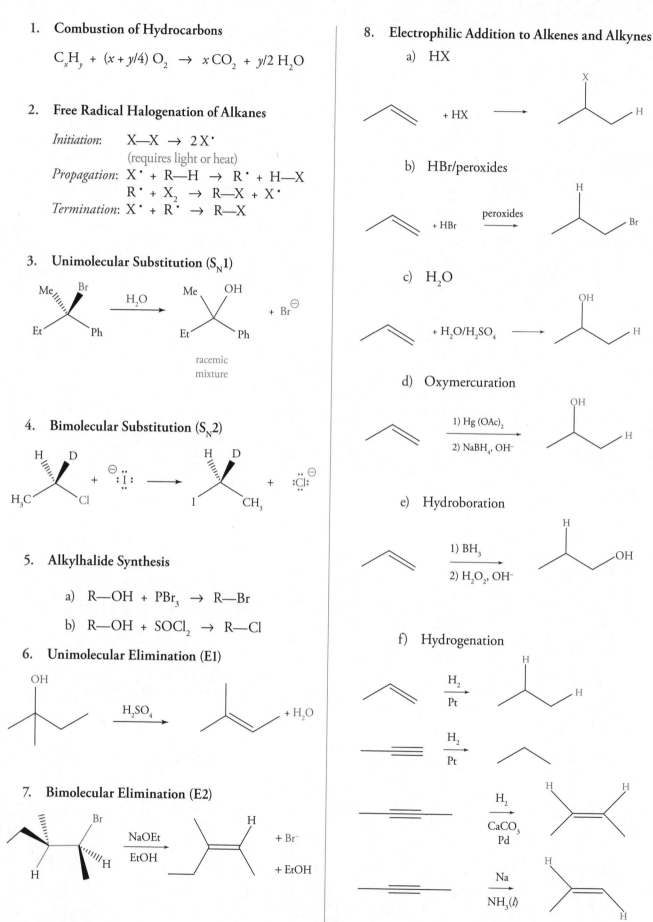

1. **Combustion of Hydrocarbons**

    $$C_xH_y + (x + y/4)\, O_2 \rightarrow x\, CO_2 + y/2\, H_2O$$

2. **Free Radical Halogenation of Alkanes**

    Initiation: $X\!-\!X \rightarrow 2\,X^{\boldsymbol{\cdot}}$
    (requires light or heat)
    Propagation: $X^{\boldsymbol{\cdot}} + R\!-\!H \rightarrow R^{\boldsymbol{\cdot}} + H\!-\!X$
    $R^{\boldsymbol{\cdot}} + X_2 \rightarrow R\!-\!X + X^{\boldsymbol{\cdot}}$
    Termination: $X^{\boldsymbol{\cdot}} + R^{\boldsymbol{\cdot}} \rightarrow R\!-\!X$

3. **Unimolecular Substitution (S_N1)**

    racemic
    mixture

4. **Bimolecular Substitution (S_N2)**

5. **Alkylhalide Synthesis**

    a) $R\!-\!OH + PBr_3 \rightarrow R\!-\!Br$

    b) $R\!-\!OH + SOCl_2 \rightarrow R\!-\!Cl$

6. **Unimolecular Elimination (E1)**

7. **Bimolecular Elimination (E2)**

8. **Electrophilic Addition to Alkenes and Alkynes**

    a) HX

        + HX

    b) HBr/peroxides

        + HBr   peroxides

    c) H_2O

        + H_2O/H_2SO_4

    d) Oxymercuration

        1) Hg (OAc)$_2$
        2) NaBH$_4$, OH$^-$

    e) Hydroboration

        1) BH$_3$
        2) H$_2$O$_2$, OH$^-$

    f) Hydrogenation

        H$_2$
        Pt

        H$_2$
        Pt

        H$_2$
        CaCO$_3$
        Pd

        Na
        NH$_3$(l)

SUMMARY OF REACTIONS

g) Halogenation

h) Epoxidation

i) Oxidation

9. Ozonolysis

10. Electrophilic Aromatic Substitution

11. Nucleophilic Addition

a) Hydride Reduction

b) Acetal Formation

c) Imine Formation

d) Grignard Reaction

e) Aldol Condensation

f) Michael Reaction

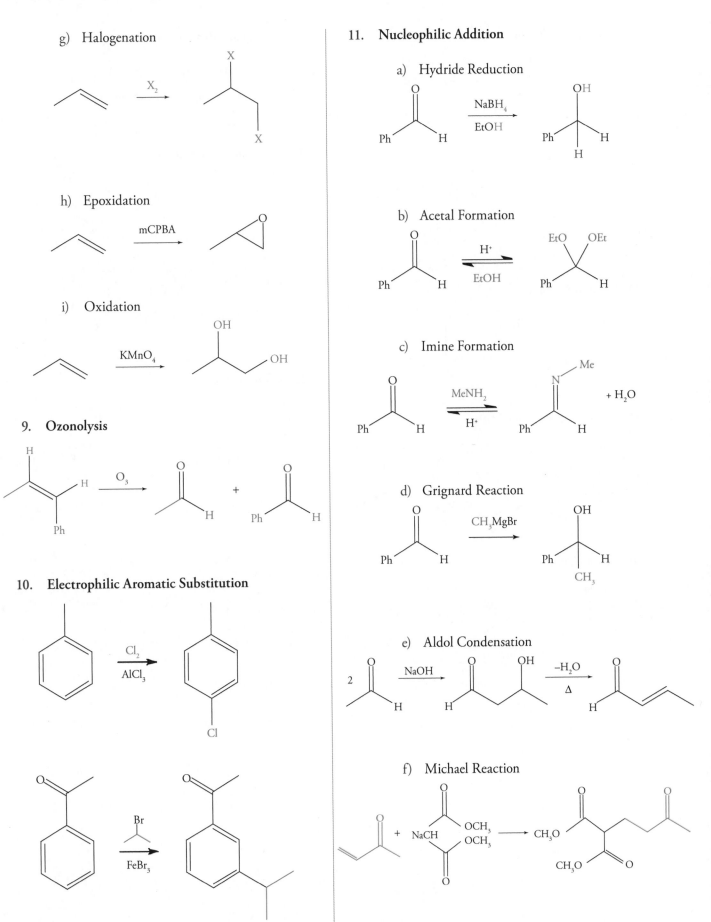

12. **Decarboxylation**

13. **Esterification**

14. **Saponification**

15. **Diels-Alder Cycloaddition**

16. **DCC Coupling**

17. **Grignard Reagent Formation**

$$R—Br + Mg \rightarrow R—MgBr$$

18. **Lithium Reagent Formation**

$$R—Br + 2\,Li \rightarrow R—Li + LiBr$$

19. **Oxidation of Alcohols**

20. **Wittig reaction**

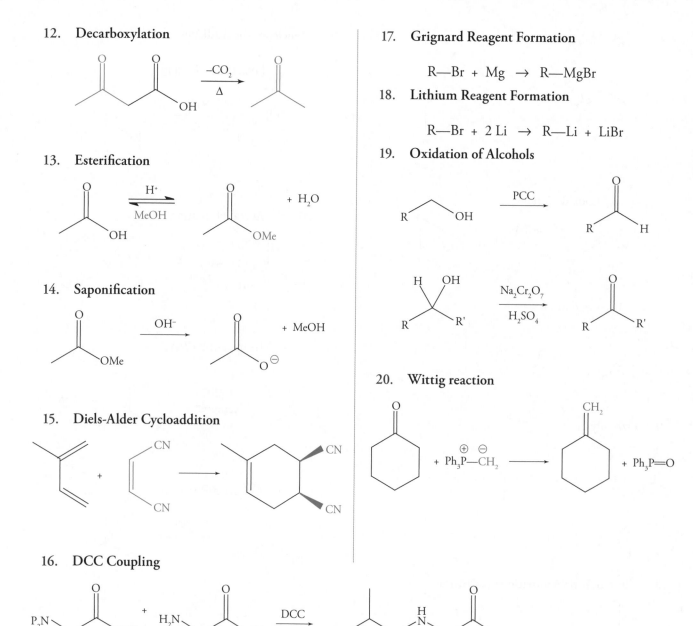

NOTES

NOTES

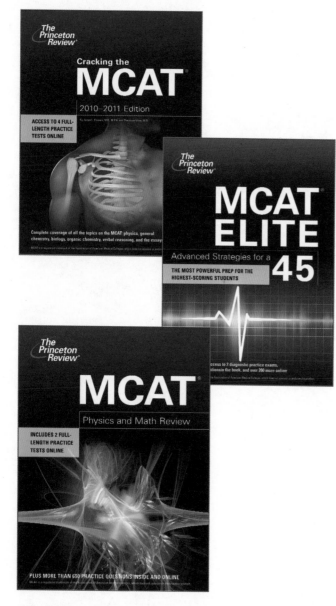